SPIRAL GUIDE

LISBON

CW00969354

AA

Publishing

Contents

the magazine 5

✦ A Melting Pot – The Colonial Legacy
✦ Henry the Navigator and the Age of Discoveries
✦ The Taste of Lisbon ✦ Saudade – That Certain Feeling
✦ Azulejos – Tiles Rule ✦ The Stones of Lisbon
✦ 1st November 1755 – A Day to Remember ✦ Up and
Down and Round and Round ✦ The Carnation Revolution
✦ Calouste Gulbenkian ✦ Best of Lisbon

Finding Your Feet 29

✦ First Two Hours
✦ Getting Around
✦ Accommodation
✦ Food and Drink
✦ Shopping
✦ Entertainment

North from the Central Waterfront 41

Getting Your Bearings
In a Day
Don't Miss ✦ The Baixa ✦ Chiado and Santa Justa ✦ Rossio,
Figueira and Restauradores ✦ Museu Calouste Gulbenkian
At Your Leisure ✦ 8 more places to explore
Where to... ✦ Eat and Drink ✦ Shop ✦ Be Entertained

The Heart of Medieval Lisbon 67

Getting Your Bearings
In a Day
Don't Miss ✦ Sé ✦ Museu-Escola de Artes Decorativas
✦ Castelo de São Jorge ✦ São Vicente de Fora ✦ Alfama
✦ Museu Nacional do Azulejo
At Your Leisure ✦ 7 more places to explore
Where to... ✦ Eat and Drink ✦ Shop ✦ Be Entertained

The Western Slopes 95

Getting Your Bearings
In a Day
Don't Miss ✦ Bairro Alto ✦ Basílica da Estrela
✦ Museu Nacional de Arte Antiga
At Your Leisure ✦ 6 more places to explore
Where to... ✦ Eat and Drink ✦ Shop ✦ Be Entertained

Belém 115
Getting Your Bearings
In a Day
Don't Miss ✦ Torre de Bélem ✦ Padrão dos Descobrimentos
✦ Museu de Marinha ✦ Mosteiro dos Jerónimos
✦ Museu Nacional dos Coches
At Your Leisure ✦ 5 more places to explore
Where to... ✦ Eat and Drink ✦ Shop ✦ Be Entertained

Parque das Nações 141
Getting Your Bearings
In a Day
Don't Miss ✦ Oceanário ✦ Centro da Ciência Viva
At Your Leisure ✦ 3 more places to explore
Where to... Eat and Drink ✦ Shop ✦ Be Entertained

Excursions 159
✦ The West Coast
✦ Sintra and Queluz
✦ Mafra

Walks and Tours 173
✦ **1** Chiado and the Bairro Alto
✦ **2** Alfama
✦ **3** Ferry to Cacilhas and the
Santuário do Cristo Rei

Practicalities 183
✦ Before You Go ✦ When To Go
✦ When You Are There
✦ Useful Words and Phrases

Streetplan 191

Streetplan Index 201

Index 203

Written by Sally Roy

Verified by Emma Rowley Ruas
Project editor Karen Kemp
Designer Catherine Murray
Cartographic editor Anna Thompson

Published by AA Publishing, a trading name of Automobile
Association Developments Limited, whose registered office is
Fanum House, Basing View, Basingstoke, Hampshire, RG21 4EA.
Registered number 1878835.

ISBN: 978-0-7495-5712-6

The contents of this publication are believed correct at the time
of printing. Nevertheless, AA Publishing accept no responsibilty
for errors, omissions or changes in the details given, or for the
consequences of readers' reliance on this information. This does
not affect your statutory rights. Assessments of the attractions,
hotels and restaurants are based upon the author's own experience
and contain subjective opinions that may not reflect the publisher's
opinion or a reader's experience. We have tried to ensure accuracy,
but things do change, so please let us know if you have any
comments or corrections.

A CIP catalogue record for this book is available from the
British Library.

Cover design and binding style by permission of AA Publishing

Colour separation by Keenes, Andover
Printed and bound in China by Leo Paper Products

Find out more about AA Publishing and the wide range of services
the AA provides by visiting our website at www.theAA.com/travel

A03005
Maps in this title produced from mapping © MAIRDUMONT/
Falk Verlag 2008
Transport map © Communicarta Ltd, UK

the magazine

A MELTING POT
the Colonial Legacy

Who are the *lisboetas*? The inhabitants of Lisbon clearly, but walk down any city centre street and you'll see an ethnic diversity that rivals that of London. Outside the capital, the Portuguese population is one of the most homogenous in Europe; an amalgam of Iberian and Celt with a dash of Roman and Moorish blood. It's a different story in Lisbon, and the explanation lies in Portugal's imperial past.

The great voyages of the 15th and 16th centuries not only opened up the world trading routes, they also heralded the start of Portuguese colonisation – in India, South America and the Far East. By 1560, Portugal controlled huge areas along both the west and east African coasts, Cape Verde, Goa and other parts of west India and modern Sri Lanka; there were settlements further east in the islands that were to become New Guinea and Timor, others in China and Japan and a vast tract in Brazil. Time passed and these possessions were gradually lost, broke away or gained independence; the last Portuguese colony, Macau, was handed back to China in 1999.

Take a stroll through Lisbon and this colonial aftermath is all around you, in the faces, the sights, the sounds and the scents from Africa, Asia and Brazil. There are estimated to be well over 200,000 Africans in the capital, mainly from Cape Verde, Angola, Mozambique and Guinea Bassau as well as a huge number of *retornados*, the name given to white Portuguese who returned home from the African

colonies in the 1970s. They all keep the culture alive – the food, the dance, the music. So do the Brazilians, who've been flocking here since the 1990s, bringing their music and their punchy *caiparinhas* (a cocktail made with lots of lime) with them, and converting a large slice of the Lisbon dwellers to all things Brazilian. There's a fondness, too, for the Indians from Goa, who've been an element in Portuguese consciousness since Vasco da Gama discovered the sea route to India in 1498, and the smaller numbers of Timorese who first came during the Indonesian occupation of this ex-

Above: Detail of the emblem on the Portuguese national flag

Top right: Traditional costume

Bottom right: The statue of Dom Pedro IV presides over the Rossio

Portuguese colony. Throw in a good helping of eastern Europeans, a sprinkling of Chinese from Macau and some Malays from Indonesia, and you've got the classic ingredients for the type of multi-cultural melting pot that gives a major city that extra cutting-edge allure.

Naturally, there's a flip side to this. Despite a tradition of tolerance towards migrants, with everyone on the whole rubbing along, discrimination certainly exists, alongside what's called the *exclusão social*, which makes foreigners of many young blacks in their own country. Poverty and drug abuse keep some ethnic groups near the bottom of the heap, and the number of illegals, particularly from the Ukraine, has reached epidemic levels.

Henry the Navigator
and the Age of Discoveries

Only 140 years separate Portugal's first maritime foray with the triumphant coup of being granted exclusive trading rights with China and Japan. From the moment the first, tentative attack on Ceuta in North Africa was launched, little Portugal was clearly destined for big things, and Infante Dom Henrique, better known as Prince Henry the Navigator, was the man to kick start the whole process.

Born in 1394, the son of Dom João I and his English wife, Philippa of Lancaster, Henry, as the fourth son, would clearly have to carve out an occupation for himself. His chance came in 1415, when his father put him charge of organising an assault on the North African port of Ceuta. The time was right; the country was ripe for expansion, fired with avarice, lusty for adventure, imbued with religious fervour against Islam. Henry's efforts paid off. Ceuta fell, giving him the clout to set up as a trainer of mariners and maritime innovator. He redesigned the ocean-going caravel and founded a School of Navigation at Sagres in the Algarve, making long-distance exploration feasible. From here, his ships pushed west into the Atlantic, sailing to the Canary Islands in 1416, discovering Madeira around 1419 and the Azores in the 1430s. Eager for trade with the Far East, but blocked by Venice and Genoa on the overland routes, Portugal began to think in terms of a sea passage east, pushing south round the African continent. Cape Bojador on the west African coast, southernmost point on sea charts, was the ultimate challenge. This was the edge

Top left: Henry the Navigator

Top right: Map of the world in mosaic at the foot of the impressive Monument to the Discoveries

Right: Henry the Navigator and Dom Manuel I – two of the historical characters on the prow of the monument

of the known world, beyond which lay a "sea of darkness". The coast to the north, desolate and sinister, has oblique currents, heavy swells and winter sea mist, and the ocean itself is tinged red with desert sand.

Between 1421 and 1433 no fewer than 14 expeditions had failed to round the Cape, and Henry was losing patience with his lily-livered captains. In 1434 he inspired Gil Eannes with promises of rewards and riches. Eannes sailed south, doubled back from the Canaries and rounded the Cape; the deadlock of superstition was broken and the way south was open.

Henry died in 1460, but the work he'd started continued. In the mid-1470s Portuguese ships crossed the Equator and in 1488 Bartholomeu Dias rounded the Cape of Good Hope. The route east was open and nine years later, Vasco da Gama set sail from Restelo (now Belém) with three caravels, reaching Calicut in India in 1498. Mayhem and violence accompanied him and his fellow mariners, with countless Muslims being put to death as the Portuguese extended their empire ever further, while the African coast supplied thousands of slaves for the sugar plantations of the Atlantic islands – the flip side to Portugal's Golden Age.

THE TASTE OF LISBON

Poor old Portugal is still seen by critics as
a sort of gastronomic desert, where the quanti-
ties are huge but the culinary skill is small.
Lisbon doesn't deserve this, for the capital now
offers immensely varied eating, while still staying true to its roots. It's these roots that count –
a tradition of good, simple food, great fish and
seafood, a terrific coffee culture, cakes and pastries that provide the ultimate in sugar kicks
and wines that are one of the country's best-kept
secrets. So grab a table, peruse the menu and
pick up that knife and fork.

So…what to eat? There's
Portuguese cooking, cooking
from the former colonies of
Brazil, Angola, Macão and
Goa, French and Italian
cuisine, Mediterranean
fusion; there are stews and
soups rich in beans and
vegetables, tiny savoury
rissoles, crumbling tarts
oozing cream and custard,
and, above all, fish. Lisbon

Sardinhas – the
quintessential
taste of Lisbon
and Portugal
itself

remains one of the best places in Europe to enjoy fish and seafood, whether it's the quintessential grilled sardine, salt-baked *salmonetes* (red mullet), a steaming bowl of *caldeirada rica* (rich fish stew), or, in Portuguese eyes, the star of the show, *bacalhau* (dried salt cod).

More than Just a Fish

It's something of a mystery as to why the Portuguese, a maritime nation whose coasts teem with the best of the Atlantic, should be so enamoured by the wood-hard and pungent *bacalhau*. The answer dates from the times when the Portuguese caught this king of fish on the Newfoundland cod banks, bringing it home to be salted, dried and thus preserved. It wormed its way into hearts and minds, becoming a staple, a food for everyday and celebration alike. It's said there are 365 ways to cook *bacalhau*, one for every day of the year, so you've got to give it a go – try *bacalhau à Brás*, where flaked cod is mixed with potatoes and scrambled eggs and strewn with parsley and olives.

Just a Touch of Something Sweet

For those moments when your energy flags, the range of sugary treats in a good *paste-laria* (pastry shop) should fit the bill. Lisbon's top favourite has to be the *pasteis de nata*, a crisp, deep tart filled with egg custard, but there are a myriad delights, with the *doces conventuais*, rich egg-yolk and sugar-heavy cakes originally made in convents, topping the bill. Wash them down with a nice cuppa *chá* (tea), a tipple the Portuguese claim they introduced to England when Catherine of Bragança married Charles II.

Fruit of the Vine

If you're after something stronger, Portuguese wines on their native soils will be a revelation. Reds are the most interesting, but the most famous native product is port, produced in the Douro in northern Portugal. Don't miss sampling *porto branco* (white port), a great aperitif, or how about a glass of Madeira, *the* other fortified wine, or a chilled goblet of sparkling, light *vinho verde*. The choice is yours – just get in there and enjoy.

Pasteis de nata (rich custard tartlets)

Saudade
That Certain Feeling

They may live in southern Europe, but it has to be said that, at first glance, the Portuguese lack the light-hearted temperament of other southern nations. Not for them high displays of temper, mirth or grief. Guardedness seems to be the watchword, though some would call it downright bolshiness. Scratch the surface and there's kindness and friendliness, but all too often, the stranger is left feeling slighted and ignored.

It's a harsh judgment and, in some ways, unfair. The explanation may be simple: the Portuguese are not Mediterranean, and neither is their temperament nor their emotions. Basically phlegmatic, they get on with life with little song and dance, hugging to themselves that enigmatic and quintessentially Portuguese emotion, *saudade*. The word is untranslatable, encapsulating nostalgia and yearning for something no longer at hand, something impossible to attain, be that a place, a person, even an object. Mariners feel it as the months away from home slip past. It's felt by emigrants abroad, determined to return, by those left at home for those who have departed, by a constant backward desire for

Fado – music from Portugal's very soul

Musical-themed tile-work on a *fado* house in the Bairro Alto

the great days of Portuguese triumph. It's *saudade* that fosters the tightly knit Portuguese communities in the world's great cities, and *saudade* that brings migrants home after years of working overseas. You'll see it in the fierce love of all Portuguese for the home patch, and above all, hear it in Portugal's own music, *fado*.

Fado means "fate", and, at its purest, this elegantly melancholic music, performed by a singer, a Spanish guitar and the 12-stringed Portuguese guitar, deals with

life's great mysteries and passions – love, jealousy, death and betrayal. It can also be light-hearted, and *fado* styles range from flirtatious and sentimental to dark and intense. Where it came from is a mystery; some say its roots are Arabic, some that it's inherited from the Provençal troubadours, some that it crossed the ocean from Brazil. Whatever. It appeared in the 1850s, flourished, peaked in the 1940s, slipped out of favour in the 1970s and finally re-emerged in the late 1990s.

Queens of the Scene

Fado's greatest exponent was Amália Rodrigues, born in poverty in 1920. She took *fado* out of the dark, smoky taverns of its birthplace, her wonderfully expressive voice gaining an international audience for the genre. When she died in 1999 the nation mourned, and she lies buried in the Panteão Nacional (► 89). Her house is now a museum, **Casa-Museu Amália Rodrigues** at Rua de São Bento 193 (tel: 213 971 896, Tue–Sun 10–1, 2–6), a shrine to Portugal's best-loved *fadista*. Hot on her heels comes Mariza, a beautiful and stylish singer for the 21st century, with an extraordinary voice. Her mission is to show that *fado* is not a fossilised style but, just like the blues or flamenco, it is alive and well. She stresses that *fado* is not just about *saudade* and melancholia but can cover many moods, and her intensity and artistry have attracted a new audience. At her best heard live, she sings new songs, choosing poetry for her lyrics and sometimes augmenting the traditional guitar and viola accompaniment with a wider range of instruments.

Azulejos –
TILES RULE

Most countries brighten their walls with carvings, frescoes, tapestries or just good old paint – Portugal uses *azulejos* (tiles), and there's no better place to enjoy this beautiful decoration than Lisbon. From its churches and palaces to its fountains, shop fronts and ordinary houses, the city enchants visitors with the singing purity of these acres of blue and white.

It's fitting that blue and white predominate; the very word *azulejo* probably derives from the Persian word *azraq*, meaning blue. If it's not *azraq*, it's the Arabic *zalayja*, "polished stone", and both words put the Portuguese tile's origins firmly back in the country's Moorish past. It was in the 14th century that tiles were bought to the Iberian peninsula by the Moors, and *mudejar* (Christian Moorish) artists, working in Seville, sent their wares to neighbouring Portugal – you can still see some of these in the Palácio Nacional de Sintra (➤ 164). Two hundred years later, Italian skill created the majolica technique, allowing artists to paint directly onto the tile without the risk of the colours mixing during the firing process. It was the impetus needed by Portuguese craftsmen, and tile-making took off with a bang. These tiles were first used principally on churches and cloisters to depict biblical scenes and favourite saints – São Roque (➤ 109) has some fine examples. By the 17th century, tile-makers were really branching out,

Where to See the Best Azulejos
- Igreja de São Roque (➤ 109)
- Linha Vermelha metro line
- Museu da Cidade (➤ 63)
- Museu Nacional do Azulejo (➤ 85–86)
- Palácio dos Marquêses de Fronteira (➤ 111)
- Palácio Nacional de Queluz (➤ 167)
- Palácio Nacional de Sintra (➤ 164)
- São Vicente de Fora (➤ 80–81)

producing huge pictures composed of hundreds of individual tiles, such as those at São Vicente de Fora (▶ 80–81) and the Palácio dos Marquêses de Fronteira (▶ 111).

Following the 1755 earthquake (▶ 20–21), Lisbon underwent a construction boom, and the first massproduced tiles were churned out by the Real Fábrica do Rato, established by the Marquês de Pombal in 1767. More neoclassical in style, these tiles were increasingly used to decorate and weatherproof facades as well as interiors, and there are plenty of examples all over Lisbon today. By the 19th century the ubiquitous tile was used on factories, apartment blocks, shops and even railway stations. It's a tradition that continues, and you can see some of Lisbon's most striking modern tile work at stations throughout the metro system, the work of the best contemporary artists.

Left: Tiles in the gardens of the Palácio dos Marquêses de Fronteira
Right: Traditional tiles in the Belém district

Where to Buy the Best Tiles
Ratton (Rua Academia das Ciências 2c, São Bento, tel: 213 460 948). Contemporary tiles by modern Portuguese and international artists.
Sant'Anna (Rua do Alecrim 95, Chiado, tel: 213 422 537). Handmade copies of 17th- and 18th-century tiles.
Solar (Rua Dom Pedro V 68–70, Bairro Alto, tel: 213 465 522). Antique tile specialists.

The Stones of Lisbon

Much of the appeal of beguiling Lisbon lies in its physical reality – its position on a great river, its hills, the contrast between its narrow streets and open spaces. Trek up to any of the *miradouros* (look-outs) that are scattered throughout the city and spread before you is a vista encompassing a mishmash of churches, palaces, civic buildings and private housing, all jumbled together. Portugal's capital wins hearts and minds, and much of its allure lies in its real sense of individuality, its lack of the sort of modern-day homogeneity found in so many 21st-century cities.

The striking interior of the Gare do Oriente in Parque das Nações

The Best and Where to Find It
Romanesque: the Sé (► 72–73)
Manueline: Torre de Belém (► 120–121), Mosteiro dos Jerónimos (► 128–132), Igreja Madre de Deus (► 85)
Spanish: Igreja de São Vicente de Fora (► 80–81)
Pombaline: the Baixa (► 46–49)
Neoclassical: Teatro Nacional de São Carlos (► 66)
Modernist: Padrão dos Descobrimentos (► 122–123)
Contemporary: Gare do Oriente (► 30), Oceanário (► 146–149)

Much of this is due to the city's distinctive architecture. Few European capitals had a chance to completely reinvent themselves in the 18th century, so while the 1755 earthquake was a truly great catastrophe, its outcome, in urban terms, was an entirely new, rationally designed city centre, the Baixa (► 46–49). Around this grid of streets and in the outlying areas are the earlier buildings that survived, a pocketful of gems that encapsulate the best from earlier ages. Their styles cover the centuries – traces of Roman and Moorish construction, the spare and harmonious lines of Romanesque architecture, soaring Gothic arches and vaults and, above all, the magic of Portugal's own architectural speciality, Manueline.

This unique style coincides with Portugal's heyday, when mariners pushed ever further – to India, Africa, Asia and South America. National confidence in the late 15th century was high, the money rolled in, and native architects fused Gothic with elements plucked from all over to create something

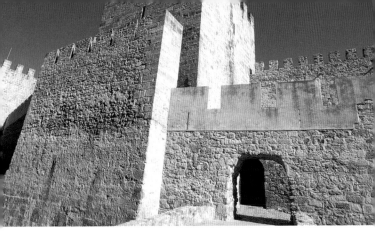

entirely new. The decorative features loved by the Christianised Moors, the Mudejars, were one ingredient, richly ornamented Spanish Plateresque another, while Italian touches added yet another component. Throw in a plethora of ornamentation celebrating the sea and those who sailed it and the result is Manueline, named after the rule of King Manuel I (1495–1521). It's identifiable by its plain walls with extravagant decoration round windows and doors. Rigging and anchors, fish and seaweed, sea creatures and ships appear time and again, intricate rope-work in stone surrounds windows, and everywhere you'll see the king's seal. This armillary sphere, with its bands repre-senting the equator and the tropics, and the Vera Cruz, the true cross, were the potent symbols of both sea power and the Christianity in whose name the mariners ostensibly set out. Miraculously, not all was lost in 1755 and you can still see Manueline at its best in the buildings at Belém, where the Torre de Belém still guards the approaches to the city.

The centuries rolled by and Lisbon grew, each gener-ation building anew, in every style popular across Europe at the time. Happily, the Portuguese never abandoned the traditions of their vernac-ular architecture, and both palaces and the houses of the ordinary people remained uniquely Portuguese – the former graceful, often colour-

The Castelo de São Jorge marks the point where the city is thought to have taken root

Cobbled Together

As your aching feet at the end of long day's sightseeing will testify, Lisbon's streets are stony indeed, made as they are of *calçada à portuguesa* – Portuguese paving. Back in the 1850s, the powers-that-be decreed that the city streets and squares should be paved with intricate cobbled designs, works of art in themselves. Look down and you'll see patterns of every description, shop names and street numbers, as well as the eight-pointed star, a good luck symbol protecting against earthquake. Every stone is cut and laid by hand by the city's calceteiros (pavers), and even if some of the old skills are disappearing as the masters are pensioned off, Lisbon's pavements continue to be an integral part of the city's identity.

washed, always richly tiled, the latter, plain and square, the elegant windows and simple balconies often the main decorative note. Tiles were everywhere (➤ 14–15) – and they still are.

Increasingly, foreign influence played a part on Lisbon's cityscape, particularly after the 1974 Carnation Revolution (➤ 24–25) restored democracy. The final architectural proof that Portugal was, once more, very much part of mainstream Europe, came with the development of a heavily polluted eastern riverside area for Expo 98. International and Portuguese architects were involved in designing the streamlined modern buildings that now form the Parque das Nações (➤ 142–155),

accessed from all over the country via Lisbon's most stunning modern public building, Santiago Calatrava's Gare do Oriente (East Station).

Lisbon's Sé (Cathedral), with its twin-battlemented towers and rose window

1 November 1755
A Day to Remember

It was a Sunday morning, the feast of All Souls, and most of Lisbon's population of 250,000 were praying in the city's magnificent churches and cathedrals when the worst earthquake ever to hit western Europe struck. It destroyed the great city-port and seat of learning, capital of Portugal and the vast Portuguese empire. The shocks killed thousands, the subsequent tsunami killed thousands more, and a huge fire raged for five days, completing the destruction of the city.

At 9:30am, an eyewitness reported that there was a "strange, frightful noise, resembling the hollow, distant rumbling of thunder" and churches and buildings began to sway. Everywhere, the panicked population rushed onto the streets, only to be crushed as the second, longer and more powerful shock caused the collapse of thousands of buildings. Fissures up to 3.5m (11.5 feet) opened in the ground. Many people fled towards the river, seeking the open spaces of the great Terreiro do Praça and the waterside promenade, others surged out of the city to the surrounding

fields. Forty minutes later, a series of tsunami waves swept up the Tejo, crashing over and destroying the quays, submerging the lower part of the city and destroying every boat moored in the harbour. An estimated 20,000 of the terrified inhabitants who had sought safety here were drowned. Whatever the shocks and tsunami waves had spared was engulfed over the next five days by fire, as a monstrous inferno, fanned by northeast winds, burned out of control. It destroyed Moorish and medieval buildings, Renaissance palaces, libraries whose contents documented the country's

Drawings depicting the earthquake of 1755

Left to right: The ruins of the church of St Paul;

General destruction of the city;

The remains of the Cathedral

history, the royal palace and thousands of works of art. Many of those who had survived the shocks and waves were burnt to death.

Into this chaos stepped King Dom José I's chief minister, Sebastão José de Carvalho e Melo. The dust had barely settled when he decreed "Bury the dead, and feed the living", a course of action that spared the city both starvation and epidemic. He was tireless, spending the next fortnight driving and riding round the city, night and day; sending out fire-fighters; arranging the collection and burial of corpses; setting up posts for soldiers to guard against looting and pillage and safeguarding what little remained. Within months, he had drawn up plans for an entire new city centre, today's Baixa, and in 1769, was rewarded with the title of Marquês de Pombal. He also sent out question-naires throughout Portugal, asking for answers that might shed light on the disaster and give warning for future cata-strophes – how long did the earthquake last? Were there aftershocks? What kind of damage was there? Did animals behave strangely? Questions that have earned him recognition as the "father of seismology".

The Earthquake in Statistics

- **Epicentre**: 200km (125 miles) west-southwest of Cape St Vincent, the most south-westerly tip of Europe, at around 36°N 10°57'W
- **Force on Richter Scale**: 8.2, possibly more
- **Time before tsunami hit**: 40 minutes
- **Height of tsunami**: 6m (19.7 feet)
- **Death toll in Lisbon**: 90,000
- **Buildings destroyed**: 18,000 – 85 per cent of the total
- **Financial cost**: £20 million
- **Area where shocks were felt**: 3,367,000sq km (1,300,000 square miles)
- **Other affected countries**: severe shocks and extensive damage in Portugal and western Spain; bad shocks in southern France, Algeria and Morocco; shocks felt in Switzerland and Germany; tsunamis observed in England and France and wave surges as far north as Norway and Sweden

Up and Down and
Round and Round

Lisbon wouldn't be Lisbon without its trams. They may be slow, they're often infrequent, but a clanking ride on a tram or funicular is an essential city experience, which will certainly save your feet in this hilly city. Other European cities may have modern stream-lined tram services, but Lisbon has retained both its historic routes and its old-style vehicles, a much-loved convenience for both locals and visitors.

Trams run on rails, their power transmitted from an overhead electric cable and fed through connecting rods to the vehicle. Unlike trains, tram tracks are laid in streets, which they have to share with cars, lorries and pedestrians. They were common everywhere in the late 19th and early 20th centuries, but fell out of favour in the 1950s. Not in Lisbon; it never abandoned the tram, and the old-fashioned trolley car grinding up the hills is one of the city's most iconic images.

The first prototypes, made in New York, appeared in 1873 – unwieldy vehicles drawn by horses which ran along the riverside between Santa Apolónia and Santos.

The *americanos* were an immediate success, and Carris, the public transport company still in operation today, was off to a good start. More lines were built, a depot constructed, and within two years over 1 million passengers were using the system. Increased business was the impetus behind the 1902 decision to electrify the system, and by 1924 Lisbon's trams were assembled in the CARRIS workshops. Some of these old stalwarts were still trundling up and down the hills in the early 1990s, but today's fleet is made up of *remodelados* (remodeled trams) and up-to-the-minute articulated Siemens trams.

Lisbon's tram hub is the Baixa (► 46–49), from

Right: Passing the Cathedral at night

Below: Trams make getting around Lisbon easy

where different lines serve the hilly neighbourhoods of the Alfama (▶ 82–84) and the Bairro Alto (▶ 100–101) and run along the flat riverside ground out to Belém (▶ 116–140). The downtown trams are splendid vehicles, their design unaltered since the late 19th century, with charmingly boxy exteriors and old-fashioned fixtures and wood panelling inside. They don't move fast, but they negotiate the steep streets and tight corners with ease, though progress is less than smooth and can be frequently halted by recalcitrant cars blocking the tracks – an essential part of the whole experience and a great way to bond with your exasperated fellow travellers. If you want 21st-century comfort, just hop on the super-smooth number 15 and head out towards Belém.

Some city areas are too steep even for trams, and here the three *elevadors* (funiculars) come into their own, hauling their fixed carriages up and down between the Baixa and the Bairro Alto, like some unlikely alpine transport far from its snowy slopes. Most perpendicular of all is the Elevador de Santa Justa, a straightforward, albeit wonderfully picturesque lift.

The Tram Museum

You can learn more about the history of trams at:

Museu da Carris

✉ Rua de Maio, 101–103 ☎ 213 613 087; www.carris.pt ◉ Mon–Sat 10–1, 2–5

For how to use the tram and funicular network, ▶ 32.

Carris also operates a sightseeing tram service.

From 1928 until 1974 Portugal was a reactionary, right-wing dictatorship, under the control of António Oliveira Salazar. For four decades, backed by his sinister political police, the PIDE, he clamped down on every type of progress, keeping the country closed to outside influences and the population fed with the 3 F diet – Fátima (the cult of the Virgin much favoured by the regime after she supposedly appeared to three peasant children), Football and *Fado*. By the late 1960s Salazar was failing, and there was student unrest and colonial problems. The time was ripe.

The Carnation
REVOLUTION

Salazar died in 1970. His successor, Marcello Caetano, although a reformist, was unable to deal with Portugal's mounting crisis, particularly the growing colonial problems. By spring 1974, a group of left-wing military officers formed a conspiracy – the Movimento das Forças Armadas (MFA), to overthrow the government by military coup and install General António Spínola as leader of a reforming government. The MFA was led by Major Otelo Saraiva de Carvalho, whose task was to direct the seizure of strategic points in Lisbon and throughout the country. Without the backing of the majority of the army, his plans had to be laid in utter secrecy, and his supporters alerted without giving the game away. On 25 April, at 12:15am, the national radio broadcast Zeca Afonso's folk song, "Grândola, Vila Morena", its lyric far too progressive normally to be heard on Portuguese radio. This was the MFA's signal to begin the *coup d'état*, which changed the Portuguese regime from an authoritarian dictatorship to a liberal democracy. Six hours later it was over; Caetano surrendered, Spínola took charge

Left: António Salazar

Below and right: Tanks on the streets during the Spínola "Revolution"

and the longest authoritarian regime in western Europe was ended. Despite repeated radio appeals that the people should stay at home, huge crowds hit the streets, mingling with both the MFA and ordinary troops, still uncertain which way to lean. They massed outside the PIDE headquarters, from where shots were fired, killing three, the only casualties of the entire day.

The crowds were thickest in the city centre, and the story goes that it was a flower-seller on Rossio who handed a seasonal red carnation to a soldier. Carnations were plentiful, and more and more troops were handed flowers, which they stuffed down their gun barrels. It was a powerful image, flashed around the world within hours by the news agencies. Portugal's revolution had found its name, the *Revolução dos Cravos*, the Carnation Revolution.

Spínola's Junta didn't last, but it was the beginning of Portugal's journey back to mainstream Europe, which culminated with its entry to the European Union in 1986. Today, the Revolution is celebrated by a public holiday, when old ladies still sell carnations to remind a new generation of Portugal's most important day in the 20th century.

Calouste Gulbenkian
The Great Philanthropist

Just who was Calouste Gulbenkian? Few people have heard of him before they come to Lisbon, yet this name, synonymous with the best of Lisbon's arts scene, is hardly Portuguese. There's a wonderful museum (▶ 55–59) named after him, but what's such a superb collection of private art doing in Lisbon? Music *aficionados* may take in a concert given by the Gulbenkian Orchestra or the Gulbenkian Choir, but what's behind all this?

This dazzling range of culture is funded by the Gulbenkian Foundation, an organisation that can claim to have done as much for the arts in Portugal as the state itself. It was set up in 1956 under the terms of the will of Calouste Sarkis Gulbenkian, an Armenian Christian, born in Istanbul in 1869. He studied at King's College, London, graduating in 1887 and headed for the embryonic petroleum industry, becoming a British citizen in 1902. Over the following decades he amassed a huge fortune from his role in the development of the industry in the Middle East, where he was involved with the founding of Royal Dutch-Shell company and negotiated in the establishment of the Turkish Oil Company. He had the golden touch, helped by his habit of retaining a percentage of the value of virtually every company and deal he was involved in – not for nothing was he nicknamed Mr Five Percent.

Gulbenkian was superrich; he was also passionately interested in art, first acquiring works of art in the 1890s and purchasing on a grand

Below and right: Calouste Gulbenkian from the age of 20 onwards

scale, always going for what he liked, with a perfect provenance and in perfect condition. What he bought, he used, living surrounded by many of his fabulous acquisitions in his Paris home. By the late 1930s he was toying with the idea of creating a London institution to display his collection publicly, but World War II saw him declared a "technical enemy" by the British government, and London lost its chance. So, later, did the United States, for by this time Gulbenkian had given his heart to Portugal, the country that gave him refuge when he fled Nazi-occupied France in 1942. He died in Lisbon in 1955, leaving his collection, and his vast fortune, to the country where he received a welcome that "I have never felt anywhere else". By 1960 his entire collection was in Lisbon, and one of the world's greatest charitable arts foundations was established.

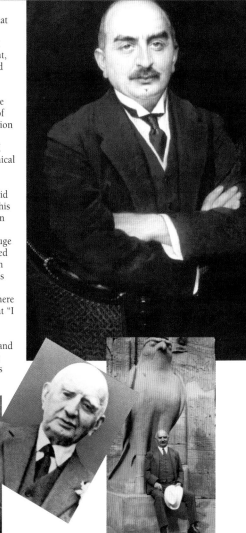

Best of Lisbon

Best *Miradouros*

Castelo de São Jorge: Sweeping views of the city centre (➤ 77–79, below and right).

São Pedro Alcântara: Views of the city centre – from the other side (➤ 174).

Santa Luzia: The Alfama and the river (➤ 178).

Esplanada da Igreja da Graça: The best sunset views (➤ 94, 179).

Santa Catarina: The river and the western neighbourhoods (➤ 110).

Best Public Transport Rides

Number 12 tram from Praça da Figueira to the Largo das Portas do Sol.

Number 25 tram from Rua da Alfândega to the Basílica da Estrela.

Number 28 tram from Graça to Chiado.

Train downriver to Cascais (➤ 161).

Ferry across the Tejo to Cacilhas (➤ 180).

Best Outdoor Cafés

Café Martinho da Arcada: Grab a table under the arcades (➤ 64).

Café A Brasileira: Lisbon's most famous café in the heart of classy Chiado (➤ 60–61).

Café Nicola: Historic café, right on the Rossio, with some of the best people-watching in Lisbon (➤ 64).

Esplanada da Igreja da Graça: Wonderful views and plenty of locals (➤ 94, 179).

Best Excursions

A day in Sintra: For palaces, gardens, hills, great views, high-class shopping and the best *queijada* (sweet cheese tart) in town (➤ 164).

An outing to Queluz: Picture-postcard palace with a beautiful garden (➤ 167).

A bit of beachcombing: Head for Cascais and the wild coast of Guincho and Cabo da Roca (➤ 162).

A taste of architectural splendour: The vast monastery-palace complex of Mafra (➤ 170–172).

If You Only Go To One

Church: São Vicente de Fora (➤ 80–81), for stunning architecture, beautiful *azulejos* and stupendous views.

Museum: It has to be the Museu Calouste Gulbenkian (➤ 55–59), one of the world's finest collections.

Bar: Cerca Moura (➤ 94), where there's the choice of an interior built within the Moorish city walls or an *esplanada* on one of the best lookout squares in Lisbon.

Restaurant: You'll find delicious Portuguese cooking in the super-cool Pap' Açorda (➤ 113), in the heart of the Bairro Alto.

Finding Your Feet

First Two Hours

Arriving by Air

Aeroporto de Lisboa (Portela)
- **Lisbon's airport** (tel: 218 413 500; flight information tel: 218 413 700; www.ana-aeroportos.pt) handles international and domestic flights.
- There are **flights direct to Lisbon** from London Heathrow, London Gatwick and London Luton.
- TAP, Portugal's national airline, and Continental each have a **daily direct flight from Newark, NY.**

Airport Transfers
- **Portela** lies 7km (4 miles) northeast of Lisbon centre and is connected to the city by airport buses, normal city buses and taxis, all of which leave from outside the arrivals level of the airport. Before exiting the terminal pick up a copy of *Your Guide*, an information-packed booklet on Lisbon displayed in racks throughout the airport.
- **Taxis** (beige or black and green) are the fastest and most expensive way of reaching downtown Lisbon; expect to pay between €15 and €20 for up to 4 people with an additional charge for extra-large pieces of luggage. The journey time is 20–40 minutes.
- The No 91 **Aerobus**, run by Carris, the city transport company, departs every 20 minutes for the centre between 7:40am and 8:45pm. Tickets are purchased on board. You can opt for a single ticket or a 1-day city transport ticket which is valid for buses and trams throughout Lisbon for the rest of your arrival day. The Aerobus stops at the Avenida da Liberdade, Rossio and Praça do Comércio before terminating at Cais do Sodré.
- **Regular city buses** (Nos 5, 21, 22, 44, 45 and 83) leave the airport for various areas of Lisbon with a similar fare structure to the Aerobus.

Arriving by Train
- Passengers arriving by **train from northern Portugal**, Spain or France will arrive at **Santa Apolónia** (tel: 808 208 208) to the east of the city centre. There is a **taxi rank** outside the station and bus stops for regular Carris services.
- Alternatively, passengers can alight at the **Gare do Oriente** station at the Parque das Nações and connect with the **metro system**.
- If you are arriving from the **south of Portugal**, trains terminate at **Gare do Oriente**.
- Alternatively, or you can get off at **Entrecampos** station, which is more central. You can connect here with the **metro system**.

Arriving by Road
- If you are driving to Lisbon, **all routes run through Spain**. The best and safest option is the **E90**, which runs from Madrid via Badajoz. Once in Portugal, it becomes the A6/A2 and heads through the Alentejo to Palmela, where you can choose to continue on the A2 to reach Lisbon via the Ponte 25 de Abril to the city's west, or take the A12 and cross the Tejo on the Ponte Vasco da Gama to the east.

- Alternatively, you can take the **E80** from Salamanca, which becomes the A25 at Vilar Formosa, then the A23 at Guarda, and approaches Lisbon via Castelo Branco and the A1 Porto–Lisbon motorway.
- **Parking** in Lisbon is at a premium, very few hotels have private car parks.
- **Underground car parks**, run by the council and marked with a white "P" on a blue background are the best bet, but charges can mount up. If you park on the street downtown, you may be met by *arrumadores*, who will expect a tip in return for guiding you to a place and keeping an eye on your car; it is advisable to pay.

Tourist Information Offices

You can get tourist information toll-free free on tel: 808 781 212. The best offices are the Lisboa Welcome Centre and Palácio Foz; the latter also has information for the rest of Portugal.

- ✉ Aeroporto (arrivals) ☎ 218 450 660 🕓 7am–midnight
- ✉ Baixa, Rua Augusta (kiosk) 🕓 213 259 131 🕓 10–1, 2–6
- ✉ Lisboa Welcome Centre, Praça do Comércio, Loja 1 🕓 210 312 810 🕓 9–8
- ✉ Restauradores, Palácio Foz 🕓 213 463 314 🕓 9–8
- ✉ Santa Apolónia 🕓 218 821 606 🕓 Tue–Sat 8–1, 2–4
- ✉ Belém, Mosteiro dos Jerónimos 🕓 213 658 435/6/7 🕓 Tue–Sat 10–1, 2–6

Getting Around

Lisbon's transport system includes the metro, buses, trams, funiculars and elevators. Carris runs Lisbon's overground services, an integrated network that includes buses, trams and elevators, all fairly frequent, cheap and reliable. You will be able to see everything you want by using just a few routes – though make sure one of these includes an iconic tram ride.

Carris

You can get information on Carris services at the Carristur booth at the foot of the Santa Justa elevator, at the kiosks in Praça da Figueira, Restauradores, Cais de Sodré or at any tourist office (tel: 213 613 000; www.carris.pt). Transport details, ticket information and free transport maps are available.

Metro

Lisbon's metro (Metropolitano), radically restructured for Expo 98, is a slick and efficient way of getting around much of the city. There are four lines, with interchanges between them at Baixa-Chiado, Marquês de Pombal, Alameda and Campo Grande (www.metrolisboa.pt).

- **Trains** run 6:30am–1am.
- **Entrances** are marked with a white "M" on a red background.
- **Tickets** cost €0.70 per journey or €6.65 for the 10-trip ticket (*caderneta*). You can also buy a 1- or 5-day (€3.35 or €13.20) rechargeable *Cartão 7 Colinas* card, valid for both Carris and metro services.
- **Validate** or swipe your ticket in the box beside the entrance barrier.
- **Clear information boards**, corresponding in colour to the line you're on, indicate direction of travel by the name of the end-of-line station.
- **Metro maps** are available at main stations.

Buses

■ Single-decker **buses** (*autocarros*) cover the whole city, and can be very crowded. There are few seats, so be prepared to stand and, although Lisbon has a very low crime rate, watch your pockets and belongings.

■ **Bus stops** show the route number and list the stops along the line. The stop where you are is indicated.

■ **Board** at the front and validate or swipe your ticket. Exit towards the rear.

■ Carris operates a **night service** (*madrugada*) along the main routes; this runs 11:45pm–5:30am, depending on the route.

Trams and Funiculars

■ Lisbon's wonderful **trams** (*eléctricos*) are worth taking for the pleasure of the ride. They run along five routes and ascend some of the steepest city gradients in the world. The old-fashioned, traditional trams, numbers 28, 12 and 25, cover the heart of the old city, with 18 running west towards Belém and a new "supertram", number 15, heading along the river from Cais do Sodré through Belém to Algés.

■ There are three useful **funiculars** (*elevadores*), Bica, Glória and Lavra, which offer quick routes from the Baixa up to the Bairro Alto. The Santa Justa lift links the Baixa with the Largo do Carmo.

Taxis

■ Lisbon **taxis** are either cream or black-and-green; **a green light indicates they are free** and the **red number indicates the tariff in force**. All have meters – check to see it's switched on – and tips are discretionary.

■ There are various **city-centre ranks**, including Rossio, Fluvial, Praça da Figueira, Chiado, Largo da Misericórdia and Avenida da Liberdade.

■ Taxis are **inexpensive**, with fares rising after 9pm and at weekends and public holidays. You can call a cab by phoning Autocoope (tel: 217 932 756), Rádio Taxis (tel: 218 119 000), or Teletaxis (tel: 218 111 100).

Ferries

Ferries across the Tejo leave from various points throughout the day. **Terreiro do Paço (Praça do Comércio) river station** links Lisbon with Montijo, Seixal and Alcochete. **Cais do Sodré river station** links Lisbon with Cacilhas. There's also a service from the **Parque das Nações** to Cacilhas, and from **Belém** to Trafaria. Buy your tickets at the ferry point; a single costs between €0.74 and €2.20 depending on the crossing (returns are not available).

Car Rental

If you want to **rent a car** while in Lisbon, all the major international firms have outlets at the airport and in the city, though it may be cheaper to arrange a deal before you leave home. To contact a car hire firm call:
Avis (tel: 800 201 002; www.avis.com)
Budget (tel: 808 252 627; www.budget.com)
Europcar (tel: 219 407 790; www.europcar.com)
Hertz (tel: 219 426 300; www.hertz.com)

Tickets and Travel Cards

Buy tickets before boarding at the Carris kiosks and at shops and kiosks displaying the Carris logo. Single-journey tickets can be bought on board.

Types

■ **Cartão 7 Colinas**: travel passes valid for either 1 day (€3.25) or 5 days (€13.20) for buses, trams, elevators and the metro.

- **Bilhete Simples Rede**: 1-day travel pass (€3.25) valid from purchase time until midnight on buses, trams, elevators and the metro.
- **Bilhete de Bordo**: Single journey tickets (€1.30) available on board and only valid in one zone.
- **Bilhete Metro**: Single €0.75, return €1.35.
- **Bilhete Simple Urbano**: Single ticket valid for unlimited bus travel and one metro journey over the course of one hour €1.15.
- If you have any sort of **combination ticket**, it must be validated the first time you use it; the **Cartão 7 Colinas** will automatically validate the first time it's swiped.

Travellers with Disabilities

Portugal has considerable problems providing facilities for travellers with a disability in Lisbon, where the difficulties lie in the very nature of this ancient and hilly city, and the overall picture lags far behind that in northern European countries and north America.

- **Taxis** can take wheelchairs folded and stored in the boot, but getting in and out may be difficult for passengers.
- There is a Dial-a-ride **bus service for people with disabilities** (tel: 213 613 141; www.carris.pt). It operates Mon–Fri 6:30–10, Sat–Sun 8–10. Each trip costs €1.30. Rides require 1 days' notice, but before using the service you must present a medical certificate, ID and photo at the Carris headquarters in Santo Amaro so they can issue a users card.
- Buses do **not** have wheelchair access.
- Some **metro** stations have lifts to the platforms.
- **Guide dogs for the blind** travel free.
- **Book well ahead** and be specific about your requirements when booking accommodation.
- **Secretariado Nacional de Reabilitação**, Conde de Valbom 63, 1069–1178 Lisboa (tel: 217 929 500; www.snripd.pt). This Government-run site provides information on transport facilities (Portuguese only). It also publishes an *Accessible Tourism Guide* with comprehensive listings of hotels, travel agents, restaurants, clubs etc.

Local Trains

If you're visiting Cascais, Estoril, Queluz or Sintra you can get there by **local train**. Trains run from Cais do Sodré to Estoril and Cascais and also stop at Belém. For Queluz and Sintra, catch the train at Sete Rios station. The Lisbon Card includes travel on these trains.

Lisbon Card

If you're planning a lot of travelling and sight-seeing in Lisbon, consider investing in the Lisbon Card (*Cartão Lisboa*), available at tourist offices. This gives unlimited travel on buses, trams, elevators and the metro and free, or substantially reduced, entry to many of the main sights (1-day card €14.85, 2-day card €25.50, 3-day card €31).

Admission Charges

The cost of admission for museums and places of interest mentioned in the text is indicated by the following price categories.

Inexpensive under €3 **Moderate** €3–€5 **Expensive** over €5

Accommodation

As Lisbon becomes an increasingly year-round destination, you can ensure peace of mind and a better choice by booking in advance, bearing in mind that prices may soar during the peak months. There's accommodation to suit everyone, ranging from historic, luxury hotels to modern establishments catering for business travellers, and a huge range of modest *pensões*, many of them right in the historic heart of the city. Choose somewhere in the Baixa, Chiado or Alfama areas to be in the heart of the action, though be warned that rooms overlooking the street here can be very noisy – central, quieter possibilities exist in the streets below the Castelo. For something more peaceful and with plenty of choice, check out the hotels on and around the Avenida de Liberdade or head out to the prosperous suburb of Lapa, where some of Lisbon's best hotels, often housed in elegant and historic buildings, are found.

Tips
- **Advance booking** is vital in July and August.
- Hotels in Portugal are graded from between **one to five stars**, with comfort, facilities and service reflected in the price and rating.
- *Pensões* and *residenciais* are a good budget choice, their main distinction being that *residenciais* are unlikely to serve meals other than breakfast. They are classified from 1 to 3 stars, a 3-star *pensão* costs roughly the same as a 1-star hotel.
- Portuguese hotels and *pensões* are legally **required to post the room rates** on the back of the bedroom doors. This should also include IVA (VAT).
- Rates **vary according to season**, sometimes by as much as 40 per cent.
- **Agree a price** before you make a reservation, and ask for written confirmation if you're booking ahead from home.
- Hotels will often quote their most expensive rates; **ask if they have cheaper rooms**.
- Hotels will put an **extra bed** in the room for a small charge; ideal for families with children.
- It's perfectly acceptable to **ask to see the room** before you take it.
- If you're considering a city-centre *pensão*, remember that many are accessed **several flights of steps** above street level and lifts are rare.
- You'll be asked to **leave your passport** when you check in at reception. Don't forget to collect it later.
- **Check-out time** is normally noon, but some hotels will keep your luggage until the end of the day.
- It's worth **looking at Internet sites** such as www.lastminute.com, www.expedia.com and www.laterooms.com to see if they are offering a good price for your chosen hotel.
- If you are interested in **self-catering** in a city-centre apartment check out www.holiday-rentals.co.uk for a wide variety of properties.

Information
- **Lisbon's tourist offices** will not book accommodation for you, but they do have lists of hotels which you can then telephone yourself.
- There's an **information desk** at the airport and the main office is in the Praça do Comércio (daily 9–8; tel: 210 312 810/15; www.visitlisboa.com).
- Many Lisbon hotels have their own **websites** with photos, prices, general information and an on-line booking service.

Prices

Prices are for a double room with private bathroom per night:
€ Under €100   €€ €100–€150   €€€ €151–€300   €€€€ over €300

Albergaria Senhora do Monte €–€€

The atmospheric Graça quarter, close to the city centre, is home to this cosy little hotel, whose south-facing rooms, some with private terraces, are well worth the extra price for the splendid views across the city and the Tejo. All are clean and comfortable, the owners friendly, and you can enjoy coffee with a view from the rooftop breakfast bar.

➕ 198 B3/4 ✉ Calçada do Monte 39, Graça ☎ 218 866 002; www.maisturismo.pt/sramonte.html
🚋 Tram 28, 12

As Janelas Verdes €€€

This charming hotel is housed in an antique-crammed 18th-century mansion, where the public rooms feel more like those of a private house. Rooms are well-equipped and pretty, the staff combine professionalism with friendliness, and the honour-bar, breakfast patio and lovely top-floor terrace and library add to the feeling of home as it should be.

➕ 196 B1 ✉ Rua da Janelas Verdes 47, Lapa ☎ 213 968 143; www.heritage.pt 🚇 Santos

Duas Nações €

Book in advance to ensure a room with its own bathroom in this excellent-value hotel in the heart of the pedestrianised Baixa. It occupies a 19th-century town house which has been refurbished to provide modest, impeccably clean rooms, some of which have shared bathrooms. Avoid those overlooking the Rua Augusta, which can be noisy. The price includes a good buffet breakfast served in an airy Portuguese-style dining room characterised by bright tiled panels and dark wood.

➕ 198 A2 ✉ Rua da Vitoria 41, Baixa ☎ 213 460 710; www.duasnacoes.com
🚇 Baixa-Chiado

Hotel Métropole €€–€€€

Stay in the heart of the action on the west side of Rossio in this elegant and traditional hotel, which first opened its doors in 1917 and underwent a huge makeover in 1993. This restored many of the original features, such as the marble bathrooms, while adding essential modern comforts like the efficient double glazing that ensures a restful night. The top-floor rooms overlooking the square have superb views of the Castelo.

➕ 198 A2 ✉ Praça Dom Pedro IV 30, Rossio ☎ 213 219 030; www.almeidahotels.com 🚇 Rossio

Lapa Palace €€€€

The Count of Valenca built this 19th-century palace in the fashionable Lapa neighbourhood, overlooking the broad stretch of the Tejo. Guests can relax in the peaceful gardens or use the pool before heading for the beautifully restored opulence of the interior. Rooms and suites are decorated in a variety of styles ranging from oriental to art deco, but all justify the hotel's reputation as one of Lisbon's most luxurious and expensive places to stay.

➕ 196 A2 ✉ Rua do Pau da Bandeira 4, Lapa ☎ 213 949 494; www.lapapalace.com 🚇 Santos

Lisboa Regency Chiado €€€

You'll find yourself in the heart of Lisbon's smartest shopping area in this modern boutique hotel with its fabulous views towards the old Alfama quarter and the Castelo. Bedrooms are a heady fusion of Portuguese and oriental design, combining rich colour, dark woods and clean-lined design, and all have up-to the-minute comfort and facilities. You can enjoy what's considered to be one of Lisbon's best breakfast buffets while gazing over the rooftops from the huge bay windows of the dining room.

➕ 198 A2 ✉ Rua Nova do Almada 114, Chiado ☎ 213 256 100; www.regency-hotels-resorts.com Ⓜ Baixa-Chiado

Palácio de Belmonte €€€€

Once the home of the earls of Belmonte, this beautiful 16th-century palace is one of the world's great luxury hotels. State-of-the-art comfort combines with understated luxury and elegance in each individual suite, where superb 18th-century *azulejos* and rich colours echo the hues of Lisbon, seen at its best from the terraces. The garden is peaceful and elegant, with a black marble pool for cooling off after a day's sightseeing.

➕ 198 B2 ✉ Páteo Dom Fradique 14, Alfama ☎ 218 816 600; www.palaciobelmonte.com 🚋 Tram 28

Pensão Alegria €

Book ahead at this welcoming guest house to ensure one of the rooms at the back, overlooking the aptly named "happiness" square, with its rows of palm trees. Rooms are spare and airy, with wooden floors, cheery fabrics and spotlessly clean private bathrooms. Breakfast is served but no other meals.

➕ 197 E4 ✉ Praça de Alegria 12 ☎ 213 220 670 Ⓜ Avenida

Pensão Residencial Royal €

One of the best budget deals in town, the Royal is housed over three floors in the heart of the Baixa, with restaurants and cafés all around. No breakfast is served, but all the freshly decorated, bright, clean rooms have their own bathrooms and many are decorated with lovely antique tiles. The upper floor of the same building is home to the even cheaper Galicia (tel: 213 428 430), a simpler establishment which may have rooms if the Royal is full.

➕ 198 A2 ✉ Rua do Crucifixo 50, 3rd floor, Baixa ☎ 213 479 006 Ⓜ Baixa-Chiado

Residencial Avenida Parque €

The rooms of this great value *residencial* overlooking Parque Eduardo VII wouldn't disgrace a 3-star hotel, with modern, light furniture, colour-coordinated soft furnishings and double glazing to ensure quiet nights. From the modern marbled entrance hall an elegant wooden staircase leads up to the rooms, some of which have balconies, while breakfast is served in the ground-floor dining room.

➕ 194 C3 ✉ Avenida Sidónio Pais 6 ☎ 213 532 181; www.avenidaparque.com Ⓜ Parque, Marquês de Pombal

VIP Inn Veneza €

The facade of this palatial town house gives a taste of the delights within. Wrought iron and polished wood highlight the colourful mural of Lisbon that adorns the monumental staircase, while the colour-coordinated bedrooms are spacious, comfortable and well equipped. The staff are friendly and efficient. As prices are lower than those at many similar hotels, and good transport links, this hotel represents excellent value for money.

➕ 197 E4 ✉ Avenidade da Liberdade 189 ☎ 213 522 618; www.viphotels.com Ⓜ Avenida

York House €€€

Climb the steps to the flower-filled courtyard of this former Carmelite convent and discover one of Lisbon's classiest hotels, which gets its name from the Yorkshire ladies who first ran a guest house here in the 1880s. Rooms range from traditional to minimalist-chic, and there are deep sofas and artwork and antiques to add to the atmosphere. Breakfast is served outside in summer and the hotel's restaurant deserves its excellent reputation for its traditional Portuguese cuisine.

➕ 196 B1 ✉ Rua das Janelas Verdes 32, Lapa ☎ 213 962 435; www.york-houselisboa.com ℝ Santos

Food and Drink

Sampling local food and drink is one of the major pleasures when you're abroad and Lisbon, whose restaurants serve food from every corner of the country, has something for every taste. The range of foods and dishes reflects the country's history and culture, with the accent firmly on fresh, seasonal, local produce – and plenty of it. Foreign invaders left their mark on Portugal's food and drink, while the coast and great sea voyages of discovery produced a passion for fish and seafood, and spices and ingredients from across the globe. If it's good, it's excellent, though pick and choose your eating place; anywhere, at any price level, that's patronised by the locals should more than fit the bill.

Meals in Lisbon

- **Breakfast** (*pequeno-almoço*) is usually eaten 8–9am and is often taken at a café; hotels serve the usual buffet-style international breakfast.
- **Lunch** (*almoço*), served 12–3, is normally a 2- or 3-course meal
- **Dinner** (*jantar*) normally starts around 7:30pm; the pattern of the meal is similar to that of lunch.
- Menus will sometimes advertise the *ementa turística*: this is not a tourist menu, but the **set meal of the day**. The price includes two courses and beer or wine and can be excellent value.
- Once you are seated, bread and a selection of small starters will be placed on the table. These range from butter, fish paté and olives, to cheese, *chouriço* and more elaborate little dishes. They are **not complimentary** and you will be charged for what you eat.
- Only the more expensive restaurants take reservations, and **you should book ahead** during the peak season or at weekends.
- Except in top-of-the-range restaurants, there is **no need to dress up**.

Culinary Terms

Sopa/ensopado soup/stew
Marisco shellfish
Peixe fish
Carne meat
Aves e caça poultry and game
Legumes vegetables
Sobremesa pudding
Fruta fruit
Queijo cheese

Types of Restaurant

- *Restaurantes* are straightforward restaurants and are normally open 12–3pm for lunch and 7–10pm for dinner; they are more likely to take credit cards than other eating places.
- A *casa de pasto* or *tasca* is a cheap, often family-run, local dining room, offering budget three-course meals, mainly at lunch time only.
- A *marisqueira* is a seafood restaurant, where both shellfish and fish are served. Menu prices are in kilos, and will add up fast.
- *Churrasqueiras* are family-style restaurants that specialise in *frango no churrasco* (char-grilled chicken), served with piri-piri (hot chilli sauce) though they do serve other grilled food.
- *Cervejarias* primarily serve beer, simple meals and snacks, and are open all day and late into the evening.

Drinks and Snacks

■ **Cafés** and **bars** are open from early morning until late, serving excellent coffee – *bica* or *café*, a short black espresso; *meia de leite* or *galão,* a long milky coffee; and *garoto,* espresso with a dash of milk, are the types to remember. Tea, soft drinks and alcohol are also served. Prices are generally higher if you sit down. Cafés also serve a variety of snacks, from breakfast pastries to lunch-time specials and sandwiches (*sandes*).

■ *Casas de chá* could have been invented to supply that essential sugar hit so loved by the Portuguese. They serve a range of excellent teas, including herbal infusions, coffee and a sometimes overwhelming range of sweet goodies.

■ *Pastelarias* are pastry shops, and you should look for the words *fabrico próprio* (home production) on the facade or window.

■ **Beer** (*cerveja*) is widely drunk in quantity. The main brands are Sagres, and Super Bock.

■ **Wine** (*vinho*) comes in a bewildering range; Portugal has over 50 wine regions and many wines are unavailable overseas. The country is divided into eight official regions; more specific is the DOC denomination, which guarantees the provenance. Look out too for *vinhos de mesa* (table wines) which are less expensive.

■ **Spirits** are known by their generic names, while Portugal's own spirit is *aguardente*, a type of brandy that can be made from a wide variety of fruits and is also distilled from the leftover grape skins and pips. Very high in proof (50 per cent), it should be handled with care – Lisbon's own *aguardente* is *ginjinha* (cherry spirit).

■ **Port** (*vinho do Porto*) makes a superb after-dinner drink, though don't miss the chance to try white port (*porto branco*) as an aperitif. Varieties of port include vintage, late bottled port (LBV), tawny and ruby.

■ **Madeira** (*vinho da Madeira*) is made by fermenting and fortifying grape juice before heating it; the varieties are Sercial, Verdelho, Bual and Malvasia.

Special Requirements

■ **Vegetarians** and those on a **gluten-free diet** may find it difficult to find suitable meals in Portugal. Even seemingly innocuous soups, rice and bean dishes will be based on meat stock or enlivened with small pieces of bacon or sausage and bread is an integral part of cooking. If you eat fish there's no problem, but otherwise you may find there's little on the menu except cheese, an omelette or salad. Even straightforward vegetable dishes may contain pork fat, so it's always best to ask. The waiter will do his best to help get the message through to the kitchen, but bear in mind that vegetarianism is a totally alien concept to the meat-loving Portuguese.

The Best For...

Traditional Portuguese – Gambrinus (➤ 64–65)
Coffee and cake – Café Nicola (➤ 64)
Food with a view – Mercado de Santa Clara (➤ 93)
Food and style – Pap' Açorda (➤ 113)
Portuguese ambience – Trindade (➤ 65)

Prices

Expect to pay for a three-course meal for one, excluding drinks:
€ under €20   €€ €20–€40   €€€ over €40

Shopping

Lisbon has everything from the country's biggest and best malls to a great range of idiosyncratic specialist shops, and boutiques crammed with cutting-edge fashion. They sell goods from all over the country, making it a great place to buy artisan work or ceramics. The same goes for food gifts, with port, wines and delicacies from around Portugal all on sale. Don't miss the chance to browse the city's markets, where you'll find everything from fresh food to clothes, antiques and bric-à-brac.

Local Specialities

■ **Ceramics and pottery**: Domestic and decorative earthenware from all over Portugal; Vista Alegre porcelain, hand-painted *azulejos* (tiles).

■ **Textiles**: Superb table linen, curtains, silk-embroidered linen bedspreads (*colchas*) from Castelo Branco and rugs from Arraiolos.

■ **Leather**: Competitively priced shoes and leather goods, including gloves.

■ **Jewellery**: Exquisitely worked, traditionally designed jewellery and quirkier modern pieces.

■ **Woodwork and basketware**: This Portuguese speciality is available in artisan shops throughout the city.

■ **Food and wine**: Specialist food and wine from all over Portugal; cheese, *presunto* (cured, dried ham), honey, olive oil, piri-piri sauce, *doces conventuais* (convent sweets), port and Madeira make excellent souvenirs.

Shopping Areas

Chiado and Baixa: Trendy shopping, designer names and traditional shops.
Bairro Alto: Boutiques and quirky shops of all description.
Avenida da Liberade: International big-name designer clothes and shoes.
Campo de Ourique: Chic boutiques, furnishings and household goods.
São Bento: Antiques, ceramics, glass and classy housewares.
Rua de Escola Politénica: Traditional handicrafts.

Shopping Centres (Malls)

Armazéns do Chiado 🚇 Baixa-Chiado
Centro Comercial Amoreiras 🚇 Marques de Pombal/Rato
Centro Comercial Colombo 🚇 Colégio Miltar
Centro Comercial Vasco da Gama (► 154) 🚇 Oriente
Galerias Saldanha 🚇 Saldanha
El Corte Inglés 🚇 São Sebastião

Markets

Feira da Ladra (► 89) 🚊 Tram 28
Praça de Espanha: Cut-price general goods 🚇 Praça de Espanha)
Mercado do Campo de Ourique: Food market 🚊 Tram 25/28
Mercado da Ribeira (► 60) 🚇 Cais do Sodré
Feira de Carcavelos: Clothes and household goods 🕐 Thu 8–1 🚆 From Cais do Sodré to Carcavelos

Tax-Free Shopping and Shipping

Residents of non-EU states can claim back IVA (value-added tax) for goods purchased at shops that are part of the Tax-free scheme. These stores will have a sticker displayed in the window. You claim by filling in a form available at the Tax-free counter at the departure airport. Many stores will pack and ship overseas, but costs can be high.

Entertainment

Lisbon has the country's widest range of entertainment with something to suit every taste and budget. Options range from theatre, music and cinema to late-night clubbing and traditional *fado*, while sports fans could catch a football match or head towards the coast for a round of golf.

Information and Ticketing

■ The best **listings** magazine is the *Agenda Cultural*, a free monthly that's published in Portuguese only, though much of its information also appears in the *Follow Me Lisboa* booklet (in English) produced by the tourist board. You can pick up them up at city tourist offices.

■ The **Gulbenkian** and the **Belém Cultural Centre** publish a monthly schedule.

■ The *Diário de Notícias* and *O Independente*, publish **Friday supplements** with full entertainment listings.

You can book ahead for different events at the following ticket outlets:

ABEP (Agência de Bilhetes para Espectáculos Públicos)
✉ Praça dos Restauradores ☎ 213 425 360 🕒 Mon–Sat 9am–9:30pm Ⓜ Restauradores

Fnac Chiado
✉ Armazéns do Chiado, Rua do Carmo 2, Loja 407, Chiado ☎ 213 221 800; www.fnac.pt 🕒 Daily10–10 Ⓜ Baixa-Chiado

Entertainment

■ **Cinema**: All films are shown in their original language with Portuguese sub-titles; there are afternoon and evening performances. The main shopping malls all have multi-screen cinemas.

■ **Classical music, ballet, dance**: Lisbon has three orchestras, a ballet company and a contemporary dance company. The season runs Oct–May.

■ **Contemporary music**: International stars and artists from Brazil, Africa and Cape Verde.

■ *Fado*: Catch it in *fado* clubs in the Bairro Alto.

■ **Theatre**: There are occasional runs of international musicals, but most performances are in Portuguese.

Nightlife

■ **Bars and nightclubs:** Most bars open around 8pm and nightclubs at midnight, with things getting going near 2am and continuing through till 5am or later. Many bars **feature live music** some nights of the week

■ The traditional place for night-time action has always been the **Bairro Alto**, though this area now concentrates more on late bars than **dance venues**. The most exciting dance venues are down by the waterside, around **Santa Apolónia** and the **Doca de Santo Amaro** beneath the Ponte 25 de Abril. Other hot spots are around **Avenida 24 de Julho** and in **Alcântara**.

■ Many clubs operate on a "*consumo mínimo*" system which refers to the minimum amount that you have to spend while in the club and acts as a type of admission charge; it may include one or more drinks.

Gay and Lesbian Nightlife

To check out what's what, pick up a copy of the quarterly men's magazine *Korpus* or, for women, *Zona Livre*. Most gay bars and clubs are found in the Bairro Alto and Príncipe Real. The **Centro Comunitário Gay e Lesbico de Lisboa** (tel: 218 873 918; www.portugalgay.pt) is a good starting point for contacts and information.

North from the Central Waterfront

Getting Your Bearings 42 – 43
In a Day 44 – 45
Don't Miss 46 – 59
At Your Leisure 60 – 63
Where to... 64 – 66

Getting Your Bearings

The Baixa, the elegant grid of 18th-century streets built to replace the old downtown area destroyed in the catastrophic earthquake of 1755, stretches back from the waterfront to central Lisbon's main squares, the beguiling trio of Praça Dom Pedro IV, known as Rossio, Figueira and Restauradores. Fronted by the huge sweep of the riverside Praça do Comércio and approached through a triumphal arch, this superb example of rational design occupies the flat land between two hills. To the east lies old Lisbon, to the west, the Chiado *bairro*, home to historic buildings, museums, theatres, cafés and some of the city's most elegant shops. These western slopes rise steeply, and 19th-century engineers linked the highest point of Chiado to the Baixa by means of the Elevador de Santa Justa, whose upper platform gives glorious views of the city and river.

The furthest of the three squares, Restauradores, heralds the start of the Avenida da Liberdade, a tree-lined boulevard completed in the late 19th century, which acts as an axis connecting the 18th-century Baixa with the new 19th-century city areas. Home to smart hotels and upmarket shops, the avenida ends with a flourish at the Praça Marquês de Pombal, behind which stretches the Parque Eduardo VII, named in 1903 in honour of King Edward VII's visit to Portugal. From here, it's a few long city blocks to the Museu Calouste Gulbenkian, Lisbon's most stunning museum, which ranks among the greatest in the world.

Previous page: View from the Elevador de Santa Justa

Below: Statue of Dom Pedro IV in Rossio Square

★ **Don't Miss**

1 The Baixa ➤ 46
2 Chiado and Santa Justa ➤ 50
3 Rossio, Figueira and Restauradores ➤ 52
4 Museu Calouste Gulbenkian ➤ 55

Off the Beaten Track

11 Museu da Cidade ➤ 63
12 Museu Bordalo Pinheiro ➤ 63

Islamic art at the Gulbenkian

At Your Leisure

5 Cais do Sodré and Mercado de Ribeira ➤ 60
6 Museu do Chiado ➤ 60
7 Café A Brasileira ➤ 60
8 Museu Arqueológico do Carmo ➤ 61
9 Parque Eduardo VII ➤ 62
10 Centro de Arte Moderna ➤ 62

This iconic central area is home to the elegant 18th-century streets of the Baixa, which surround the city's main squares, and give access to the 19th-century avenues leading to Lisbon's finest museum – the Museu Calouste Gulbenkian.

North from the Central Waterfront in a Day

9:00am

Start your exploration of **❶ The Baixa** (► 46–49) in the Praça do Comércio, strolling through the arcades before passing under the Arco Triunfal (left) into Rua Augusta. Explore this atmospheric grid of streets before heading to Rua do Ouro and taking the **Elevador de Santa Justa** (► 50, 176) up to the Largo do Carmo, for superb views over the city and the Tejo.

10:00am

Stroll downhill towards Rua Garrett, one of 19th-century Lisbon's most fashionable streets, and pause for coffee at the historic **❼ Café A Brasileira** (► 60–61), before spending time either visiting the **❻ Museu do Chiado** (► 60) or the **❽ Museu Arqueológico do Carmo** (► 61), or indulging in some retail therapy. Keen shoppers will find tempting modern stores in the Armazéns do Chiado mall (► 65) and some of Lisbon's quirkiest and most individual shops in Rua Garrett and Rua do Carmo.

12:00 noon

Head down the Rua do Carmo towards the iconic **❸ Rossio** (► 52–53), downtown Lisbon's crossroads, with its cafés and hurrying crowds, from where it's just a few paces to the area's other main squares, the **❸ Praça da Figueira** and **Restauradores** (► 53–54).

1:00pm

You'll find plenty of choice for lunch in the Rua das Portas de Santo Antão and the surrounding alleys, which stretch north behind Rossio – a good bet would be to head for Bonjardim (► 64), grab a table outside and soak up the sun while you eat succulent chicken and some of the best chips in town.

2:30pm

Allow yourself half an hour or so to get up to the **4 Museu Calouste Gulbenkian** (► 55–59); spare your feet by taking a taxi or hop on the metro from Baixa-Chiado to S Sebastão. Spend a couple of hours marvelling at the treasures in this intimate, varied and superb collection, the gift of an oil-magnate to Portugal.

4:30pm

You could relax after your visit either in the museum's own lovely gardens, with their pools and cool greenery, or head down to the formal green spaces and parterres of the **9 Parque Eduardo VII** (► 62; left), a garden-lover's delight.

6:00pm

Join the late afternoon crowds in **3 Rossio**, and enjoy either tea and a mouth-watering pastry or drink at Café Suíça (Praça Dom Pedro IV 96–100, tel: 213 214 090) or Café Nicola (► 64) which has been in business since 1929.

8:00pm

There's a huge choice of places to eat in this central area, but be sure to return to the Baixa (left) later and enjoy the wonderful late-night atmosphere, when the years roll away and the sense of its historical elegance is strongest – you could round off your day with a nightcap at the Café Martinho da Arcada (► 64) in the Praça do Comércio.

◻ The Baixa

The Baixa, a superb example of 18th-century town planning, lies at the heart of Lisbon. Its arrow-straight streets, the huge space of its main square, the clean, regular lines of its houses, the tiled fronts of its idiosyncratic little shops and its street life all combine to encapsulate the city's spirit. This is architecture on an inspired scale, whose construction changed the face of the city and created a central area that draws both *lisboetas* and every city visitor.

The Baixa – literally lower area – owes its existence to one of Europe's worst natural disasters, when, in 1755, Lisbon suffered one of the most catastrophic recorded earthquakes (▶ 20–21), which, besides killing thousands, destroyed much of the historic centre, including the entire area behind the waterfront Terreiro do Paço, site of the Royal Palace. Drastic times called for drastic measures, and the Marquês de Pombal, Portugal's First Minister, was commissioned by the king to rebuild the area along the most up-to-date lines. He envisioned a grid of ordered streets, 12m (40 feet) wide and lined with elegant, classical buildings, and called on Eugénio dos Santos, a military engineer, to help him realise the dream. The design was based on a military encampment, with specific thoroughfares for specific activities, and the street names and occupants continue to echo this – you'll still find jewellers in the **Rua do Ouro** (Gold Street) and the **Rua da Prata** (Silver Street), shoe menders in the **Rua dos Sapateiros** and textile and fabric merchants in the **Rua dos Fanqueiros**.

Looking down on the Baixa at night

One of the best ways to comprehend Pombal's grandiose scheme is to take the short ferry trip across the river from the Estação Fluvial on the Praça do Comércio's eastern side simply to enjoy the return journey and a sight of the square as it was designed to be approached.

The Baixa lies tucked between Chiado, rising to the west, and the Alfama to the east, and is bounded on the north by the square known as **Rossio**, properly called Praça Dom Pedro IV (➤ 52–53), and the waterfront **Praça do Comércio** to the south. This great square, lined with arcades, occupies the site of the medieval expanse of the Terreiro do Paço, destroyed, as was everything around, during the earthquake. Post-earth-quake, Pombal called for a majestic square, fit to rival anything in Europe, which would act as a grand theatrical arrival stage for kings, presidents and ambassadors. Its buildings were designed to house government ministries; some still do, and Lisbon's town hall, the **Câmara Municipal**, continues to occupy its purpose-built classical 19th-century building in the elegant **Praça do Município**, just off the west side of the square. It was from its grand balcony that the Portuguese republic was proclaimed in 1910, and the square is still used

Arcade in
the Praça do
Comércio

for the annual Republic Day celebrations on 5 October. Lording it over Comércio is the 14m-high (46-foot) **equestrian statue of Dom José I**, who reigned at the time of the earthquake and commissioned Pombal's reconstruction. Joaquim Machado de Castro was the sculptor, and the base is decorated with figures representing the "Victory" of the new buildings over the "Destruction" caused by the earthquake. The arcades are home to the historic Café Martinho da Arcada, founded in 1782, where Lisbon's favourite poet, Fernando Pessoa was a regular in the 1920s and 1930s. Pessoa (1888–1935) came here night after night to work on his epic poem, *Mensagem*, and his marble-topped table is still lovingly preserved. José Saramago, the Portuguese novelist who won the Nobel Prize for literature in 1998, was another frequent visitor; his best-known work for English readers is probably his homage to his native country, *Journey to Portugal.*

Artwork for sale along pedestrianised Rua Augusta

At the north end of the square a grandiose neoclassical triumphal arch, the **Arco Triunfal**, leads into Rua Augusta. The topmost statue is Glory, holding laurel wreaths above the heads of Genius and Bravery seated on either side of the royal coat of arms, while below, figures represent Viriatus, Nun'Alvares Pereira, Vasco da Gama, the Marquês de Pombal and Portugal's two great rivers, the Tejo, on the left, and the Douro.

Running up from under the Arco Triunfal is **Rua Augusta**, the main axis of the Baixa, a handsome thoroughfare bursting with charm and liberally endowed with tiled facades, mosaic pavements and wonderfully picturesque old shopfronts. Like some of the other streets in the grid, it's been pedestrianised, and abounds in café *esplanadas*, where you can sit people watching and enjoying the street theatre of buskers, roast-chestnut ladies and the Baixa's ubiquitous shoe-shine boys. The stalls just through the arch are known by the locals as the Mercado dos Hippies – browse the stuff on sale and the reason becomes obvious. From Augusta, stroll over to the **Rua da Conceição** to take in the splendid art nouveau shopfronts of the haberdashers and trimmings stores, looking for a rectangular manhole cover between the tram lines near the junction with the Rua da Prata. Below lie remnants of Roman Lisbon in the shape of ancient tanks, once thought to be the ruins of baths, but more probably the foundations of a large public building. To catch a glimpse of more of the **Roman city**, head for the back of the Banco Comercial Português, beneath which a 1991 reconstruction, known as the **Núcleo Arqueológico da Rua dos Correeiros**, unearthed the remains of a Roman *garam* (fish-sauce) factory, where rotted fish was mixed with salt and spices to make the Rome's favourite condiment, exported throughout the Empire.

Three blocks east of here is the Baixa's other main drag, the Rua do Ouro, once the Rua Aurea. It's home to the **Elevador de Santa Justa** (➤ 50), the 19th-century solution to getting up the steep slopes to Chiado. Walk south and you'll find yourself back at the waterfront; better still, head for a café, sit down and let the everyday life of the Baixa flow around you.

TAKING A BREAK

Pause at any of the street cafés or head for **Café Martinho da Arcada** (➤ 64), which is both a restaurant and café serving up some of the best *pastéis de nata* (custard tarts) in town.

➕ 198 A2

Núcleo Arqueológico da Rua dos Correeiros
✉ Rua dos Correeiros 9 ☎ 213 211 700 🕐 Tours Thu 3, 4; Sat 10, 11, noon, 3, 4
💶 Free 🚇 Rossio, Baixa-Chiado

Sculpture in
the Praça do
Município

THE BAIXA: INSIDE INFO

Top tips If you're in Lisbon in winter, be sure to buy **roast chestnuts** from the street vendors.
• It's worth starting your visit to the area by popping in to the **tourist office** in the **Praça do Comércio** for free city maps and information leaflets.
• **Late afternoon** is a good time to explore the area and get the best of the street life.

② Chiado and Santa Justa

Spreading up the hill to the west of the Baixa, and linked to it by the iconic Elevador de Santa Justa, Chiado is among Lisbon's most loved neighbourhoods. Scene of the city's thriving literary and cultural life throughout the 19th and early 20th centuries, it's home to museums and theatres, historic shops and cafés and grandiose churches, rich in artworks and decoration. The central core of its main streets was devastated by fire in 1988, but new buildings rose phoenix-like from the ashes to ensure Chiado retained its attractions, characteristic and elegant shops, and above all, its atmosphere. Come here to wander the streets, take in the view from the top of Santa Justa and indulge in some serious retail therapy.

It makes sense to gain height by taking the **Elevador de Santa Justa** up to the Rua do Carmo, a quintessential Lisbon experience. This wonderful iron structure, complete with Gothic-style tracery that echoes that of the ruined **Convento do Carmo** (▶ 61), was inaugurated in 1902 and built to save locals' legs between the Baixa and the higher parts of downtown Lisbon. Its architect was Raul Mesnier de Ponsard, a Porto-born engineer of French descent and a keen fan of Eiffel, that great French designer. Mesnier de Ponsard was responsible for all nine of the original city lifts and elevators, of which four still survive, but Santa Justa is the only vertical one, its internal elevators whisking passengers up the 45m (148 feet) to the walkway that connects the top with the Largo do Carmo. There are splendid views from here – across the Baixa to the Castelo de São Jorge, north to the central squares and down to the river.

The walkway leads into **Largo do Carmo**, one of Chiado's prettiest squares, dominated by the ruins of the Convento do Carmo,

Fernando Pessoa

Born in Rua Serpa Pinto in the Chiado in 1888, Fernando Pessoa, Portugal's greatest modern poet, spent his entire life in his beloved Lisbon, producing his greatest works. His poems are written under 72 alter egos and are imbued with melancholy and mystery; only one, *Mensagem*, was published in his lifetime. By day he worked as a translator, spending his evenings writing at one of his two favourite cafés, A Brasileira (► 60–61) or the Café Martinho da Arcada (► 64). The absinthe he consumed here hastened his death, in 1935, from cirrhosis.

destroyed in the 1755 earthquake and now home to the **Museu Arqueológico do Carmo** (► 61). From here, you can walk downhill to **Rua Garrett**, once Lisbon's most fashionable street, and still buzzing with people and lined with shops. The church at the top is the **Igreja dos Mártires** (Our Lady of the Martyrs) built in the 1770s on the site of an earlier one. Here you'll find **Café A Brasileira** (► 60–61), or cross the road and head further downhill to the **Museu do Chiado** (► 60) and the facades of two of Lisbon's main theatres, the **Teatro Nacional de São Carlos** (1793) and the **Teatro Municipal de São Luiz**, dating from the 19th century.

Rua Garrett and the surrounding streets were the epicentre of the 1988 fire, which raged for over 20 hours, destroying 18 buildings, including two historic department stores, the Grandella and the Chiado. Reconstruction was entrusted to the Porto architect, Alvaro Siza Vieira, whose highly successful scheme kept the original street layout and ensured the new buildings would meld into the existing cityscape. The department stores were replaced with a state-of-the-art mall, the **Armazéns do Chiado**. From the entrance, head downhill, to the right, along **Rua do Carmo** to the Rossio at the bottom.

TAKING A BREAK

If you don't stop at **Café A Brasileira**, head for **Café no Chiado** (Largo do Picadeiro 10am–midnight, tel: 213 460 501).

➕ 197 F2

Left: The iron Elevador de Santa Justa

Elevador de Santa Justa
➕ 197 F3 ✉ Rua do Ouro–Rua do Carmo ☎ 213 613 000 (Carris); www.carris.pt 🕐 Daily 8–9 💰 Inexpensive 🚇 Baixa-Chiado

CHIADO AND SANTA JUSTA: INSIDE INFO

Top tips Many of the shops in Chiado have beautifully restored late 19th- and early 20th-century facades – worth a photo opportunity.
• If you want a quick, inexpensive snack try one of the food outlets on the top floor of the **Armazéns do Chiado** mall.

In more depth Head uphill to the two churches at the top of the Largo do Chiado. On the right is **Igreja da Encarnação** (Church of the Incarnation), inaugurated in 1708 and rebuilt after the earthquake in 1784; it has beautiful *azulejos* in the sacristy. On the left is **Nossa Senhora do Loreto** (Our Lady of Loreto), built in the 16th century by Lisbon's Italian community and reconstructed post 1755. The main altar, with its marble statues, was brought from Italy.

❸ Rossio, Figueira and Restauradores

Just north of the 18th-century grid of streets built by Pombal, lie three squares – the Rossio, Figueira and Restaudores. Thronged with people, fringed with swirling traffic, they are a natural focus and meeting point, through which you're bound to pass several times a day. Rather than hurrying through, make time to stop, look, and take in the buildings, the street life, the sights and sounds. This is crossroads Lisbon, with a history that echoes that of the entire city, while the shifting and diverse crowds reflect both Portugal's erstwhile role as an imperial power and the multi-ethnicity of this tolerant and open-minded city.

The Rossio, properly called **Praça Dom Pedro IV**, is the largest of the three, and has occupied the same area since medieval times, when it was the city's trading and gathering place. Military parades, *autos-da-fé* and bullfights were held here, despite the fact that it flooded at higher-than-average tides. Things changed radically after 1755, when many of its buildings were destroyed or badly damaged in the earthquake.

Eugenio dos Santos, the architect of the Baixa, and his fellow designers, visualised the city's focus moving away from the Rossio to the new expanse of the waterfront, Praça do Comércio. The Rossio was heightened to avoid flooding, redesigned and rebuilt, and it wasn't until the 19th century that it regained its role as the hub of city-centre life, which it retains. When the tanks rolled into downtown Lisbon on 25 April 1974, it was reputedly a Rossio flower seller who gave a carnation to a soldier, earning the Revolution the nickname Revolução dos Cravos, the Carnation Revolution (► 24–25).

Today, it's a bustling, wide space, fringed with historic cafés and sombrely elegant buildings. The **statue** in the square's centre depicts **Dom Pedro IV**, proclaimed King of Portugal in 1826. That's the official line, but many claim the statue

Right: The statue of Dom Pedro IV stands at the heart of the Rossio

---

Ginjinha – The Cherry on Daily Life

Clustered around the northeast end of Rossio are a handful of hole-in-the-wall bars that survive by selling just one drink – *ginjinha*. This sticky and potent number is made from cherries and much loved by *lisboetas*, who knock it down from dawn to midnight. It comes with or without whole cherries, and is served in plastic cups – try Ginja Sem Rival, the biggest-selling brand, or Espinheira, or go for Eduardino, a herbal liquer that's been around since the 1840s.

started life in 1870 as a portrayal of the Emperor Maximilian of Mexico. It had got as far as Lisbon to await shipment across the Atlantic when news broke of Maximilian's assassination, and the statue ended up 23m (75 feet) above the Rossio, from which height any lack of resemblance to Pedro IV is a somewhat academic question. The grand neoclassical building on the north side is the **Teatro Nacional de Dona Maria,** inaugurated in 1846 on the site of the old Inquisitor's palace – heretics were once burned in the Rossio. It's a piece of architectural re-cycling – the six Ionic columns of the portico came from the Church of St Francis, destroyed in the 1755 earthquake. West of here, on the **Largo de São Domingo**, an extension of the Rossio, is the church of the same name, originally the monastery church for the city's Dominicans. It's been built and re-built since its foundation in 1242, and for many years was central to the Inquisition, which was based across the square and run by the Dominicans. In recent years São Domingo traditionally had a black priest, and the Largo is still popular with Africans from the former Portuguese colonies in Guinea-Bissau and Angola who gather here to catch up on news.

From São Domingo, you can head south into **Praça da Figueira**, the other square built to bound the northern end of the Baixa after the earthquake. It's lined with four-storey facades and gets its name from the street market that occupied the space until 1949. It's not as elegant as the Rossio, but it serves much the same purpose; the statue in the centre portrays **João I**, who came to the throne in 1385 and signed the Treaty of Windsor with England, one of the oldest extant treaties in the world.

If you head north from the Rossio, skirting the side of the Teatro Nacional, you'll come to Lisbon's third central square, **Restauradores**. It's heralded by the architectural flourish of the splendid neo-Manueline facade of the Rossio station, completed in 1887 as the terminus for Sintra, but currently shut while new tunnels are constructed. The obelisk in the centre of Restauradores commemorates the 1640 restoration of Portugal's independence from Spain; from it the Avenida da Liberdade stretches north. Built to link 18th-century downtown Lisbon with the growing 19th-century city, and completed in 1886, it was modelled on Paris' Champs-Elysées. On the west side you'll see the facade of the art nouveau **Eden building**, once a cinema. Just up from here is the **Palácio Foz**, home to Lisbon's main tourist office.

TAKING A BREAK

The splendidly restored **Café Nicola** (► 64) on Praça Dom Pedro IV, 24 is an ideal place for a snack and a spot of people-watching.

🔡 198 A2 (Rossio and Figueira); 197 F4 (Restauradores)
🚇 Rossio, Restauradores

Above: The art nouveau Eden building

Left: The commemorative obelisk in Restauradores

ROSSIO, FIGUEIRA AND RESTAURADORES: INSIDE INFO

Top tips A late afternoon drink at **Café Nicola** (► 64) or **Suiça**, Rossio's most famous cafés, is a must.

• The **Carris kiosk** on Praça da Figueira is a good place to buy **travel cards**.

4 Museu Calouste Gulbenkian

If you only see one museum in Lisbon, the Museu Calouste Gulbenkian should be it, for this is one of the world's great collections, a comprehensive, but manageably sized, selection of the best, from every century, from all over the world. Factor in a visitor-friendly building and 7ha (17 acres) of lovely gardens and it's easy to see what puts the Gulbenkian head and shoulders above any other city museum.

Top: Outside the Gulbenkian

Above: Modern sculpture in the gardens that adjoin the Centro de Arte Moderna

The buildings of Portugal's great cultural body, **Fundação Calouste Gulbenkian**, surround the museum itself. The Foundation funds both the art collection and the nearby Centro de Arte Moderna, supports an orchestra and a choir, and runs three concert halls and two exhibition galleries in Lisbon alone. It's active all over Portugal, funding museums and libraries, and also giving charitable grants to a huge range of projects. All this is possible thanks to Calouste Gulbenkian (1869–1955) (► 26–27), who made millions in the Middle East and spent some of it on amassing this superb collection, only to bequeath everything to Portugal, his adopted country. The accent is personal; Gulbenkian had three great passions – Venetian painting, French furniture and silver – but he also had an eye for the best of the rest, and it's the sheer quality and conservation condition of every piece that takes the breath away. The exhibits are arranged more or less chronologically, a stunning stroll through four thousand years of great art and craftsmanship.

The Ancient World, Rooms 1–3

This is a small collection of superlative quality, focusing first on **Ancient Egypt**, from where there is a translucent **alabaster bowl** dating from around 2,500 BC, a **relief** *stela* carved with an offering being made to the pharaoh (1580 BC), and a black and white **bowl**. Most visitors though, will warm to the stunningly tactile and realistic **bronze cat with her kittens** (664–525 BC), possibly made to mark a pet's grave. Pick of the Greek collection is the terracotta **Attic vase** (*c*440 BC), its black ground decorated with red figures of satyrs, fleeing maidens, horses and chariots – the story of Castor and Pollux. Roman gods appear too, on the stunning and intricate **Roman jewellery** set with gems, while from the same date is a set of fragile, iridescent **glassware**. Next door, there's an **Assyrian bas-relief** from the palace of Assurbanipal in Nimrud showing a bearded warrior wearing a feather-trimmed cape, from the 9th century BC.

Rembrandt's celebrated *Portrait of an Old Man*

Treasures of the East, Rooms 4–6

Two inter-connecting galleries house the Eastern Islamic and Armenian collections, providing an overview of all that's best from these regions, with particular emphasis on 15th- to 17th-century works. The silk and wool **carpets**, some laid flat, others used as wall hangings, are a highpoint, as are the numerous examples of **wall tiles** from the Ottoman Empire – one particularly beautiful **15th-century panel** of faience tiles with a turquoise, blue-and-white underglaze stands out for its almost art deco style. Take in too, the **Persian and Turkish ceramics**, especially the mainly blue-and-white **Turkish Izmet bowls** and tile panels. These have a definite Ming influence and were made as goods were traded into Europe from Asia across the Silk Road. An entire case is filled with exquisite Egyptian glass **mosque lamps** made in the 14th century – gilded, translucent and iridescent, they represent staggering technical expertise for their age. Dating from a century later is the **white jade tankard**, made in Samarkand, and owned over the centuries by Tamerlane's grandson and members of the Mughal imperial line. Moving on, exhibits in the Far Eastern room include deep **Ming bowls** with a translucent celadon green glaze, though more eye-catching by far are the **Chinese porcelain vases and covered pots**, dating mainly from the 17th to 18th centuries. Two outstanding sets are made of enamelled porcelain, one decorated with chrysanthemums in pinks, turquoise and greens on a white underground, the other with pink and green flowers and natural motifs on a black glaze. Don't miss either, the intricate 14th-century Chinese **coromandel screen**, inlaid with lacquer and paper designs – on the right as you leave the gallery.

European Art, Rooms 7–15

The European art collection focuses on painting, sculpture, ceramics, furniture and gold- and silverware, with pictures and *objets d'art* either hung or exhibited in separate rooms or displayed with contemporary furniture. It's an overwhelming selection, spanning nearly a thousand years, and most visitors concentrate on what appeals personally.

There are wonderful examples of **ivories** and **illuminated manuscripts**, but many people are drawn straight to the paintings, a collection that's rich in portraits and landscapes, Gulbenkian's own favourite genres. Renaissance highlights here include a lovely Venetian *Holy Family* by **Vittore Carpaccio**, rich in the colour and detail so typical of this painter, and **Ghirlandaio's** *Portrait of a Young Woman*; she's wearing a pink dress with green sleeves, while her coral necklace draws attention to the delicate wisps of hair around her face. More pretty girls feature in a trio of portraits by the English artists **Gainsborough**, **Romney** and **Lawrence**, while **Rembrandt's** *Pallas Athene*, a dark depiction of the god with a superb shield and plumed helmet, brings a more sombre note. Three portraits represent **Rembrandt, Rubens and Van Dyck**; all have superbly rendered textiles – you can almost feel the silk and velvets just by looking. You can feel the misty air too in **Turner's** *The Mouth of the Seine*, all swirling water and pearly tints. Venetian fans shouldn't miss the side room devoted to **Guardi** – no fewer than 19 real or imagined Venetian scenes, including one showing Palladio's *Design for the Rialto Bridge*. **Corot, Manet, Renoir** and **Degas** represent

Gulbenkian's world-class museum is housed in a sleek building

Top 10 at the Gulbenkian
Greek Attic vase – Room 2
Egyptian Mosque lamp – Room 4
Iznik footed bowl – Room 4
Famille Rose garniture – Room 6
Portrait of a Young Woman by Domenico Ghirlandaio – Room 8
Writing table by Martin Carlin – Room 10
Silver mustard pots by Antoine-Saebastien Durant – Room 12
The Feast of the Ascension in the Piazza San Marco by Francesco Guardi –
   Room 14
Chalice with Vines and Figures by René Lalique – Room 17

the French Impressionists; outstanding here are two winter scenes: a Millet pastel of *Snow-Covered Haystacks* which contrasts finely with Monet's *Ice Floating*.

Backtrack from the pictures to enjoy the superb **French Louis XV** and **Louis XVI furniture**, laid out in a series of "rooms". These display chairs, cupboards, sideboards and inlaid tables, set off by wall hangings and tapestries. Top of the pops here are the **commode** made in 1750 by Deforges and inlaid with Japanese lacquer panels, the **Boulle armoire**, with its inlay of bronze, pewter and brass into precious woods, and the **Carlin writing table** (1772) decorated with plaques of **Sèvres porcelain** and made for Madame du Barry. There's more French pre-Revolutionary opulence in the shape of silver and gold table ware and a large display of Sèvres porcelain, some with blue, some with green background glaze.

Equally magnificent is the museum's collection of **silver**, unrivalled pieces made in 18th-century France by masters such as **Durant** and **Germain** for the Russian imperial court.

Left: The Far Eastern collection includes exceptional pieces of Chinese porcelain

Gulbenkian acquired them between 1928 and 1930 and they are considered the world's most important of their type. Decorated with realistic fish, shells, fruit, vegetables and animals, gilded and embellished with fine exotic wood, such pieces represent a level of ostentation and extravagance that has rarely been rivalled.

The final room is devoted to the work of the art nouveau jeweller and designer **René Lalique**. It includes 169 pieces of his **jewellery**, intricate and sinuous designs embellished with enamel, gold, diamonds, pearls and other gems – look out for the *Orchid* **diadem**, a beautiful hair ornament where horn, ivory, gold and topaz are used to create a supremely tactile piece, and the exquisite *Peacock* **pectoral**, where gold, enamel, opals and diamonds are sinuously entwined.

TAKING A BREAK

The museum has an excellent **café**, where you can enjoy anything from coffee and cakes to a full lunch.

Below: Islamic art in the museum

194 C4
Avenida de Berna 45A ☎ 217 823 000; www.museu.gulbenkian.pt
Tue–Sun 10–5:45 Moderate Bar and restaurant in museum
São Sebastião, Praça de Espanha 746 from centre Audio guides (moderate), combined ticket with Centro de Arte Moderna (expensive)

MUSEU CALOUSTE GULBENKIAN: INSIDE INFO

Top tips Allow around 2 to 3 hours for a **leisurely visit**.
• Leave time to enjoy the **gardens** that surround the Fundação's buildings.
• You could combine the Gulbenkian with the **Centro de Arte Moderna**, also part of the Fundação.
• Learn more about the Foundation, Gulbenkian, the Museum and the collections by using the **touch-screen computers**.

In more depth The museum also features changing exhibitions in its downstairs rooms, and focuses on a changing number of art works in small "**Work in Focus**" shows upstairs, where the history and provenance of a single piece from the collection are examined in detail. There is also a short and informative **exhibition on Gulbenkian's life** and the order in which he acquired his treasures, complete with old photographs showing the exhibits as they were originally housed in his Parisian home.

At Your Leisure

⑤ Cais do Sodré and Mercado da Ribeira

From the Praça do Comércio a walk-way leads west along the Tejo to **Cais do Sodré**, a former red-light area. In the Salazar years, this was the only place with late drinking and seedy bars, and the Rua Nova de Carvalho still boasts scruffy sex bars. The hookers are still here too, but they've moved back from the water-front, which is now home to bars, trendy clubs and some of the best seafood restaurants in town. Across the road from the station is the **Mercado da Ribeira**, Lisbon's main central food market, in an 1182 building – though the market dates from medieval times. With fish stalls lining the sides and the fruit, vegeta-bles and produce in the main hall, it's a feast for the senses. Here are home-grown sweet potatoes, dried beans, chillies, coriander, cabbage and peppers, alongside mangos from Brazil and okra and yams from Africa, ingredients that tell the story of the Portuguese colonies. By lunchtime, the flower sellers are opening up along one aisle, while on the upstairs floors restaurants serve traditional Portuguese fare; book and craft fairs take place here too and there is often live music and dancing.

🚩 197 E2 🖂 Avenida 24 de Julho
☎ 213 462 966; www.espacoribeira.pt
🕐 Market Mon–Sat 6–2; flower market Mon–Fri 6–2, 3–7, Sat 6–2 🍴 Bars and restaurants in market 🚇 Cais do Sodré

The ferry leaving Cais do Sodré

⑥ Museu do Chiado

Redesigned along streamlined modernist lines after the 1988 Chiado fire (► 51), the Museu do Chiado, founded in 1911, re-opened in 1994. The **permanent collections** cover Portuguese art from 1850 to 1950, showcasing works by the natu-ralist painters working in Lisbon in the last quarter of the 19th century, whose street and river scenes portray corners of Lisbon that remain unchanged. The collection covers every movement from romanticism, through naturalism, modernism and surrealism to abstractionism. Artistically, works such a *A Sesta* by Almada Negreiros and *O Desterrado* by Soares dos Reis take the prize, but most visitors find Lisbon scenes such as Carlos Botelho's *Lisboa e o Tejo* more appealing. The museum stages regular temporary exhibitions, and there's a great view over Chiado from the terrace to further tempt visitors.

🚩 197 F2 🖂 Rua Serpa Pinto 4
☎ 213 432 148; www.museudochiado-ipmuseus.pt 🕐 Tue–Sun 10–6
🏛 Moderate 🍴 Café no Chiado
(► 51) 🚇 Baixa-Chiado

⑦ Café A Brasileira

This great Lisbon institution first opened its doors in 1905, when the Brazilian Adriano Teles set up a busi-ness selling the superb coffee beans from Minas Gerais. Buyers were given a free *bica*, the tiny cup of the strong coffee *lisboetas* favour, and within three years the enterprise had become a café. From the start it attracted writers and artists, and at its 1920s peak, was renowned as a centre for philosophers and dissi-dents. The interior matched the sparkle of the conversation and the wood panelling, mirrors and gilded ceiling fans, installed in the 1920s, have all been retained. Inevitably, A Brasileira today is firmly on the

Pessoa statue outside Café A Brasileira

The ruins of the Convento do Carmo

tourist trail, with visitors flocking to be photographed beside the life-size bronze of Fernando Pessoa, Portugal's greatest modern poet (➤ 51) and an A Brasileira regular, represented sitting at one of the outside tables.

🕂 197 F3 ⊠ Rua Garrett 120 ☎ 213 469 541 🕔 Daily 8am–2am 🚇 Baixa-Chiado

8 Museu Arqueológico do Carmo

One side of Largo do Carmo, with its central, classically inspired fountain, is occupied by the majestic Gothic ruins of the **Convento do Carmo**, now home to an eclectic collection of archaeological finds from around Portugal and Europe. The **Convento de Nossa Senhora do Monte Carmel** (Convent of Our Lady of Mount Carmel) was built in the 14th and 15th centuries on the orders of Nun'Alvares Pereira, constable to Dom João I. Pereira was instru-

mental in consolidating the rule of the House of Avis and had vowed to construct a church if successful in a key battle. Despite the difficulties of construction, he insisted on the hillside location, which caused problems for the builders who had to contend with a nearby precipice and collapsing foundations. Despite this, a magnificent church went up, which soon became a much-loved city emblem. The church's site was possibly instrumental in its catastrophic collapse during the earthquake, when the roof fell in, killing many worshippers and leaving only the walls and some rib vaulting standing. Today, the nave is grass covered and the walls are open to the sky, while the soaring lines of these beautiful ruins serve as a reminder of the events of 1755.

🕂 197 F3 ⊠ Largo do Carmo ☎ 213 478 629 🕔 May–Sep Mon–Sat 10–6; Oct–Apr 10–5 💰 Inexpensive 🍴 Leitaria Academia, Largo do Carmo 1–3 🚇 Baixa-Chiado

9 Parque Eduardo VII

Following the construction of the Avenida da Liberdade, the next city must-have was and urban park where people could stroll and take the air. Planning began in 1888 and today's Parque Eduardo VII took shape over the next 50 years. It's named after British King Edward VII, who visited Lisbon in 1903. Swathes of grass, shrubs and trees run on either side of a more formal central area, where you'll find impeccable parterres, sculpture, fountains and rose gardens. Follow the contours uphill from the entrance on the Praça Marquês de Pombal and superb city and river views open up as you approach the Estufa Fria – three greenhouses that house plants from all over the world. Look for the ferns and orchids, or simply enjoy the oasis of green peace provided by the park.

🔁 194 C2 ⊠ Praça Marquês de Pombal ⊚ Daily 9–5:30 🎫 Park: free;

Estufa Fria: inexpensive 🍴 Café in park ⊚ Marquês de Pombal

10 Centro de Arte Moderna

On the other side of the grounds surrounding the Museu Calouste Gulbenkian (➤ 55–59) is another of the Foundation's enterprises, the Centro de Arte Moderna. The collection highlights Portuguese modern art in particular, housed in a modernist building, which should be high on the list for lovers of 20th-century painting and good design. A highlight is José Almada Negreiros' *Self-Portrait in a Group*, and there are works by Portuguese modernists like António Pedro and António da Costa. Outside, are sculptures from the collections, including works by Henry Moore.

🔁 194 C4 ⊠ Rua Dr Nicolau de Bettencourt ☎ 217 823 474;

A statue is the focal point of a pool in the Estufa Fria in Parque Eduardo VII

For Kids

This is a good city area to visit if you've got kids with you. They might enjoy the short **ferry ride** across the River Tejo and back (➤ 180–181), a hunt for picnic provisions in the **Ribeira market** (➤ 60), or a **tram ride** from the Praça do Comércio. There are delicious **ice-creams** to enjoy at Suíça in Rossio and plenty of grass in the **Parque Eduardo VII** on which to let off steam. Older children might enjoy an hour or so at a museum – the **Museu da Cidade** might be of interest, and the buildings and garden at the **Gulbenkian** (➤ 55–59) might persuade them to take a look at the actual collection. Back in town, let them loose in the **Baixa** to see how many **"old-fashioned shops"** they can find (➤ 48) or whisk them up on the **Elevador de Santa Justa** (➤ 50) for a ride with a difference and **fabulous views** of where they've been.

www.camjap.gulbenkian.org
🕐 Tue–Sun 10–6 💷 Moderate
🍴 Cafeteria in museum 🚇 São
Sebastião, Praça de Espanha
❓ Combined ticket with Gulbenkian:
moderate

Off the Beaten Track

⑪ Museu da Cidade

To put Lisbon's history into context,
head for the Museu da Cidade, which
traces the city's development from
prehistoric times to the 20th century.
Housed in the beautiful 18th-century
Palácio Pimenta – worth the trip
on its own – it comes complete with
splendidly tiled old kitchens and a
garden humming with bees. The
displays may seem daunting, so pick
and choose the best to get an overall
view of Lisbon's history. Don't miss

Eye-catching exhibits in the state-of-the-art Centro de Arte Moderna

⑫ Museu Bordalo Pinheiro

The ceramicist
Rafael Bordalo
Pinheiro
(1846–1905),
was born in
Lisbon and
moved to Caldas da Rainha in the
Ribatejo, where he set up a workshop
specialising, above all, in caricatures.
He invented a peasant figure, **Zé**

the scale reproduction of pre-earthquake Lisbon or the portrait of the
Marquês de Pombal, responsible for
the construction of the Baixa post
1755.

Other insights on the past come
in the form of a vast canvas of the
Terreiro do Paço, forerunner of the
Praça do Comércio, and a painting of
Torre de Belém (► 120–121) in the
days when it was surrounded on all
sides by water.

➕ 195 off E5 ✉ Campo Grande 245
☎ 217 513 200 🕐 Tue–Sun 10–1, 2–6
💷 Inexpensive 🚇 Campo Grande

Povinho, who came to the city and
made a habit of saying exactly what
he thought. Jugs, bowls and stat-
uettes feature this forthright figure.
Pinheiro also created fantastically
designed bowls and platters, often
featuring animals – look for soup
tureens with lids in the shape of pigs'
heads, platters ornamented with
wonderfully lifelike frogs and beetles
and ceramic baskets complete with
resident lobster.

➕ 195 off E5 ✉ Campo Grande 382
☎ 217 550 468 🕐 Tue–Sun 10–6
💷 Inexpensive 🚇 Campo Grande

Where to...
Eat and Drink

Prices

Expect to pay for a three-course meal for one, excluding drinks:

€ under €20   €€ €20–€40   €€€ over €40

Bonjardim €

In an area crammed with tourist traps Bonjardim stands out for one of best plates of chicken you'll ever eat – grilled over charcoal, embellished with home-made chips and served by the half-bird. Order a side salad, dab on the fiery piri-piri sauce you'll find on the table and enjoy the buzzing atmosphere generated by the loyal locals and speedy, professional staff. There are other dishes on offer, including a well-hung steak, and vast slices of home-made cakes and tarts to round it all off.

➕ 198 A3 ✉ Travessa de Santo Antão 12 ☎ 213 427 424 Ⓜ Daily noon–11 Ⓜ Restauradores

Café Martinho da Arcada €

Like the Café Nicola on the Rossio and A Brasileira in the Chiado, this old coffee house, founded in 1782, was a gathering place for Lisbon's 19th-century literati, and found favour with Fernando Pessoa, who came here to enjoy his daily absinthe. The adjoining restaurant has smartened itself up in recent years and is now fairly expensive, but the bar, with its fine age-old

wood-panelled counter, is still a good spot for a coffee and light snack – try one of the *pastéis de nata* for an instant mid-morning sugar fix.

➕ 198 A/B1 ✉ Praça do Comércio 3 ☎ 218 879 259 Ⓜ Mon–Sat 7am–11pm Ⓜ Baixa-Chiado

Café Nicola €

There's been a café here since the 18th century, and Nicola too, is an example of one of Lisbon's haunts of both the literati and political intriguers. The marble, steel and glass interior, splendidly restored in the late 1990s, is a great place for a snack, or watch the world go by at one of the outside tables. Food here is straightforward, veering towards the meat and fries school, but the ambience makes up for that. It's one of the city's more popular cafés, so finding a table can sometimes be difficult.

➕ 198 A2 ✉ Praça Dom Pedro IV 24 ☎ 213 460 579 Ⓜ Mon–Sat 8am–10pm, Sun 9–7 Ⓜ Rossio

Confeitaria Nacional €

There's a plethora of choice for the sweet-toothed in the way of pastries, cakes and biscuits at this long-established cake shop, where the glass cases and painted panelling bear witness to its 19th-century origins. The first floor serves lunches and afternoon tea. Service is brisk and friendly, and you can buy biscuits and cakes to take away; they make great gifts to take back home.

➕ 198 A2 ✉ Praça da Figueira 18B–C ☎ 213 424 470; www.confeitarianacional.com Ⓜ Mon–Sat 8–8 Ⓜ Rossio

Gambrinus €€€

Of all the restaurants and eateries in this street, Gambrinus is the most expensive and by far the best for a memorable meal. The interior, with its wood-beamed ceilings and huge fireplace, suggests well-heeled comfort – no surprise that it's popular with politicians, journalists and public figures. Sit at the bar counter or in one of the two dining rooms and choose from a huge selection of seafood, fresh fish, meat and game in season. Service is, miraculously, both helpful and discreet and you can round off dinner with a glass of port from the huge range.

+ 198 A3 ⊠ Rua Portas de Santo Antão 23 ☎ 213 421 466 ◉ Daily noon–1:30am ⓖ Restauradores

Solar dos Presuntos €€–€€€

You'll recognise the Solar, another highly recommended establishment in this street full of eating places, by the air-cured hams hanging in the window. Inside, the walls are covered with football memorabilia and tributes from famous patrons. The kitchen specialises in traditional dishes from the Minho region of northern Portugal, including roast kid and, when in season, the highly prized lampreys, an eel-like freshwater fish, as well as fish and seafood stewed as a *caldeirada* or simply grilled. Service is friendly and professional.

+ 198 A3 ⊠ Rua das Portas de Santo Antão 150 ☎ 213 424 253; www.solardospresuntos.com ◉ Mon–Sat noon–3:30, 7–11 (closed Aug) ⓖ Restauradores

Solmar €€

The untouched 1960s décor, with its neon, murals, sinuous lines and curving staircase, would make this big, bustling restaurant, once a beer hall, worth a visit; factor in professional staff, an extensive menu and a couple of nightly specials and it's clear why it's popular with locals and tourists alike. Choose your lobster from the tanks, opt for a salt-baked fish or a plate of coriander-infused rice and seafood, before choosing pudding from the groaning pastry trolley, where chocolate profiteroles are the star turn. There's a comprehensive wine list and the house wine is more than acceptable.

+ 198 A3 ⊠ Rua das Portas de Santo Antão 108 ☎ 213 460 010 ◉ Daily noon–11:30 ⓖ Restauradores

Terreiro do Paço €€€

Located in the heart of downtown, this stylish venue, with a reputation as one of the top restaurants in Europe, offers a creative modern take on traditional Portuguese cuisine, particularly seafood. The wine list is also superb.

+ 198 A/B1 ⊠ Praça do Comércio ☎ 210 312 850. ◉ Mon–Fri 12.30–3, 8–11, Sat 8–11 ⓖ Baixa-Chiado

Trindade €

This beautiful old beer hall, on the edge of the Bairro Alto and lined with blue-and-white *azulejos*, is one of the most famous in Lisbon, crammed with people throughout the evening. Head for the first room for a drink and a snack or peruse the menu in the quieter second space for good, straightforward Portuguese cooking and a plate of more than reasonable seafood.

+ 198 A2 ⊠ Rua Nova da Trindade 20C ☎ 213 423 506; www.cervejaria-trinidade.pt ◉ Daily noon–1am ⓖ Baixa-Chiado

Where to... Shop

There's no better place to experience the two contrasting Portuguese shopping experiences than in the Baixa and Chiado; on the one hand, state-of-the-art malls, like the **Armazéns do Chiado** (Rua do Carmo 2, tel: 213 210 600; www.armazensdochiado.com), with the full range of international outlets on six floors, on the other, tiny individual specialist stores, many unchanged for decades.

Head for these if you're looking for something special, such as a great range of tea, coffee and chocolate at **Casa Pereira da Conceição** (Rua Augusta 102, tel: 213 423 000), or other gastronomic goodies at **Manuel Tavares** (Rua da Betesga 1A–1B, tel: 213 424 209;

Where to...
Be Entertained

Early evening is prime relaxation time in the Baixa and Chiado, as later the action moves upwards into the Bairro Alto (▶ 100–101). So have a drink anywhere in the area before eating or perhaps taking in a performance.

Three of Lisbon's major venues are in downtown Lisbon, and there's the chance to catch anything from a rerun of the *Sound of Music* to grand opera.

The beautiful **Teatro Nacional de São Carlos** (Rua Serpa Pinto 9; tel: 213 253 045; www.saocarlos.pt), a feast of 18th-century rococo decoration, dates from 1793 and is Lisbon's premier opera house; it also hosts symphony concerts; ticket prices vary depending on the event.

Up on Rossio, the classical facade of the **Teatro Dona Maria II** (Praça Dom Pedro IV, tel: 213 250 800/213 250 835, www.teatro-dmaria.pt) hides two separate venues, staging plays and classical music.

Behind here, on the Rua Portas de Santo Antão, the **Coliseu dos Recreios** (tel: 213 240 585, www.coliseulisboa.com) is noted for the variety of its offerings – everything from ballet to musicals and contemporary music.

Also in the same area, just west of the Teatro Nacional, is the council-owned **Teatro Municipal de São Luiz** (Rua António Maria Cardosa 40, tel: 213 257 640), a 1,000-seater venue that stages a varied programme of entertainment from theatre to world music.

www.manueltavares.com), an institution in the Baixa for over a hundred years.

Retrosaria Bijou (Rua da Conceição 91, tel: 213 425 049) sells every kind of trimming, ribbon, button and bow, while **Luvaria Ulisses** (Rua do Carmo 87; tel: 213 420 295) is a treasure trove of luxurious gloves in suede, lace, leather and silk, and **Casa Havanesa** (Largo do Chiado 25, tel: 213 420 340), established in 1861, still sells Cuba's finest Havana cigars.

Fashionistas should head for **Ana Salazar**, Rua do Carmo 87, tel: 213 472 289; www.anasalazar.pt), Portugal's best known women's designer, or indulge in classy fabrics to make up from **Casa Frazão** (Rua Augusta 259–265, tel: 213 421 639). Men are catered for at **Alfaiataria Nunes Corrêa** (Rua Augusta 250, tel: 213 240 930), a high-class tailor and outfitter who once kitted out the Portuguese royal family, and there's every type

of hat at **Azevedo Rua** (Praça Dom Pedro IV, 72–73, tel: 213 470 817), elegantly displayed and sold with a flourish from wooden cabinets beneath stuccoed ceilings.

Book-lovers should explore **Livaria Bertrand** (Rua Garrett, 73–75, tel: 213 468 646, www.bertrand.pt), a splendidly old-fashioned shop, founded in 1773, which carries a good range of illustrated coffee table books on Lisbon and Portugal.

The **Armazéns**, besides outlets such as **Fnac, Intimíssimi, Massimo Dutti, Sephora** and **L'Occitane**, also houses **Casa Batalha** (level 4, 10; tel: 213 427 313), founded in 1665 and still selling quality costume jewellery and accessories.

Sports fanatics should head for the lower level, which houses **Sport Zone** (tel: 213 230 730), a vast selling space devoted to every conceivable type of sports equipment, including fishing tackle and riding gear.

The Heart of Medieval Lisbon

Getting Your Bearings 68 – 69
In a Day 70 – 71
Don't Miss 72 – 86
At Your Leisure 87 – 91
Where to... 92 – 94

Getting Your Bearings

The settlement that was to become Lisbon was sited on the hill of the Castelo de São Jorge, and the castle still dominates the oldest part of the city. It's the focal point of this fascinating area, whose delights range from the huddled, higgledy-piggledy streets of the Moorish Alfama to splendid churches, wonderful panoramas and a handful of the city's most characteristic museums. This is one of the most densely inhabited parts of Lisbon, packed with shops, restaurants and bars; its occupants range from the urban poor to well-heeled professionals, all very passionate about the area's varied charms.

From the east side of the Baixa, the hill rises sharply towards the castle, whose walls and terraces give marvellous views over city and river. Below here, graceful streets, rebuilt after the 1755 earthquake and lined with elegant houses, are punctuated by some of Lisbon's finest *miradouros* (look-outs). These give bird's-eye views over the rooftops of the Alfama, old Lisbon's most

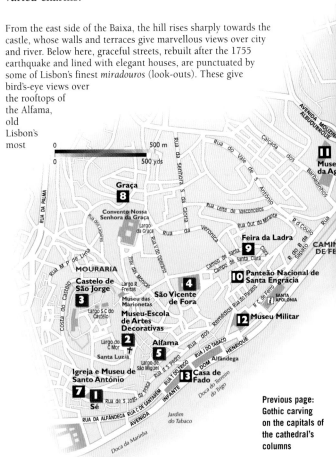

Previous page:
Gothic carving
on the capitals of
the cathedral's
columns

★ Don't Miss

1 Sé ➤ 72
2 Museu-Escola de Artes Decorativas ➤ 74
3 Castelo de São Jorge ➤ 77
4 São Vicente de Fora ➤ 80
5 Alfama ➤ 82
6 Museu Nacional do Azulejo ➤ 85

Below: View
from the
Cathedral's
cloisters

Bottom: The
ramparts of
Castelo de São
Jorge

At Your Leisure

7 Igreja e Museu de Santo António ➤ 87
8 Graça ➤ 88
9 Feira da Ladra ➤ 89
10 Panteão Nacional de Santa Engrácia ➤ 89
11 Museu da Agua ➤ 90
12 Museu Militar ➤ 90
13 Casa de Fado ➤ 91

6 Museu Nacional
do Azulejo

RUA N D BARROS
Pedra
HENRIQUE
DOM

compelling area, whose stairs and alleys drop down towards the Sé (Cathedral) and its surrounding buildings, some of the oldest in the city. North from here stand the great churches of São Vicente de Fora and Santa Engrácia and the wonderful Museu-Escola de Artes Decorativas. Follow the streets uphill to discover Graça, a beguiling *bairro* with a strongly individual atmosphere, or head downhill towards the river and more museums illuminating different aspects of national life.

Lisbon's castle broods above the labyrinthine streets of the city's oldest area, packed with museums, churches, fascinating streets and *miradoures*, the lookout points above the River Tejo.

The Heart of Medieval Lisbon in a Day

9:30am
Start your day at the **①Sé** (Cathedral, ► 72–73); take in the cloister (left), where an archaeological dig tells Lisbon's history. You could also peek at the **⑦Igreja de Santo António** (► 87), dedicated to St Anthony.

10:30am
Climb up Rua do Eléctrico da Sé to the Largo das Portas do Sol, passing the lovely *miradouro* of Santa Luzia (► 178). Take in the view from the Portas do Sol balcony, before visiting the magical **②Museu-Escola de Artes Decorativas** (► 74–76).

11:30am
Go up the steep streets behind the museum to the iconic **③Castelo de São Jorge** (► 77–79), before heading up to the Igreja da Graça (► 88), set on one of the highest points of Lisbon.

1:00pm
You could have lunch at the café on the Esplanada da Igreja da Graça (► 94) then head further up Rua Damasceno Monteiro and the Calçada do Monte for the *miradouro* of Nossa Senhora do Monte, the highest in the city. Alternatively, relax over lunch at the Mercado de Santa Clara (► 93) set above the **⑩Panteão Nacional de Santa Engrácia** (► 89).

2:30pm

Take tram 28 to **4 São Vicente de Fora** (➤ 80–81), with its beautiful cloister, great views and some of the loveliest *azulejos* in the city. If you're here on a Tuesday or Saturday, browse the stalls of the **9 Feira da Ladra** (➤ 89) behind the church; things pack up around 3–3:30.

3:30pm

Walk downhill and wander the narrow streets of the **5 Alfama** (➤ 82–84; bottom); heading downhill, you'll eventually hit the Largo Chafariz de Dentro, home to the **13 Casa de Fado** (➤ 91), dedicated to Lisbon's own music.

4:45pm

Take bus 794 or a taxi to head east to the **6 Museu Nacional do Azulejo** (➤ 85–86; above), housed in an old convent, and its adjacent church, rich in beautiful blue-and-white tiles.

6:00pm

You'll be ready for a drink, so why not head back to one of the *miradouros* and relax as the light changes and evening falls.

8:00pm

You could spend the evening in the Alfama (right), dining at Malmequer Bemmequer (➤ 93) before heading for Parreirinha de Alfama (Beco do Espirito Santo 1, tel: 218 868 209) to hear some of the best *fado* in the *bairro*.

❶ Sé

Among Lisbon's rich variety of religious buildings, there's none where the weight of history is felt more strongly than the Sé (Cathedral). Standing on the site of some of the city's earliest buildings, it's redolent with the past – the Romans, Visigoths and Moors all left their mark on this spot, while today's great church echoes the history of Portugal itself. Its soaring interior bears witness both to its founders and the religious fervour of the city through the centuries.

In 714 Lisbon fell to the Moors, who established a rich city and built a great mosque. Christians and Jews lived amicably together and the city thrived. But in the north, Portugal was emerging as a country in its own right, and the Portuguese and their crusading allies swept south to retake the city in the name of Christ. In 1147, Moorish Lisbon fell to Afonso Henriques, King of Portugal, who appointed his English follower, Gilbert of Hastings, as the city's first Christian bishop. Gilbert supervised the construction of a **fortress-like cathedral** on the site of the mosque, and today's **Sé** still includes much of this Romanesque building. The severe **facade**, with its twin battlemented towers, dates from a 14th-century reconstruction, carried out after an earthquake, when the cloister was added and the interior Gothic elements put in place. Over the following centuries, there were numerous facelifts, the most major following the 1755 earthquake, when the baroque high altar was added and the entire cathedral "modernised". These trappings were removed in the 1930s,

Romanesque arches in the nave lead the eye to the high altar

Save your legs by taking a tram up to the Sé

when the beautiful **rose window** was reconstructed from fragments, and today's interior, dark, sombre and mystical, probably reflects the original appearance of the building more closely than at any other date.

As you walk round the inside of the Sé, don't miss the **ambulatory** behind the high altar, an open processional space designed to facilitate the flow of pilgrims – there would have been plenty in the 14th century when it was built, for the Sé contained the relics of St Vincent, patron saint of Lisbon. The urn holding his remains was destroyed in the 1755 earthquake. Off the south aisle is the **treasury**, crammed with a selection of glittering religious artefacts and ornately embroidered vestments, and nearby is the entrance of the **Romanesque-Gothic cloister**, with its vaulted roof and pointed arches. In the centre, once a grassy space, is one of Lisbon's most evocative sights; layer upon layer of **archaeological excavations** which reveal the buildings that lie beneath the cathedral. Here is the entire history of Lisbon, from the Iron Age to early medieval times, and you can follow the walkway built around the whole site. There's a Roman street, complete with steps, drainage and shops, later Roman walls, the remnants of the medieval buildings levelled off when the cathedral was built, and a medieval well. The special-interest prize has to go to a courtyard, built in Moorish times, that's still surrounded by the walls of a pink-painted Islamic public building.

TAKING A BREAK

The **Alfama** has many atmospheric cafés and restaurants.

➕ 198 B1 ✉ Largo da Sé ☎ 218 876 628; www.ippar.pt ◑ Daily. Cathedral 9–7; cloister 10–6; treasury 10–5 💷 Cloister and treasury inexpensive 🍴 Bar at Largo de Santa Luzia 🚊 Trams 12, 28

SÉ: INSIDE INFO

Don't miss The Gothic altarpiece in the **Chapel of Bartolomeu Joanes**, attributed to Portugal's greatest painter, Grão Vasco (1480–c1543).
• The **view** from the southeast corner of the cloister, a beautifully framed **panorama** of the jumbled roofs of the Alfama and the river beyond.
• The beautiful **tomb of Lopo Fernandes Pacheco** to the right of the ambulatory.

2 Museu-Escola de Artes Decorativas

The 17th-century Palácio Azurara, delightfully set on a panoramic square above the Alfama, is home to the Museu-Escola de Artes Decorativas (Museum of Applied Arts), a treasure house of furniture, paintings, porcelain and textiles. The collections are arranged, in a series of sumptuous and beautifully decorated rooms, as if this were still a private house, giving an unforgettable impression of how the wealthy lived as the gold flowed back home from Portugal's overseas possessions.

In 1947, Ricardo do Espírito Santo Silva, banker, Salazar supporter, lover of the *fadista* Amália (► 13) and builder of the Ritz hotel, purchased the **Azurara Palace** to house his important collection of **Portuguese applied arts**. His passion was **furniture**, particularly that of the 17th and 18th centuries, but he understood that it was best seen as it was first used, surrounded by **paintings, textiles, porcelain, silver** and *objets d'art*, and set against an aristocratic background. To this end, the entire building was restored and decorated in contemporary 17th- and 18th-century style, Silva even going to the lengths of buying additional *azulejos* panels for the walls from other Lisbon palaces. The result is stunning, a lovingly tended sleeping beauty of a palace, with an overwhelming feeling that the owners have just gone away for

The elliptical Music Room has exceptional acoustics

a few days and could be back at any time. Six years later, the **Escola** was founded, **a training school** that teaches every branch of the applied arts. Products from its workshops are commissioned from all over the world, and the scale of expertise is among the highest in Portugal.

From the **entrance hall**, graceful flights of shallow treads lead past 18th-century blue-and-white tiles to a series of three, low-ceilinged rooms, filled with elegance and charm. Precious rugs from Arraiolos, the traditional centre of Portuguese carpet manufacture in the Alentejo, are scattered on the polished floor, which is dotted with light, perfectly proportioned furniture. These rugs, usually made of linen or burlap with woollen embroidery, range from the very simple to intricate in the extreme; they are still made in the town today. The scale of this room is intimate, and side tables hold Chinese export ware, made for the Portuguese market, dating from the T'ang dynasty. The furthest room has a floor entirely covered in straw matting, often used in 17th- and 18th-century Portuguese houses, particularly during the hotter months.

The next floor holds the far grander **main living rooms** of the palace, all with high ceilings, shining wooden floors, sumptuous textiles and intricate painted decoration. The **Main Hall** is vast, with its own tiny chapel tucked into one wall, while another displays a 17th-century Franco-Flemish tapestry representing the Portuguese arrival in India. The furniture, inlaid with ivory and rosewood and decorated with scenes of the hunt, is Indo-Portuguese, while the country's trading links with China are echoed in the pair of huge vases and the Chinese export porcelain, many pieces featuring Portuguese coats of arms. Through here, you'll

Your carriage awaits – an unusual exhibit in the museum's entrance hall

come to the **Store Window Hall**, its walls half-tiled and lit by a glittering 19th-century chandelier. In the centre, there's a uniquely Portuguese seat known as a *duchesse brisée*, composed of two armchairs with a footstool between, allowing two people to recline intimately face to face.

More comforts are found in the next room, hung with red damask, in the shape of travelling beds and folding furniture. You'll notice that not every bed has ruffles round the canopy – these were strictly reserved for men. The **corridor** next to this has another practical piece, the 18th-century equivalent of a sofa bed, whose brocaded cushions lift off to allow the seat to be extended. Next door, in the **Dom José Hall**, look for the exquisite gaming table, a multi-purpose number ideal for a gambling-obsessed society. Folded, it looks like a normal

table, but open it up and it can become a velvet-covered card table, a plain tea table or a chess, chequers and backgammon board, complete with ivory receptacles for the gaming chips. Hidden inside is a mirror. Further on is the **Music Room**, its elliptical shape designed for the best possible acoustics; the walls are magnificently decorated with musical motifs. Don't miss the glass case containing the miniature chamber music ensemble – such pieces were popular with the high-spenders of the 18th century. More stairs, much narrower, lead to the top floor and four darker rooms, the gleaming wood contrast-ing with the painted coffered ceilings. One is a **dining room**, tiled, painted and hung with red brocade. The central table holds 17th- and 18th-century silver, but the chief treasure is perhaps the Ch'ing dynasty 17th-century cutlery case, made in China to a Portuguese model, and enamelled in cobalt blue, fiery red, green and gold.

The vast Main Hall, with its fine Indo-Portuguese furniture

TAKING A BREAK

Pause for coffee or a drink with a view across the river at one of the **cafés** on the **Largo das Portas do Sol**.

➕ 198 C2 ✉ Largo das Portas do Sol 2 ☎ 218 881 991 ⏰ Tue–Sun 10–5
💰 Moderate 🍴 Café with courtyard in museum 🚌 37; trams 12, 28

MUSEU-ESCOLA DE ARTES DECORATIVAS: INSIDE INFO

Top tips Many of the staff **speak excellent English** and are passionate and knowledgeable about the collection – so pick their brains.
• Call ahead if you want to **visit the workshops** where student artisans and restorers are taught every technique involved in the decorative arts.
• Bags etc **must be left** in rather small lockers during your visit so don't bring anything too large.

❸ Castelo de São Jorge

From the moment you arrive in Lisbon, the honey-coloured walls of the Castelo de São Jorge (St George's Castle) will act as a magnet, drawing you up the hill to explore this historic complex. Here are mighty fortifications, watch-towers and ramparts, shady courtyards and beguiling squares, while the terraces and promenades provide some of the city's best views, with Lisbon's heart laid out at your feet.

Castelo de São Jorge, Lisbon's ancient fortress

The steep hill on which the **Castelo** stands was the obvious place for a defensive stronghold, and an Iron Age fort stood here even before the arrival of the Romans in 138 BC. They built a citadel here, and the Roman city, Olispónia, spread outwards down the hill to the river below. Roman rule throughout the Iberian peninsula came to an end in 409 and, after 300 turbulent years of Visigothic occupation, the Moors arrived in Lisbon in 714. Adapting the remnants of the Roman stronghold, they built a fortress here, whose centre was the Alcáçova, the palace still existing today. The Muslims held Lisbon for over 400 years, their occupation ending with the siege of the Castelo by Afonso Henriques in 1147. He had appealed to a group of French and English Crusaders on their way to Jerusalem to stop off and help him oust the Moors, a suggestion seized eagerly by the northerners, ever ready for pillage and murder. They threw in their lot with Afonso, embarking on a 17-week siege of the Castelo and the surrounding inner city. The walls were finally breached in October amid scenes of devastating destruction, rape and murder of Muslims and Christians, who had lived peacefully side by side with the Moors for centuries. From 1279 to 1511 the Portuguese kings lived in the old

Moorish palace, only moving after the construction of the Palácio da Ribeira. Later centuries saw construction of houses, palaces and government offices in and around the castle complex. Much of this was removed in the 1930s, when the walls and battlements were restored, but there's much more to the Castelo than a mere castle.

Some of the oldest segments are the **outer walls**, thought to be Roman, which enclose both the castle and the *intra-muros* (within the walls) neighbourhood. This comprises narrow streets, approached through the **Arco de São Jorge**, where elderly tenants living in rent-controlled flats rub shoulders with the high-earning professionals who've paid steeply to live in this desirable enclave. To the northeast is the **Igreja de Santa Cruz do Castelo**, built on the site of a mosque, while the entrance to the castle proper lies ahead. Once inside, you'll find yourself on a broad square, with its **statue of Afonso Henriques**, and cannons lining a parapet, part of the outer walls. From here, a perfect viewpoint for getting your bearings, the hill drops down to the Baixa (► 46–49) and its squares, with Lisbon's hills and its river lying beyond. Follow the **ramparts** and **well-tended gardens** to the inner walls and you'll be in the heart of the medieval castle, a series of **courtyards** and more walls. These splendid and surprisingly pristine structures embody everything a castle should be. Topped with authentic-looking battlements – part of the 1930s face-lift – and crowned with ten towers, they surround two courtyards, from where stairs give access to the wall-top walkways. From these you can climb the towers, one of which houses the **Câmara Escura**, an old-fashioned camera obscura which gives bird's-eye views via a series of lenses onto the streets and people far below.

Also within the castle complex is the **Alcáçova**, the original Moorish palace, which acted as the royal residence from the 13th to 16th centuries. Little remains today, and what there is has been heavily restored, but you'll get a good idea of

You can walk around the ramparts of the fortress for superb views over Lisbon

Right: Grim carving on the walls

its original dimensions in the series of chambers now housing the **Olisipónia, a multimedia exhibition** focusing on the history of Lisbon. A series of screens and sound effects lead you through a 25-minute rundown of the city's past, with some good information on Portugal's 15th- to 16th-century Golden Age and some insights into the earthquake of 1755. Outside this inner core, more stairs lead down the hill to the outlying **Torre de São Lourenço**. The entire complex had a thorough face-lift before Expo '98, as did the surrounding gardens, one of the loveliest spots in central Lisbon. The combination of plants and trees, terraces, pools and fountains provide the perfect backdrop to the wide views over the city.

TAKING A BREAK

There's a **café** and **restaurant** in the castle complex, or buy a drink from the kiosk to enjoy looking out across the city.

Trees line the cobbled ramparts of the Castelo

🔧 198 B2 ✉ Costa do Castelo ☎ 218 800 620; www.castelosaojorge.egeac.pt (in English) 🕐 Castle and Olisipónia Mar–Oct daily 9–8:30; Nov–Feb daily 9–5:30. Câmara Escura Mar–Oct daily 10–5; Nov–Feb daily 11–2:30 💷 Castle free; Olisipónia moderate 🍴 Restaurant and café within castle complex 🚌 37; trams 12, 28

CASTELO DE SÃO JORGE: INSIDE INFO

Top tips The **Castelo and its gardens** are a great place to spend a couple of hours during the hottest part of the day.
• Surfaces underfoot are often uneven and there's plenty of walking, so **wear comfortable, flat shoes**.

Must see The Olisipónia for a **state-of-the-art overview** of Lisbon's history.
• The **views** from the **ramparts**.
• The **medieval quarter of Santa Cruz** within the Castelo's outer walls.

❹ São Vicente de Fora

The beautiful Italian-style church of São Vicente de Fora (St Vincent Without the Walls) forms only one part of this stunning complex, set high above old Lisbon and the Tejo. The adjoining monastery, with its double cloister and fabulous blue-and-white tiling, is one of the city's loveliest, while its pantheon of royal tombs is a link with Portugal's past.

A church dedicated to **St Vincent, patron saint of Lisbon**, was first built on this site to commemorate the ousting of the Moors from the city. Afonso Henriques, first King of Portugal, had vowed to build Christian places of worship on all the sites where Portuguese soldiers and Christian crusaders were buried. The date was 1147, and the area stood outside the existing city walls – hence the name, St Vincent Without. The church was completed in 1629, but was severely damaged by the great earthquake of 1755 when the cupola collapsed, killing hundreds. It was restored by all the major contemporary architects and sculptors and is now **one of Lisbon's finest examples of the baroque**. Approached by an elegant stairway, the facade was the first of its type to be built in Portugal and was to be immensely influential, copied throughout the country and in its overseas possessions as far apart as Brazil and Macao. The **interior**, built to the Greek-cross pattern, has a soaring nave with classical pilasters supporting a fine coffered vault, which leads the eye up to the gilded high altar with its baldachino, while the walls are decorated with 17th- and 18th-century *azulejos*.

The dome allows light to filter through to the nave

Leaving the church, head left for the **cloisters**, once the focus of the church's monastery. These two **adjoining courtyards** are in Italian Mannerist style, the graceful stone arches of the ground floor supporting a harmonious grey and white second storey. Step beneath the arches, though, and you're very firmly in Portugal, for the lower half of the walls are sumptuously tiled in blue and white, providing a superb

Top: The former refectory now serves as Portugal's Royal Pantheon

Above: The church of St Vincent once stood outside the walls of the city

contrast of classicism and the finest of vernacular decoration. Between the two cloisters you'll find the **sacristy**, totally covered in opulent polychrome marble panels. Next comes the monastery refectory, converted in 1885 to serve as a **pantheon** for the monarchs of the House of Bragança, Portugal's last ruling dynasty. Outside here, head for the elegant staircase, lined with tiles rich in naturalistic detail of foliage, animals and birds, which leads to the **upper storey**. The main draw upstairs are the tiled panels illustrating the Fables of la Fontaine, moralistic and lively tales written in France in the 1660s and based, to some extent, on Aesop's Fables. From here you can climb up and up to the **terrace** above the church; this gives access to the tower, where you'll find one of the best views in Lisbon.

TAKING A BREAK

There's a **tea room** near the museum entrance, where you can have a coffee and home-made cakes or enjoy a light lunch.

➕ 198 C3 ✉ Largo de São Vicente ☎ 218 824 400, www.ippar.pt ⏲ Church Tue–Sat 9–4, Sun 9–12:30; cloisters Tue–Sat 10–5, Sun 10–11:30 💰 Church free, monastery moderate 🍴 Café in monastery 🚌 37; trams 12, 28

SÃO VICENTE DE FORA: INSIDE INFO

Top tip Although the **view from the tower** is one of best in the city, it's a long way up steep and narrow steps. You could just climb as far as the **terrace**, which **also has fine views** – though naturally not as wide.

Don't miss The **monastery entrance hall**, with its solid marble balustrade, inlaid marble columns, domed frescoed ceiling and chequered floor of pink, black and white; the *azulejos* are by Emanuel dos Santos.

5 Alfama

Labyrinthine, narrow streets, flights of steps, blind alleys and tiny squares are the hallmarks of the wonderfully atmospheric Alfama, Lisbon's oldest *bairro*. Densely inhabited, vibrant with ebullient street life and packed with interest, it's one of the city's most compelling areas. Its heady mix of sights, sounds and smells evoke the past so strongly that few other neighbourhoods can equal it for bringing home the weight of Lisbon's history and the peoples that have shaped it.

The Alfama is the most ancient *bairro* of Lisbon, a densely built, well-watered and historic quarter that was inhabited in Roman times. The Visigoths lived here too, and some of today's buildings still stand on Visigothic foundations, but it was the Moors who left the biggest mark. The very name Alfama probably comes from the Arabic "Al-Hama", meaning springs or fountains, and two local fountains, the **Chafariz del Rei** (King's Fountain) and the **Chafariz del Dentro** (Interior Fountain) have been in use since medieval times. Under the Moors, this was the grandest area of the city and continued to be so during the early years of Christian rule, but a succession of earth tremors caused the nobility to move out, leaving the Moorish character of the *bairro* untouched. The street pattern is entirely Moorish, a web of streets designed as a defence system and

Top right: Narrow cobbled street in the Alfama

Left: Largo de São Miguel

Bottom: Detail of an *azulejo* panel depicting the fight to win the Moorish castle in Lisbon

Right: Looking east from the Largo das Portas do Sol

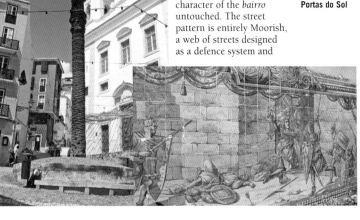

modelled on the *kasbahs* of North Africa. Narrow streets keep out the great midday heat, the latticed window shutters are still modelled on Islamic designs, and hidden behind the houses are patios and gardens where citrus trees and grapevines grow. The area, built on rock tight against the Castelo (➤ 77–79) hill, escaped much damage in the great earthquake and remained a vibrant, heavily populated working class area. It continues to be so today, though some commercialisation is creeping in with the influx of tourists, and top-floor apartments are becoming increasingly desirable to well-off young professionals, though the lack of vehicle access – the streets are too narrow – may act as a brake on whole-scale gentrification.

The heart of the area is perhaps the **Largo de São Miguel**, where the facade of the **Igreja de São Miguel** (St Michael's), a post-earthquake reconstruction of a much earlier church, overlooks a single, stately palm tree. From here, you have a couple of choices; cut one street down to take in the weekday morning fish market in the **Rua de São Pedro**, complete with raucous fishwives straight out of central casting, or head along **Rua de São Miguel**. If the Alfama can be said to have a main street, this is it, as the

St Vincent and His Ravens

Presiding over the Largo das Portas do Sol and the slopes of the Alfama is a statue of St Vincent, patron saint of Lisbon. Legend tells that, back in the 12th century, Afonso Henriques heard of the whereabouts of the saint's relics, hidden far to the south in the Algarve and guarded by ravens. He sent his ships to retrieve the relics; second time round they were lucky and the ship, encircled by ravens, reached Lisbon in September 1173. St Vincent was declared the city's patron and the image of a boat and ravens has been Lisbon's emblem ever since.

butchers' shops, tiny
grocers, and cramped
little bars and *tascas*
testify. Narrow alleys
run off from either
side, and it's these
you should explore –
they lead to twisting
staircases, low arch-
ways, patios, streets
and gardens, the
essence of the
Alfama. Both these
main streets lead
to the **Beco do
Spirito Santo** and
on to church of
Santo Estêvão
(St Stephen's), whose
veranda gives great
views down into
nearby gardens and
across the surround-
ing red roofs to the
harbour beyond.

Red roofs and
whitewashed
walls are
keynotes of
domestic
architecture
in the Alfama

West from São Miguel, the alleys lead to the Sé (➤ 72–73)
and the area between it and the river. Here you'll find the
Casa dos Bicos, a merchant's house and warehouse built in
1523 by Brás de Albuquerque, whose name comes from the
pyramidal spikes (*bicos*) which decorate the facade. West
again, near the Praça do Comércio (➤ 47), is the sublime
portal of the **Igreja da Conceição-a-Velha** (Church of the
Conception), a Manueline doorway showing Our Lady of
Mercy sheltering nobles, rich and poor under her cloak, while
flights of cherubim swarm up the side column, all that's left
of the pre-earthquake church.

TAKING A BREAK

Choose one of the many **bars** or **cafés** you'll pass as you
explore the Alfama.

➕ 198 C2 🍴 Numerous throughout area 🚋 Trams 12, 28

ALFAMA: INSIDE INFO

Top tips If you get lost in the Alfama don't worry, just **head downhill** to get
your bearings.
• The **best time to visit is the morning**, to get the best of **street life**, or **evening**,
when the restaurants and *fado* houses open up.
• Pickpocketing can be a problem in the Alfama, so **watch your bag**, **wallet** or
camera. Parts of the area are best avoided after dark.
• To avoid walking uphill, **catch the tram** up to the São Vicente de Fora and
walk downhill

❻Museu Nacional do Azulejo

Azulejos (tiles) are everywhere in Lisbon, but there's no better place to see them than at the Museu Nacional do Azulejo (National Tile Museum), where some of the most historic and beautiful tiles ever made are displayed in one of the city's loveliest monastic complexes. Against a backdrop of courtyards and cloisters are thousands of tiles, seen at their best in the opulent interior of the Igreja de Nossa Senhora da Madre de Deus (Church of Our Lady Mother of God).

The Church of Madre de Deus is filled with exquisite gilt woodwork and *azulejos*

The Franciscan convent of **Madre de Deus** (Mother of God) was founded in 1509 by Queen Leonor, and remained part of the queen's household until 1834, when religious orders were suppressed in Portugal. Over the centuries major construction work was carried out, financed by the gold brought from Brazil. The sacristy was altered and the church covered in gilded carvings, tiles, paintings, polychrome marbles and exotic woods, turning the convent into one of the most exuberantly baroque buildings in Portugal. It was this that prompted the authorities to choose the complex as the home of the National Tile Museum, founded in 1971.

The word *azulejo* has its roots in two Arabic words; *azraq*, meaning azure, and *zalayja*, polished terracotta. Blue, polished terracotta precisely describes Portugal's most ubiquitous tile, and you can learn about how they are made at the start of the museum tour. Tiles first appeared in Lisbon at the start of the 16th century; over the next 200 years designs and colours became more complex, as the Portuguese borrowed Italian, Dutch and Chinese techniques and ideas, transforming themselves into Europe's master tilemakers.

Much of the museum's charm and interest lies in the building and its decorative tiles, brought here from all over Lisbon and beyond, but there are a few unmissable exhibits. Top of the list is the **Panorama of Lisbon**, dated 1700, and thus showing the capital before the earthquake. Its 23m (75 feet) length shows 14km (9 miles) of coastline, and is rich in detail, clearly showing the hills, palaces, churches and civic buildings of a city that was laid waste only half a century later. There's charm too in the domestic tiles, made to decorate kitchens, gardens and living rooms and painted with plants, flowers, fruit, vegetables and animals; look for these in the **Santos Simões Room**. Be sure to take in too, the **Claustrim** (Small Cloister), the convent's original exercise and meditation space, whose walls are now covered with both polychrome and blue-and-white tiles, the perfect foil to the Manueline touches of the architecture. From here, there's access to the **church** itself, an in-your-face blast of over-the-top opulence, with a gilded high altar, paintings, woodcarving, marble and, above all, tiles, whose cool blue is the perfect foil for the richness of the décor.

Below: Example of colourful tilework

Bottom: Azulejo panorma of the waterfront

TAKING A BREAK

The museum has a **café** and **restaurant** where you can sit and relax: refreshments are often served outside in the garden in summer.

🚌 199 F5 ✉ Rua da Madre de Deus 4 ☎ 218 100 340; www.mnazulejo-ipmuseus.pt 🕐 Tue 2–6, Wed–Sun 10–6 💷 Moderate
🍴 Café and restaurant in museum 🚍 794

MUSEU NACIONAL DO AZULEJO: INSIDE INFO

Must see The **cloisters** – two contrasting courtyards.
• The **church** and **altarpiece** – quintessential baroque splendour.
• The **Hunting Room** – green, blue and yellow tiles with a distinctly Far Eastern flavour.
• The **Panorama of Lisbon** – a glimpse of pre-earthquake Lisbon.

At Your Leisure

7 Igreja e Museu de Santo António

St Vincent may be Lisbon's official patron saint, but the best loved is St Anthony of Padua, born in Lisbon around 1190. He travelled to Morocco, was shipwrecked and landed up in Padua in Italy, where, following his death in 1231, his shrine became, and remains, among that country's largest and busiest. Back in Lisbon, the Igreja de Santo António (also known as Museu Antoniano) now stands on the site of his birthplace. The present church was completed in 1787 after the destruction of the original in the earthquake, and is a small, typically **baroque church**. It's busy with devotees, who pop in to light a candle, and really buzzes on 12 June, the eve of the saint's feast. The afternoon sees the simultaneous marriage of around 16 couples, drawn by lot, in a splendid celebration funded by the council, which is followed the next day by a procession from the church to the Sé. Despite being a stone's throw apart, this takes 2 hours or more to weave its way through the streets of the Alfama. The festivities end with a giant street party, complete with grilled sardines and copious amounts of red wine.

You can learn more about the life of St Anthony in the **museum** next

The Church of St Anthony

View from Esplanada da Igreja de Graça

door to the church, where there are sculptures, paintings and biographical documents.

➕ 198 B2 ✉ Largo de Santo António à Sé 24 ☎ 218 860 447 (museum) 🕐 Church 8–7:30; museum Tue–Sun 10–1, 2–6 💰 Inexpensive 🍴 Bars nearby 🚌 37; trams 12, 28

❽ Graça

The faithful tram No 28 grinds its way uphill to Graça, a neighbourhood set on the hill behind São Vicente. Part of the city since earliest times, the *bairro* expanded in the 19th century, when open lots were developed for low-cost housing for city workers. These characteristic blocks, often tiled, ensure that Graça retains a thriving population and its own distinctive, small-town atmosphere.

The centre is the bustling **Largo da Graça**, from where you can stroll across to the Esplanada da Igreja de Graça, a terraced café that has one of Lisbon's best sunset views. Up here too, is the **Igreja da Graça** (Mon–Sat 9–12, 3–7;

One of Lisbon's liveliest shopping experiences – the Feira da Ladra

Sun 9:30–12:30, 6–8), once the centre of a monastic community, founded in the 13th century. The monastery was dissolved in 1834 and the buildings handed over to the army, but the church, rebuilt after the earthquake, is still very much in use. During Lent, from its ludicrously glitzy interior, the Senhor dos Passos procession sets out, taking images of Christ and the Virgin all over the *bairro*. For another splendid *miradouro*, head up Rua Damasceno Monteiro and the Calçada do Monte for Nossa Senhora do Monte, a chapel set on the very highest of all the city hills. The chapel contains an ancient marble seat, said to have belonged to the Roman bishop St Gens; despite its original masculine ownership, the chair was thought to ease labour pains, and enjoyed great popularity with Portuguese queens awaiting childbirth.

➕ 198 C3 ✉ Graça 🍴 Numerous bars 🚌 Trams 12, 28

❾ Feira da Ladra

Campo de Santa Clara comes into its own on Tuesdays and Saturdays, when it hosts Lisbon's own **Flea Market**, the Feira da Ladra (Thieves' Market). From daybreak, stall-holders set out their wares, some simply spread out on the ground, others housed in more permanent shops set around the perimeter of the square. What's on sale is basically typical flea-market offerings, and there's plenty of junk as well. Get there early, and you may be able to pick up a bargain in bric-a-brac and

tiles, and some of the outer stalls have good furniture. The chief pleasure though, is browsing the stalls crammed with oddities – old books, postcards, African artefacts and shoes and clothing. Nearby is the **Mercado de Santa Clara**, a vibrant food market that's a great place to pick up a picnic and also home to one of Lisbon's great places to eat (➤ 93).

🔢 199 D3 ⊠ Campo de Santa Clara, São Vicente ⏱ Tue, Sat 6–4; Mercado de Santa Clara Mon–Sat 8–2 🍴 Bars nearby 🚌 34; tram 28

❿ Panteão Nacional de Santa Engrácia

You can't miss the vast white cupola of the Igreja de Santa Engrácia, nominated in 1916 by the Republican government as the national Pantheon, a burial place for Portuguese heroes. The present church dates back to 1683, when construction started on a building that was to take 285 years to complete – the dome was finally finished in 1966, and *lisboetas* still refer to anything that overruns its schedule as "the works of Santa Engrácia". Its predecessor was torn down in 1630, when a local Jew was charged with having desecrated it by robbery. Defending his innocence, he is supposed to have foretold that the new church would never be completed because of this false

The Igreja de Santa Engrácia, with its impressive dome

For Kids

Top of the list in old Lisbon for kids has to be a long ride on tram 28. Hop on at Praça Martim Moniz and sit tight for the whole journey up the hill and down again to the Sé – possible jumping off points might be Graça or the Largo das Portas do Sol. The Castelo de São Jorge is also popular; it's a good place to let off steam with plenty of opportunities to storm the ramparts or attack the walls with stealth. Most children will be fascinated by the Alfama, and enjoy exploring and watching the street life, and older ones, especially girls, might like to imagine themselves living a fairy-tale, 18th-century life in the Museu-Escola de Artes Decorativas. Whatever their ages, most kids enjoy an ice-cream with a view, so head for one of the *miradouros*, where you can identify and point things out as a family, while ice-cream drips down your arms.

Exhibits in the Vasco da Gama Room of the excellent Military Museum

accusation. Sure enough, the first rebuild collapsed in 1681; work started again, the plans heavily inspired by St Peter's in Rome. It's a mammoth building, its interior rich in coloured marble, a fitting home for the famous departed who are interred or commemorated here. Most familiar to foreigners is probably the great *fadista* Amália Rodrigues, and there are memorials to Vasco da Gama and Prince Henry the Navigator.

➕ 199 D3 ✉ Campo de Santa Clara
☎ 218 854 820; www.ippar.pt
🕐 Tue–Sun 10–5 💷 Inexpensive
🍴 Bars nearby 🚌 34; tram 28

🕦 Museu da Agua

EPAL, the Portuguese Free Water Company, has won several awards for its museum presentations, which tell the story of Lisbon's public water supply from Roman times to the present day and also provide public access to the sites connected with this branch of Portugal's industrial heritage. This museum is only one of the four sites operated by EPAL, but steam fans in particular will get enormous pleasure here. Built in 1830, and the first pumping station to supply the whole city, its cavernous **Steam Hall** houses four huge steam engines, installed in the 1880s. They're run regularly, so call ahead to ensure your visit coincides with this. Next door, there's an exhibition hall telling the history of water in the city; the staff here can also organise a trip to the 18th-century aqueduct at Alcântara, on the western edge of Lisbon.

➕ 199 E4 ✉ Rua Alviela 12
☎ 218 100 215 🕐 Mon–Sat 10–6
💷 Inexpensive 🍴 Bars nearby 🚌 794

🕧 Museu Militar

With its tranquil courtyard lined with tiles and its magnificent interior, it's hard to grasp that the Museu Militar (Military Museum) is, in fact, appropriately housed in what was once a weaponry factory. Thirty-four rooms are packed with armour, weapons, uniforms and military ephemera, tracing the history of **Portuguese warfare**. The visit starts upstairs with two rooms devoted to the Napoleonic campaigns, inextricably linked with the small town of Torres Vedras, just outside Lisbon. From here, the route runs through a series of ornately decorated rooms, complete with triumphalistic ceiling panels, displaying literally thousands of pieces –

Examples of the Portuguese guitar (*guitarra portuguesa*)

heaven for war buffs. Besides 17th- and 18th-century equipment, there's plenty of mid-20th-century armoury and weapons, equipment of the type used by the Portuguese and their adversaries in the bloody colonial campaigns in the late 1970s.

🏛 199 D2 ⊠ Largo do Museu do Artilharia ☎ 218 842 568; www.geira.pt/mmilitar ④ Tue–Sun 10–5 ⑥ Moderate 🍴 Bars nearby 🚌 794 ❓ Labelling is in Portuguese only so ask at the ticket desk for the English leaflet

🔟 Casa de Fado

To learn all you want to know about Lisbon's own soul music head for the Casa de Fado (House of Fado), an intriguing museum, opened in 2000, that explains and illustrates this quintessential Portuguese passion. Through a series of exhibits, posters, recordings and mock-ups, you'll learn the history, hear the music and gaze at the stars. If you're planning to listen to *fado* (► 12–13) at some point, this museum will provide an excellent background, and help you get more out of a live performance. Along the way, you can see clips from *fado* movies featuring the much-

loved diva, Amália, spy on a guitar workshop, where the distinctive 10-stringed Portuguese guitars are made, and visit a 1940s-style *fado* house. If you want to purchase CDs or books, the museum shop has one of the best selections in town, with the opportunity to listen before you buy.

🏛 198 C2 ⊠ Largo do Chafariz de Dentro ☎ 218 823 470; www.museudofado.egeac.pt (in English) ④ Tue–Sun 10–5:30 ⑥ Inexpensive 🍴 Café in museum 🚌 8, 28, 35, 90, 746, 759, 794

Where to...
Eat and Drink

Prices
Expect to pay for a three-course meal for one, excluding drinks

€ under €20   €€ €20–€40   €€€ over €40

Antiga Casa de Pasto Estrela da Sé €
Lisbon was once full of *casas de pasto*, cheap and simple restaurants aimed at ordinary people, and this example is one of the last. Step inside and the timewarp decor includes wonderful curtained wooden booths, a hangover from the 19th century when they allowed a touch of privacy for would-be lovers. The food is straightforward, fresh and traditional; portions generous. If you're looking for a real Lisbon eating experience that won't break the bank, this could be it.

✚ 198 B2 ⊠ Largo de Santo António da Sé 4 ☎ 218 870 455 ⓒ Mon–Fri noon–3, 7–10 🚊 Tram 28

Arco do Castelo €€
This is Portuguese Indian cooking, all the way from Goa, once a Portuguese possession, and is rich in fresh ginger, fiery spices and fish and seafood. Try the delicious prawn curry, *xacuti*, a house speciality rich with coconut milk. If you're dining, it's essential to book.

✚ 198 B2 ⊠ Rua Chão da Feira 25, Castelo ☎ 218 876 598 ⓒ Mon–Sat 12:30–10.30 🚊 Trams 12, 28

Bica do Sapato €€€
The super cool Bica do Sapato, partly owned by John Malkovich, is high on the list of Lisbon's trendiest restaurants. The setting, right on the docks just across from the Santa Apolónia train station, helps, and the decor in its three eating areas is geared to complement the food. The main restaurant concentrates on modern favourites with a twist and offers a popular *sugestão da semana* (dish of the week), and lovers of traditional Portuguese cooking will find what they're looking for in the Café. Fish is at its freshest in the Sushi Bar where, on a Wednesday, their fixed-price *Dia dos Sabores* (Day of Flavours) menu is particularly good value. There's a huge tapas buffet on Tuesday evenings.

✚ 199 E3 ⊠ Avenida Infante Dom Henrique, Armazém B, Cais da Pedra, Santa Apolónia ☎ 218 810 320; www.bicadosapato.com ⓒ Restaurant: Mon 8pm–11:30pm, Tue–Sat 12–2:30, 8–11:30. Café: Mon 7:30pm–1am, Tue–Sat 12:30–3:30, 7:30pm–1am. Sushi bar: Mon–Sat 7:30pm–1am 🚋 9, 12, 51, 81, 90

Casanova €€
If you want a change from Portuguese cooking, head for this converted warehouse opposite the Santa Apolónia train station with its good-value Italian eatery. Choose one of the myriad varieties of pizza, paper-thin and cooked to order in a wood-fired oven, if you want to keep the cost right down, or try one of the other specialities, which range from simple *crostini* or *bruschetta* to slow-cooked bean dishes if you're feeling more adventurous. No reservations, but the turnover is fast so you shouldn't have long to wait.

✚ 199 3E ⊠ Avenida Infante Dom Henrique, Cais da Pedra, Armazém B, loja 7 (warehouse B, shop No 7), Santa Apolónia ☎ 218 877 532; www.restaurantecasanostra.com ⓒ Tue–Sun 12:30pm–1am; closed Tue lunch 🚋 9, 12, 51, 81, 90

Where to... Shop

Despite the fascination of the Alfama's streets and alleys and the charm of this entire area, it doesn't rate high as a shopper's paradise. You could possibly pick up a few bits and pieces in the way of everyday items in the **Graça shops**, and burn money in the classy **antique shops** around the Sé and Castelo, but for easily portable and desirable goods it's better to head for the temples of indulgence in and around Baixa and Chiado. There are honorable exceptions though, and *fado* fans will find an excellent selection of CDs, instruments and books at the museum shop attached to the **Casa de Fado** (➤ 91).

Right on the edge of this area, in a less than salubrious square, is one of Lisbon's best tile outlets,

onions and chips, and flavoured with coriander. Leave room for one of the desserts.

➕ 199 D3 ☒ Campo de Santa Clara ☎ 218 873 986 ⏰ Mon–Sat 12:30–3, 8–10:30; Sun 12:30–3 🚋 Tram 28

Via Graça €€€

At the top of Graça you'll find one of Lisbon's most perfect restaurants for romantics, a civilised spot with beautiful views of the floodlit castle ramparts and the city below. The cooking is rooted in classic Portuguese cuisine, but there's a touch of subtlety in the combination of flavours, such as undernotes of Moscatel in a duck marinade. Service is excellent and the wine list strong on good reds, particularly from the Alentejo. The only caveat is the size of the portions which is more than generous.

➕ 198 B3/4 ☒ Rua Damasceno Monteiro 9B, Graça ☎ 218 870 830; www.restauranteviagraca.com ⏰ Mon–Fri 12:30–3, 7:30–11, Sat and Sun 7:30–11 🚋 Tram 28

Hua Ta Li €€

The clean Chinese flavours at Hua Ta Li make a great change after days of Portuguese staples. Ingredients are fresh and top quality, and service fast, and children very welcome – there are even high chairs on offer – so it's easy to overlook the less than inspired plastic décor. It fills up fast, so get here early.

➕ 198 B1 ☒ Rua dos Bacalhoeiros 109–115, Alfama ☎ 218 879 170 ⏰ Daily 11–3:30, 7–11 🚋 Trams 18, 28

Malmequer Bemmequer €€

Right in the heart of the Alfama district, this friendly little restaurant inevitably draws tourists by the score. But despite this, standards haven't slipped and the mainly Portuguese classic dishes are well cooked and nicely served – including the signature dish, charcoal-grilled *barbecue dos diabos* (devil's barbecue), mixed meat and poultry with the fiery taste of

cayenne. The rice dishes are also very good, and they do a mean line in puddings, including a distinctly English-style trifle.

➕ 198 C2 ☒ Rua de São Miguel 23–25, Alfama ☎ 218 876 535 ⏰ Tue 7–11pm, Wed–Sun noon–3, 7–10:30

Mercado de Santa Clara €

You'll have to climb to the upstairs of Santa Clara market to reach this splendid restaurant, but it's well worth with it, both for the great views across the tree tops to the dome of the Panteão Nacional de Santa Engrácia and for the food, which is excellent. Carlos Braz Lopes, the owner, also runs cookery courses at his gourmet store across town and has a passion for the best that Lisbon has to offer. Expect the traditional staples, made using high-quality ingredients – both the pork and the beef here are well prepared and properly hung. If you haven't tried *bacalhau*, go for the *bacalhau à bras*, where the dried fish is mixed with scrambled eggs,

Viúva Lamego (Largo do Intendente 25, tel: 218 852 408; www.viuvalamego.com), adorned with tiles on its exterior. Founded in 1849, it still makes tiles to order from old designs; they can also ship goods worldwide.

Near here, on Largo Martim Moniz, you'll find the **Centro Comercial Mouraria**, a bustling warren of multi-ethnic shops. Food from all the old Portuguese colonies – India, Africa and China – cheap clothing, watches and CDs are all here, and the immigrant crowds are among Lisbon's most fascinating.

If you've been visiting the Castle, keep an eye out for the nearby **Pessoa de Carvalho** (Costa do Castelo 4; tel: 218 862 413), a craft and gift shop housed in an old Alfama house, or head down the hill towards the Casa dos Bicos, next to which you'll find **Atelier** (Rua dos Bacalhoeiros 12; tel: 218 865 563), specialising in hand-painted tiles. The artists are often at work and they can ship world-wide.

Where to... Be Entertained

Along with the Bairro Alto, the **Alfama** is one of the best places to hear traditional *fado*. You can either head for a *casa de fado*, where a reasonable standard of performance is guaranteed, but where you'll have to have dinner, or take your chance on hitting something good at a bar specialising in *fado vadio*, where it's all less structured and anyone can get up and sing.

In the Alfama, good *fado* restaurants include the **Clube de Fado** (Rua São João da Praça, tel: 218 852 704), a great little place with regular traditional sessions; the **Parreirinha de Alfama** (Beco do Espírito Santo 1, off Largo do Chafariz de Dentro, tel: 218 868 209); and **A Baiuca** (Rua de São Miguel 20, tel: 218 867 284), a

family-run place that specialises in *fado vadio*.

If you're looking for cooler sounds, **Netjazzcafé** (Costa del Castelo 7, tel: 218 804 406) features an intimate, wide-ranging selection of music, with the emphasis on jazz, performed from what was originally a wash tank in this ex-laundry of a former women's prison, while nearby, the terrace of the **Bar das Imagens** (Calçada Marquês de Tancos 1, tel: 218 884 636), on the Costa do Castelo, is a great place to listen to music while you gaze out over the Baixa. Or head down towards the river to **Onda Jazz** (Arco de Jesus 7, tel: 218 873 064; www.ondajazz.com; Tue–Thu 9pm–2am, Fri-Sat 9pm–3am) where they hold live

jam sessions on Tuesdays in addition to a monthly programme (check website for details).

There are more night-time views from the esplanada of **Cerca Moura** (Largo das Portas do Sol 4, tel: 218 874 859), which also has a cosy inside bar built into the ancient Moorish city walls, or head further up the hill to the **Esplanada da Igreja da Graça** (Largo da Graça, no phone) for more great views and eclectic music in the evenings.

Clubbers should waste no time in heading for **Lux** (Avenida Infante Dom Henrique, Armazém A, Cais da Pedra, Santa Apolónia, tel: 218 820 890; www.luxfragil.com) a huge, cool club in a riverside warehouse, with a minimal post-modern interior. Local and international DJs please the stylish crowd with a mix of dance and mainstream music.

Nearby, at Doca do Jardim do Tobaco, you can head for **MUSIcais** (Pavilhão A/B, tel: 937 583 698), two bars in one, that features live music on the *esplanada*, and a DJ).

The Western Slopes

Getting Your Bearings 96 – 97
In a Day 98 – 99
Don't Miss 100 – 108
At Your Leisure 109 – 111
Where to... 112 – 114

Getting Your Bearings

West of the Baixa, the hill rises steeply to an area first developed in the 1500s, when aristocrats and merchants settled here, building around the Jesuit church of São Roque. The district became known as the Bairro Alto de São Roque – literally St Rock's High District. This is today's Bairro Alto, Lisbon's own party hot spot, where, come weekend evenings, every narrow street is crammed with revellers. Here you'll find restaurants, bars, and cafés, and the Bairro has more clubs and *fado* houses than anywhere else in Lisbon. Throw in some of the sharpest of all the city's retail outlets, and it's no surprise the Bairro Alto is a magnet for locals and tourists alike.

To the north is the Jardim Botânico, to the south Santa Catarina with its beautiful river views, while to the west lie the quieter streets of São Bento, home to Portugal's National Assembly. This is a hilly area, where the streets march inexorably up and down, leading, west of São Bento, to the *bairro* of Estrela, its high point crowned with the great Basilica da Estrela. This is prosperous, middle-class territory, where the property prices rise as you edge south towards the Tejo. Overlooking the river itself are spread the classy, mansion-lined streets and avenues of Lapa, where big money rubs shoulders with the diplomatic corps. Down by the river, Lapa runs into Santos, one of the longest-settled parts of Lisbon and home to one of Portugal's most important museums, the Museu de Arte Antiga.

Previous page: Rich gilding and carving in São Roque

Below: Neon sign in the Bairro Alto

★Don't Miss

1 Bairro Alto ➤ 100
2 Basílica da Estrela ➤ 102
3 Museu Nacional de Arte Antiga ➤ 104

At Your Leisure

4 Igreja de São Roque ➤ 109
5 Jardim Botânico and Praça do Príncipe
    Real ➤ 109
6 São Bento and Lapa ➤ 110
7 Igreja de Santa Catarina ➤ 110
8 Mãe d'Água ➤ 111

Off the Beaten Track

9 Palácio dos Marquêses de Fronteira
    ➤ 111

The dome of
the Basílica
da Estrela

This diverse area is home to the Bairro Alto, famed for its clubs and nightlife, residential areas that range from smart to distinctly edgy, fine churches, shady squares and a splendid museum.

The Western Slopes in a Day

9:30am

Start your day by getting your bearings in the ❶ **Bairro Alto** (➤ 100–101) when it's at its quietest, and you'll have time and space to browse in its quirky specialist shops and get a flavour of its private life. Save your feet on the way by taking either the **Elevador da Glória** or the **Elevador da Bica** to gain your height; a journey on one of these wonderful old funiculars (➤ 32) is an essential Lisbon experience.

11:00am

Enjoy coffee with a view from the kiosk on the *esplanada* at the Miradouro de Santa Catarina (➤ 111), from where there's a sweeping view over the river, before heading northwest uphill to join the Calçada de Estrela. This long street climbs past the **Palácio de São Bento** (➤ 110; right) to the ❷ **Basílica da Estrela** (➤ 102–103), its mighty dome one of Lisbon's most distinctive landmarks.

12:30pm

Visit the basílica and then head for a well-earned lunch, back-tracking down hill to the Bairro Alto, from where you can start your afternoon.

2:30pm

Stroll through the streets of **6 Lapa** (► 110; left) with its elegant houses, to reach the **3 Museu Nacional de Arte Antiga** (► 104–108), where you can pick and choose what you see to get an overview of all that's best in Portuguese and international painting, sculpture and the applied arts.

5:00pm

Walk down the steps below the museum entrance to catch any bus heading east to Cais do Sodré and the city centre, and head back to your hotel to put you feet up before an evening out in the Bairro Alto.

7:30pm

Head back to the **1 Bairro Alto** and kick off your evening in one of the bars on the two key streets, Rua do Diário de Notícias or Rua da Atalaia. Good bets are B'Artis (Rua do Diário de Notícias 95–97, tel: 213 424 795) and Cafédiário (Rua do Diário de Notícias 3, no phone), both on Notícias, though the action really starts here after 10:30.

8:30pm

Walk across to Rua da Atalaia for **dinner**; 1° de Maio (► 112) is a good budget choice, or splash out at the superb Pap'Açorda (► 113) for award-winning cooking in chic and minimalist surroundings.

10:30pm

Time to **hit the night scene** and there's a plethora of choice in the bars of the Bairro Alto (above), which often feature live music and are open late, late, late. *Fado* devotees could head for Adega Machado (► 114).

⬛ Bairro Alto

The Bairro Alto, the upper town, stands high above the city centre, a bohemian area that easily manages to combine its role as a down-to-earth residential district with that of a vibrant night-time mecca. By day, you'll find life proceeding at a gentle pace within this relatively small area, but at night it's a different story, when the entire *bairro* gives itself over to pleasure and buzzes until the early hours. Here you'll find narrow, hilly streets, pretty squares, one of Lisbon's great churches and some of the city's quirkiest shops, where cutting-edge fashion rules.

The area was laid out in the 1500s, when it was the first district in Lisbon whose streets were constructed with any sort of pattern. Regular they might have been in contemporary terms, but it's as easy to get lost in the alleys and dead ends here as in the Alfama (▶ 82–84). There are two main squares, the Largo de Trindade Coelho, bordering the upper Chiado, and the **Praça Luís de Camões** at the southern end of the *bairro*, where it merges into Chiado.

Take the **Elevador da Glória** up from Restauradores (▶ 174), a great journey on an iconic funicular which has been saving the leg muscles since its inauguration in 1885. As you emerge, directly opposite you'll see the **Palácio Ludovice**, built in 1747 by Johann Friedrich Ludwig, the architect of Mafra (▶ 170), as his town house. It's now home to the **Solar do Vinho do Porto** (Port Wine Institute), and a good place to sample some of Porto's best – over 200 varieties are on offer in the bar (▶ 113). Just south from here, the restrained facade of the church of **São Roque** hides one of the city's most ebullient interiors, a 16th-century classical church with a series of sumptuously gilded and decorated marble-clad side chapels (▶ 109).

Cross the road and you'll find yourself in the heart of the **Bairro Alto**, the core of the party scene and a stronghold of Lisbon's own blues, *fado* – the *bairro* has over 20 *fado* houses. These once grand streets were later occupied by small merchants, their shops then followed by newspaper offices – both the **Rua do Século**, where, in 1699, the Marquês de

Above: The colourful Restaurante Alfaia

Top right: The Bairro Alto's steep hill leads down to the sea

Right: Fresh vegetables for sale

Pombal was born in the Palácio dos Carvalhos, and the **Rua do Diário de Notícias** get their names from the papers once based here. There are few grand palaces or monuments here, and the chief pleasure of the *bairro* is simply wandering the streets, particularly **Rua do Diário de Notícias, Rua da Atalaia** and **Rua da Rosa**. Walk through the arch at the bottom of Rua da Rosa and you'll see the top of the Elevador da Bica, inaugurated in 1892, which links the Bairro Alto with Bica (► 111). Along with the bars and restaurants there are plenty of shops – alternative fashion, specialist record shops, and booksellers around the Rua Nova de Trindade, home to a theatre and one of Lisbon's most famous beer halls (► 65). At the bottom of the hill, you'll emerge into Praça Luís de Camões, named after the 16th-century poet – his 19th-century statue stands in the square's centre, surrounded by other Portuguese literary figures.

TAKING A BREAK

You'll be spoiled for choice on the Bairro's main streets – try the **Pastelaria São Roque** (Rua Dom Pedro V 45) a superb old pastry shop with a marble and tiled interior.

➕ 197 E3 ⊠ Bairro Alto
🍴 Numerous cafés, bars, restaurants 🚇 Baixa-Chiado
🚌 92; tram 28

BAIRRO ALTO: INSIDE INFO

Top tips As it's at its **most vibrant after dark,** you might prefer only to visit the Bairro Alto in the evening.

• If you're taking an *elevador* **up the hill,** check to see they're both in operation; repairs sometimes cause closures.

Hidden gems For a *miradouro* that offers a different angle on Lisbon, head for the **Jardim de São Pedro de Alcântara**, just north of the Elevador da Glória. From here, the Avenida da Liberdade, the Castelo, the Baixa and the river are all laid out at your feet (see Walk ► 174–176).

🔢 Basílica da Estrela

The ornate white dome of the Basílica da Estrela dominates Lisbon's western skyline, a much-loved symbol of the city. Set high on its hill, this ebullient masterpiece is the emblem of an era of vast wealth and confidence. Flamboyance and austerity are perfectly fused here. Few other buildings so neatly encapsulate the spirit of an age, when intellectual curiosity and high moral values went hand in hand with a deep love of ostentation.

Above: The pink, grey and black marble altar of the Basílica

In 1770, Maria Francisca, heiress to the Portuguese throne, vowed to build a basilica, dedicated to the Sacred Heart of Jesus, if she gave birth to a male heir. Within a few years two sons were born, and building started in 1779. With its enormous team of labourers, work on the project was fast, and in 1788 the bells were blessed and in place. Only a month later, they rang out to mark the death, by smallpox, of one of the heirs. The building was consecrated the following year; Maria I, who died in Brazil in 1816, is buried in a monumental tomb in the main chapel of her gift to God and the city.

Inside this huge, shadowy building, the **single nave** has six side chapels, each with its own altarpiece. Marble pilasters delineate these chapels, soaring up to the richly decorated **vaulted ceiling**. At the far end in the transept, the crossing with the apse is drenched with the light that floods in from the **two-storey dome**. Pink, grey and cream marble is everywhere; gilt drips from the high altar, statues gesticulate from all sides. It's all very grand, very austere and somewhat chilling. There's light relief in the **Sala do Presépio**, which houses a Christmas crib, entirely made of cork, by Machado do Castro, who also sculpted the Holy Ghost bas relief on the facade. The crib contains over 500 figures, the traditional Holy Family, shepherds, angels and Magi being joined by figures from every walk of life, all in incredible detail. You can also ascend to the top of the dome, one of the highest, and best, vantage points over the city.

Below: The austere facade of the basilica

Bottom right: A pleasant shaded spot in the gardens

Opposite the basilica is the main entrance to the **Jardim da Estrela**, one of Lisbon's most pleasant parks. Locals come here during the day to enjoy its shady greenery, trees, flowers and ponds, and old men pass the time on its benches. Parents can have a coffee at the café while their children head for the play area – or bring some bread and feed the ducks.

If you leave through the top gate and cross the street, you'll see the wall which encloses the **Cemitério Inglês** (English cemetery), a Protestant burial ground dating back to 1654. Surrounded by high walls, it contains the grave of the 18th-century novelist Henry Fielding, creator of *Tom Jones*, who came to Lisbon for the sake of his health and promptly died.

TAKING A BREAK

Cross the road and head into the **Jardim da Estrela**, where you can sit amidst cool greenery at the café in this tranquil park.

➕ 196 B3 ✉ Largo da Estrela ☎ 213 960 915 🕐 Daily 8–7 💷 Free 🍴 Bar in Jardim da Estrela 🚌 713, 773; trams 25, 28

Jardim da Estrela

➕ 196 B3 ✉ Praça da Estrela ☎ 213 963 275 🕐 Daily 7am–midnight

Cemitério Inglês

➕ 196 B4 ✉ Rua de São Jorge à Estrela ☎ 213 906 248 🕐 Mon–Sat 9–5, Sun 9–1 ❓ To enter, knock loudly on the main gate

BASÍLICA DA ESTRELA: INSIDE INFO

In more depth The architects who designed the basilica, Mateus Vicente Oliveira and Reinaldo Manuel, were also responsible for **Mafra** (➤ 170–172), and the two buildings have many common features. The figures topping the columns on the facade, representing Faith, Adoration, Gratitude and Freedom, were executed by Mafra's sculptors, and the entire exterior has been described as a "mini-Mafra". Inside, the same pink, grey and cream marbles are used as in the main gallery at Mafra, and the fusion of Rococo with neoclassical is entirely similar.

❸ Museu Nacional de Arte Antiga

The Museu Nacional de Arte Antiga (National Museum of Ancient Art or MNAA), is among the best places in Lisbon to enjoy an overview of Portuguese and other European painting schools and to take in a stunning collection of furniture, textiles and objects from all branches of the decorative arts. Beautifully presented in a stylishly converted 17th-century palace, the exhibits not only trace the history of the arts in Portugal, but also shed light on the impact of the country's history and empire on its way of life.

The MNAA was founded in 1884, the first large public museum dedicated to the arts to be opened in Portugal. It's housed in the old **Palácio das Janelas Verdes** (Palace of the Green Windows), which got its name from the 40 green-painted windows on the north facade, which still overlook the street of the same name. The building was considerably altered when it was converted into a museum in the 1880s, and again in 1940, when an annexe was built in the area once occupied by the adjoining Carmelite convent. The convent's **church**, rich in gilding and blue-and-white *azulejos*, was spared and now forms part of the museum. The museum's strengths are its Portuguese art, much of which was acquired following the 19th-century suppression of Portuguese monasteries and convents, and the African, Indian and Far Eastern collections, particularly the late 16th-century porcelain and Japanese Namban art, dating from the time the Portuguese first traded with Japan. There's a lot more than this, including a good and representative collection of European art, some stunning silver and 18th-century French furniture and *objets d'arts*.

Right: A gilded and jewelled monstrance, used for displaying the Consecrated Host, in the museum's ecclesiastic collection

Below: The Panels of St Vincent, by Nuno Gonçalves

Level 1 (Ground)
European Painting, Furniture and the Decorative Arts

Picture-lovers should visit the 15 galleries devoted to
European painting. The Flemish and German schools are
strong here. Pick of the pops has to be the *Temptation of St
Anthony* by Hieronymous Bosch, an outstanding example of
the artist's surrealistic style. Dating from around 1500, its
provenance is something of a mystery – it possibly arrived
here with Philip II of Spain's court when he became Philip I of
Portugal. Packed with bizarre figures and monsters, half-man,
half-beast, it shows the saint in the central of the three panels,
surrounded by the personifications of the sins of gluttony, lust
and avarice. Even today, it's a disturbing work. Look too for
work by **Cranach** and **Dürer**, incuding the latter's *St Jerome*,
painted in 1521, which shows the elderly saint, his finger
resting on a skull, reflecting on mortality, while the crucifix
on the wall behind points to Christ the Saviour. Other works
to look for are a serene and statuesque *St Augustine* by Piero
della Francesca in room 53, and the magnificent *Twelve
Apostles* by the Spanish painter Zurbarán in room 62.

The picture galleries lead to a series of exhibits of **decorative
arts, furniture and textiles**. In room 69 is a **Germain silver
table service**, made in Paris around the 1770s by a father and
son team for the Dukes of Aveiro. Here are plates, flatware,
ladles, tureens, candelabra and an entire set of 16 silver gilt
dancing figures, designed for table decoration. The huge table
centrepiece, with its intricate foliage and graceful whippets,
was probably made in the 1720s. Next door, there's a wealth
of early **glass** and **porcelain**, including some early Wedgwood
Jasperware and vividly coloured and gilded Meissen.

Level 2
Goldware, Ceramics and Far Eastern Art

Straight ahead at the top of the stairs is room 29, where you'll
find the **Belém monstrance**, commissioned for the Jerónimos
monastery (► 128–132) and made in 1506 by the great gold-

A salver,
candlesticks
and coffee
pot from the
Germain 18th-
century French
silver service

smith, Gil Vicente, reputedly from the first gold brought back from the Indies by Vasco da Gama. Rich with minutely observed detail and Manueline symbols, the actual monstrance, used to display the Sacred Host, is surrounded by kneeling figures in gold and enamel, and it's easy to see why this work of technical virtuosity is considered Portugal's finest goldware. Moving on from here, along the river side of the building, you'll come to space devoted to the museum's superb **ceramics**, much of it from the Far East. Here are **dinner and tea sets** made for the Portuguese market, many complete with the armorial markings of the great Portuguese families who commissioned them. It was a two-way process; oriental influence crept into home-produced porcelain, and there are 17th-century Portuguese copies of Chinese **blue-and-white vases and spice jars**. The cross-cultural pendulum swung the other way at times, as can be seen by the Indian and Chinese manufactured **church vestments**, where printed cotton is used to emulate the richly embroidered garments back in Portugal. Portuguese cabinetmakers had a hand in passing on designs to Indian furniture-makers, whose products fuse Indian and Portuguese design – look out for the **mahogany furniture** inlaid with rosewood, silver and ivory, a

MNAA's Official Top Ten
These are the works the museum authorities consider the finest in the collections
- Dom Sancho's processional cross, 1214
- Panels of St Vincent, Nuno Gonçalves, 15th century
- Temptations of St Anthony, Hieronymous Bosch, *c*1500
- Belém Monstrance, Gil Vicente, 1506
- St Leonard, Andrea della Robbia, 1501–1510
- St Jerome, Albrecht Dürer, 1521
- Benin salt cellar, *c*1525
- Portuguese double fountain, 16th century
- Namban screens, Japan *c*1600
- Silver service made for the Dukes of Aveiro, Thomas & François Thomas Germain, 1729–1757

Top: The statue of St Trinity

style uniquely found in Portugal. But the chief of the eastern treasures by far are the **Namban screens**, made in Japan between 1593 and 1602. These household screens, common in contemporary Japanese houses, depict the arrival of the Portuguese in Nagasaki as seen through Japanese eyes.

They're crammed with quirky observations of the European "long noses" and their activities, with the sailing ships, sailors, merchants and their trade goods all depicted, and even a group of Jesuit priests who, at this early date, were already established as missionaries in Japan. Europeans loom tall over the natives, and this eastern take on the stork-like legs of the foreigners must have come as a surprise to the Portuguese who commissioned the screens.

Level 3
Portuguese Painting and Sculpture

The painting collection covers the 15th- to 16th-century schools when Portuguese painting was moving from Gothic to Renaissance and was heavily influenced by Flemish artists such as Jan van Eyck and Rogier van der Weyden. The big names are **Nuno Gonçalves, Gregório Lopes** and **Frei Carlos**, all portrayers of strictly religious scenes. Gonçalves' star piece is the *São Vicente Polyptych*, a six-panel altar piece showing Lisbon's patron saint receiving homage from a wonderful cross-section of society. Painted between 1458 and 1464, when Gonçalves was court painter to Afonso V, it contains portraits of 60 prominent figures; the King and Queen hold centre stage, surrounded by knights, merchants and clerics, so clearly portrayed they would all have been instantly identifiable. Up here too, you'll find sculpture from the 12th to 19th centuries. The star turn is the **Benin salt cellar**, made in Africa, in what is now Nigeria, around 1525 and intricately carved in a primitive Gothic style with knights and exotic creatures – another superb example of the cross-cultural exchanges during the Age of Discoveries.

Outside the Museu Nacional de Arte Antiga

TAKING A BREAK

The **museum café** is particularly nice for a pause; you can sit outside in the peaceful garden.

✠ 196 B1 ✉ Rua das Janelas Verdes ☎ 213 912 800; www.mnarteantiga-ipmuseus.pt
🕐 Tue 2–6, Wed–Sun 10–6
💶 Inexpensive 🚌 60, 713, 714, 732; trams 15, 18, 25

MUSEU NACIONAL DE ARTE ANTIGA INSIDE INFO

Top tips Pick up a **leaflet at the ticket office**; the plan will help you find your way around this confusing building.
• Planning is essential to avoid cultural overload; bear in mind there's **no short guidebook or audio guide**.
• There are good **English-language** information panels in many rooms; you'll find laminated printed sheets in boxes to pick up as you move around.

At Your Leisure

⁴ Igreja de São Roque

Built between 1565 and 1583, São
Roque stands on the site of an earlier
church, dedicated to St Roch, patron
saint of both hopeless causes and the
plague. Its interior, with its single
nave and painted wooden ceiling,
survived the earthquake; look in
particular for the Capela de São
Roque, with its superb *azulejos*, and
the Capela de São João Baptista, a
riot of marble, ivory, gold and lapis
lazuli. It was built in Rome, blessed
by the Pope, then shipped to Lisbon,
where it took four years to re-assem-
ble. There's a **museum** beside the
church, crammed with textiles,
paintings and gold and silver vessels.

- ✚ 197 F3 ✉ Largo Trindade Coelho
- ☎ 213 235 000 🕐 Daily 8:30–5
- 🍴 Bars and cafés nearby 🚋 Elevador
da Glória

Museum

- ✉ Next to church ☎ 213 235 380
- 🕐 Tue–Sun 10–5 💲 Inexpensive

⁵ Jardim Botânico and Praça do Príncipe Real

Walk up the palm-lined avenue that
runs up one side of the Escola
Politécnica, and past the Museu de

Lisbon's fine Botanical Gardens

Ciência to reach this sprawling site,
planted between 1873 and 1878.
Shady walkways wind between the
10,000 or so plants, many of them
imported from the former Portuguese
colonies; look for *strelitzia regina*, the
Bird of Paradise plant, and the palm
ferns, an ancient species that's been
around since prehistoric times.

Cross the road outside and head
downhill and you'll come to Praça do
Príncipe Real. Laid out in the 1850s,
the central gardens are a lovely place
to pause, enjoying a drink in the
shade of the venerable cedar tree.
Elegant, pastel-washed houses ring
this lovely space, and your eye will
be drawn to No 26, a neo-Moorish
fantasy built as the Palácio Ribeiro
da Cunha and now part of the
university.

The baroque splendour of São Roque

✚ 197 D4
Jardim Botânico
✉ Rua da Escola Politécnica 58
☎ 213 921 802; www.jb.ul.pt (in Portuguese) 🕐 Mon–Fri 9–8, Sat–Sun 10–8 May–Sep; Mon–Fri 9–6, Sat–Sun 10–6 Oct–Apr ✋ Inexpensive
🍴 Pastelaria-Padaria São Roque, Rua Dom Pedro V 57 🚇 Rato
🚌 58, 790

➏ São Bento and Lapa

The neighbourhood of São Bento gets its name from the Palácio de São Bento, the ex-Benedictine monastery that now houses the **Assembleia da República**, the Portuguese Republic's national assembly. This imposing building, with its huge pediment and columns, became the seat of the government in 1834, when religious orders were abolished in Portugal. Since then it's been renovated, and you can take a tour of the interior, with its historic murals painted by Rafael Bordalo Pinheiro between 1920 and 1926. Further up the street, at No 193, is the former home of the *fadista* Amália Rodrigues (➤ 13), now a museum.

West from here is Lapa, perhaps Lisbon's classiest area, with its huge mansions and small palaces. For a glimpse of its best buildings walk down the Rua do Pau de Bandeira, where the former residence of the Viscounts of Olivais now houses part of the US embassy, or drop into the Lapa Palace hotel (➤ 35).

✚ 196 A2 (Lapa); 196 C3 (São Bento) 🚇 On Rua de São Bento
🚌 São Bento: 6, 713; trams 25, 28; Lapa: 713, tram 25

Palácio da Assembleia da República
✉ Largo das Cortes, Rua de São Bento ☎ 213 919 000; www.parlamento.pt 🕐 Guided tours only (☎ 213 919 625 the previous day to book) ✋ Free 🚇 Rato 🚌 6, 713; tram 25, 28

➐ Igreja de Santa Catarina

Santa Catarina is perched above the Bica, a diverse neighbourhood where smart eateries and bars rub shoulders with shops and taverns catering for the less well-heeled. Its steep slopes were formed when a landslide swept away a gentler rise during an earthquake in 1598. The whole area was dealt another blow in 1755, and the church of Santa Catarina, built in 1647, was then remodelled. It's a riot of 17th-century giltwork, with an astounding ceiling painted in the 18th century. From here, you can walk up to the Esplanada do Adamastor, or Esplanada de Santa Catarina, one of the finest of Lisbon's *miradouros*, with great views over the Tejo. The statue on the lawn represents the Adamastor, a mythical beast who guarded the Cape of Good Hope. Backing onto the square is the **Museu da Farmácia**, with its collection of medical artefacts that spans over 2,000 years.

✚ 197 E3 ✉ Calçada do Combro 82
☎ 213 464 443 🕐 Daily 8–7:30
✋ Free 🍴 On Esplanada de Santa Catarina 🚌 92; tram 28

Museu da Farmácia
✉ Rua Marechal Saldanha 1 ☎ 213 400 680 🕐 Mon–Fri 10–6 ✋ Moderate
🍴 On Esplanada de Santa Catarina
🚌 92; tram 28

The grand entrance to the imposing Palácio de São Bento

Tiled panels depicting 12 gallant horsemen in the Palácio dos Marquêses de Fronteira

8 Mãe d'Água

Between 1731 and 1748, the Aqueduto das Aguas Livres was built to bring water to Lisbon from 58km (36 miles) to the northwest. The main span runs across the valley of Alcântara, a 940m-long (3,100-foot), 64m-high (210-foot) series of arches supporting the water channel, and debouches into the Mãe d'Água (Mother of Water), a large stone building housing a tank capable of storing 5,500cu m (194,350 cubic feet) of water. Neither the aqueduct nor the tanks were damaged by the earthquake and the Mãe d'Água today is used for exhibitions and performances. Inside the building, you can see the arriving water cascading dramatically down over an extraordinary sculpture into the tank, and catch one of the temporary shows in this cool, echoing stone space.

➕ 196 C5 ✉ Praça das Amoreiras 10 ☎ 213 251 646 🕐 Mon–Sat 10–6 🎟 Moderate 🍴 Bars nearby 🚇 Rato 🚌 6,9, 58, 74

Off the Beaten Track

9 Palácio dos Marquêses de Fronteira

If you love the combination of *azulejos*, statuary, fountains and gardens, visit the Palace of the Marquis de Fronteira, set on the lower slopes of Monsanto Forest. It was built as a hunting lodge in 1640 and rebuilt after the earthquake. The guided tour takes you round the main halls and state rooms, notably the **Sala das Batalhas**, richly decorated with 17th-century tiles. Look too, for the Dutch tiles from Delft, some of the first to be imported. Outside, in the Italianate gardens, there are *azulejos* wherever you look. Combined with the splash of water, the neatly clipped parterres and the ebullient baroque statuary, the tiled gardens at Fronteira are among the loveliest in Lisbon.

➕ 194 off A5 ✉ Largo de São Domingos de Benfica 1, Sete Rios ☎ 217 782 023 🕐 Tours only; Palace and gardens Jun–Sep Mon–Sat 10:30, 11, 11:30, 12; Oct–May Mon–Sat 11, noon; gardens only Mon–Sat 10–6 all year 🎟 Adults expensive, children under 14 moderate 🚇 Jardim Zoológico ❓ 10- to 15-minute walk from metro; taxis are recommended or bus 70

For Kids

Older children should enjoy the **Bairro Alto** – particularly dinner and an evening stroll as it revs up for the night, and all ages might appreciate an ascent on the **Elevador da Bica** and a walk to the *miradouro* at **Santa Catarina**. If your kids are younger, you could head for Lisbon's zoo, the **Jardim Zoológico** (right) at Sete Rios (Praça Marechal Humberto Delgado, tel: 217 232 910) which has an amusement park and

the **Museu das Crianças** (tel: 213 976 007). From here, it's not far to the **Parque Recreativo do Alto de Serafina** in Monsanto (tel: 217 710 870), an adventure park with slides, swings, boats and more. Monsanto was noted for drug dealers and other undesirables, but after a massive campaign to clean up the area it is now much safer, though best avoided after dark.

Where to...
Eat and Drink

Prices

Expect to pay for a three-course meal for one, excluding drinks
€ under €20   €€ €20–€40   €€€ over €40

1° de Maio €€

Get here before 9pm or be prepared to queue at this popular and informal eatery, where the honest pricing is indicative of its value-for money reputation. Tiled walls surround the tables where locals and visitors tuck into a daily changing menu. This includes favourite Portugese staples such as fresh fish, *açorda* (bread based stew), beans and rice, and various *bacalhau* dishes.

197 E3 Rua Atalaia 8, Bairro Alto 213 426 840 Mon–Fri 12–3, 7–10:30; Sat 12–3 Baixa-Chiado

O Acontecimento – Clube dos Jornalistas €€

The innovative Catalan cooking in this pretty restaurant with its lovely, flower-filled patio draws in the crowds, making booking recommended. Kick off with *pão com azeite*, generous slices of country bread drizzled with olive oil, then move on to one of the house specialities, such as cod with rosemary and honey, onion tart or salmon with brie. The ice cream is great, but for dessert the hands-down winner has to be the *delirium de chocolate*.

196 B2 Rua das Trinas 129-r/c (ground floor), Lapa 213 977 138 Mon–Sat 12–3, 8–12 Tram 28 to Estrela, then walk

Alcântara Café €€–€€€

Located in a converted docks warehouse, this classy space, resplendent with stainless steel and red velvet, is scattered with well-spaced tables where you can enjoy Mediterranean fusion cuisine featuring seafood, meat and fresh, seasonal produce. Expect big portions, sophistication, high quality and attentive staff.

196 A1 Rua Maria Luisa Holstein 15, Alcântara 213 637 176 Daily 8pm–1am Tram 15, 18

Ali-à-Papa €€

For a change from solid Portuguese fare, head for this Moroccan restaurant, where the décor, all tent-like draperies and candles, echoes the ethnic roots of the aromatic cuisine. The menu is short, and concentrates on the quality of ingredients and care that goes into such dishes as *cuscus Tifaya* with cinnamon-spiced lamb and raisins, and *tagine Moderbel*, with aubergines and lamb. Vegetarian are well-served, with a good vegetable and chick-pea couscous, and puddings are light and refreshing. Book ahead.

197 E3 Rua da Atalaia 95, Bairro Alto 213 474 143 Wed–Mon 7:30pm–1am Baixa-Chiado

O Chá da Lapa €

Just a few minutes from the Museu Nacional de Arte Antiga, this smart and traditional *salon de chá* (tea-shop) is an excellent place for a light lunch or snack. Sink onto one of the red velvet sofas and enjoy a selection of the delicious cakes and biscuits, all freshly made on the premises, or choose from the two or three *pratos do dia* (dishes of the day) and the excellent quiches on offer at lunchtime.

196 A1 Rua do Olival 8–10, Lapa 213 957 029 Daily 9–7

A Charcutaria €€

Brick arches, light wood panelling and basketware chairs set the tone here. The more imaginative dishes feature game such as hare or partridge, though there's a sure touch with staples such as *carpaccio de bacalhão*. If you want to sample one of the sugar- and egg-rich *doces conventuais*, desserts originally made in convents, this is the place.

➕ 197 E2 ✉ Rua do Alecrim 47A, Bairro Alto ☎ 213 423 845
🕐 Mon–Fri 12:30–4, 7–11, Sat 7pm–midnight 🚇 Baixa-Chiado

Comida de Santo €€

This tiny Brazilian restaurant needs advance booking. Sip a *Caipirinha* made with white rum and limes, while you decide between such dishes as chicken *muquecas*, cooked in coconut milk, or a delicious pork-based stew like *feijoada*, made with black beans and served with toasted manioc and oranges. The atmosphere is great and the portions generous.

➕ 197 D4 ✉ Calçada Engenheiro Miguel Pais 39, Rato ☎ 213 963 339
🕐 Daily 12:30–3:30, 7:30–1 🚇 Rato

Conventual €€

Set on one of the area's loveliest squares and decorated with sacred art, the dining experience here includes Pope of Avignon snails, as well as some excellent rice dishes – try the *arroz de pato* (duck with rice). The rich and sugary egg *doces conventuais* will give you a taste of what Portuguese nuns once ate.

➕ 197 D4 ✉ Praça das Flores 44–45, Rato ☎ 213 909 246
🕐 Tue–Fri, 12:30–3:30, 7:30–11; Sat, Mon and public hols 7:30–11; closed Aug 🚇 Rato

Pap' Açorda €€

Housed in an old bakery, this fashionable restaurant's signature dish, *açorda*, is bread based – a thick egg and bread stew blended with garlic, coriander and prawns, though other combinations are also on the menu. Starters include some of the freshest

seafood you'll ever eat, and those in the know rate the chocolate mousse as the best in town.

➕ 197 E3 ✉ Rua da Atalaia 57–59, Bairro Alto ☎ 213 464 811
🕐 Tue–Sat 12–2, 8–11; closed 1st 2 weeks of Jul and Nov 🚇 Baixa-Chiado

Primavera €

If you're looking for good, straightforward Portuguese cooking, head for Primavera. Favourites include game, hearty meat dishes from the north and delicate white clams in wine, while, if you're watching the budget, an excellent dish of *bacalhau* or a *sopa alentajana* won't break the bank. Spotless surroundings, friendly service and a wine list that caters for all budgets.

➕ 197 E3 ✉ Travessa da Espera, Bairro Alto ☎ 213 420 477
🕐 Tue–Sat 12–3, 7:30–11:30; Mon 7:30–11:30 🚇 Baixa-Chiado

Solar do Vinho do Porto €–€€

The Solar is run by the Port Wine Institute, the industry's regulatory

body, and offers over 200 varieties of styles and vintages to choose from. It is housed in an elegant 18th-century palace, and you can spend a fine couple of hours here while you discover the joys of port-drinking on its native soil.

➕ 197 E3 ✉ Rua de São Pedro de Alcântara 45, Bairro Alto ☎ 213 475 707/8 🕐 Mon–Sat 11am–midnight 🚇 Funicular: Elevador da Gloria

XL €€

XL draws those in search of late-night dining. The ochre-painted walls, rustic furniture and antique curios give this popular restaurant a home-like feel. Soufflés are their forte. Also worth trying is the Camembert in breadcrumbs with raspberry sauce and traditional Portuguese dishes. Finish with a crêpe or the delicious crème brûlée for dessert.

➕ 196 B3 ✉ Calçada da Estrela 57, Estrela ☎ 213 956 118 🕐 Mon–Wed 8pm–midnight, Thu–Sun 8pm–2am
🚋 Tram 28

Where to... Shop

There's shopping for everyone in the Bairro Alto and around, ranging from quirky little shops, many of them selling stuff at fashion's cutting edge, to long-established top-end retailers with enviable reputations. Fashionistas should head for **Fátima Lopes** (Rua da Atalaia 36, Bairro Alto, tel: 213 240 546), one of Portugal's most creative designers, whose trademark, asymmetrically cut style features body-hugging fabrics and plunging necklines. Another top name, who trained under Ana Salazar, is that of **José António Tenente** (Travessa do Carmo 8, tel: 213 422 560), now one of Portugal's leading international designers – sleek clothes and accessories to die for. **Lena Aires** designs distinctive

and colourful women's wear which you'll find at **1a** (Rua da Atalaia 96, tel: 213 461 815). For your home, Rua Dom Pedro V is noted for its antique shops – one of the best is **Solar** (Rua Dom Pedro V 68–70, tel: 213 465 522), which has a vast selection of antique, hand-painted tiles, while over near São Bento there's the best of Portuguese glass ware at the **Depósito da Marinha Grande** (Rua de São Bento 234–242, tel: 213 963 234), an outlet for the vibrant tableware, vases and decanters. Lighter take-home souvenirs, such as candles, are found at **Casa das Velas Loreto** (Rua do Loreto 53, tel: 213 425 387), founded in 1789, whose glass-fronted mahogany display cases are packed with candles of every description. There's another atmospheric old interior at **A Carioca** (Rua da Misericórdia 9, tel: 213 420 377), where you can buy coffee – beans or freshly ground – as well as teas and coffee- and coffee-making paraphernalia.

Where to... Be Entertained

The main streets of the Bairro Alto are solid with bars, often spilling out on to the pavements, and half the joy of a good evening is sampling the atmosphere – and drinks – in a fair selection. *Fado* fans could try the **Arcadas do Faia** (Rua da Barroca 54–56, tel: 213 426742), a big venue where you're pretty much guaranteed to hear good *fado*, or **Adega Machado** (Rua do Norte 91, tel: 213 224 640), which has been in business since 1931. South American rhythms vibrate at **A Tasca** (Travessa da Queimada, 13–15, tel: 213 433 431), great for tequila, nachos and throbbing Latin American music, and there's more of the same – plus house and 1980s tunes – at **Keops** (Rua da Rosa 157–159). If you want

to dance along with Lisbon's rich and beautiful, head for **Kapital** (Avenida 24 de Julho 68, Santos, tel: 213 957 101), a trendy hang-out with a super-selective doorman – smart dressing may get you in. The same strip is also home to **Plateau** (Avenida 24 de Julho, Escadinhas da Praia 7, tel 213 965 116), Lisbon's original nightclub, where 1980s, pop and rock are the order of the day if you can get in. The entrance story's the same at **Kremlin** (Avenida 24 de Julho, Rua das Escadinhas da Praia 5, tel: 213 525 867); once in you can choose between techno, acid, dance and underground. **Trumps** (Rua da Imprensa Nacional 104B, tel: 213 971 059), back in the Bairro Alto, is Lisbon's best and biggest gay club.

Belém

Getting Your Bearings 116 – 117
In a Day 118 – 119
Don't Miss 120 – 135
At Your Leisure 136 – 138
Where to... 139 – 140

Getting Your Bearings

Some of Lisbon's most iconic sights, familiar from a thousand postcards, are packed into Belém, whose clutch of superb monuments and museums stands beside the water to the west of the city centre. They cover Portugal's political and cultural past, with stunning architecture spanning over 600 years and a history that resonates with echoes of the country's Golden Age. The area, originally called Restelo, was once separate from the city, a prime anchorage with easy access to the ocean. From here, throughout the 15th century, overseas expeditions set sail, and Belém, which got its new name, Bethlehem, a century later, saw the departure of the country's greatest navigator, Vasco da Gama, as he set out to discover a maritime route to India in 1497.

There's enough here to keep you busy for a whole day. Monuments and museums are scattered around a wide area beside the Tejo, with lovely views across the river and a plethora of spacious promenades, gardens and water features. Once there, plan your visit carefully to avoid cultural overdose, concentrating on what most appeals, and leaving time simply to enjoy the setting. You shouldn't miss the three main highlights, the Torre de Belém, the Mosteiro dos Jerónimos and the Padrão dos Descobrimentos, but museum visiting will depend on your taste and stamina. Start your explorations at the Torre de Belém and work your way east to the Padrão and the Mosteiro dos Jerónimos; everything else, with the exception of the Igreja da Memória and the Palácio da Ajuda, lies on the same waterside axis.

★ Don't Miss

1 Torre de Belém ➤ 120
2 Padrão dos Descobrimentos ➤ 122
3 Museu de Marinha ➤ 124
4 Mosteiro dos Jerónimos ➤ 128
5 Museu Nacional dos Coches ➤ 133

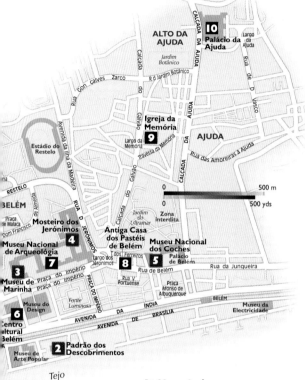

At Your Leisure

6 Centro Cultural de Belém ➤ 136
7 Museu Nacional de Arqueológia ➤ 136
8 Antiga Casa dos Pastéis de Belém ➤ 137

Further Afield

9 Igreja da Memória ➤ 138
10 Palácio da Ajuda ➤ 138

Page 115: Manueline tracery on the Torre de Belém

Far left: The Monument to the Discoveries

Left: View over Belém from the monument

Packed with monuments to Portugal's Golden Age, this beautiful riverside area is home to some of Lisbon's most iconic sights, a clutch of buildings and museums that will keep you busy for the whole day.

Belém in a Day

9:30am

Head out to **Belém** in time for the 10am opening of the monuments and museums. Either take the fast, modern No 15 tram or the Cascais train; both leave from Cais do Sodré and travel cards are valid for both. If you don't have one, buy your tram ticket on board or your train ticket from the station vending machines. Once in Belém, if you're travelling by tram, get off at the stop past the monastery complex so you can walk directly down to the **Torre de Belém** (below). Train travellers could get off at Algés, the stop after Belém, from where the walk back to the Torre is slightly shorter.

10:00am

Have your camera to hand as you explore the **❶ Torre de Belém** (► 120–121); you'll want to capture this wonderful building and the views from its upper levels. After your visit, it's worth bearing in mind that the Belém sites are quite scattered so you might want to use the **tourist train**, an open-air miniature tram which stops at hourly intervals outside all the monuments and museums (open Tue–Sun 10–5).

11:00am

Next stop is the **❷ Padrão dos Descobrimentos** (Monument to the Discoveries; ► 122–123; above), where you can put Belém in context by watching the multimedia history show before taking the lift to the top for more fabulous river views. Outside, you'll want to spend time examining the huge **map of the world**, which shows the Portuguese routes of discovery.

12:00 noon

Continue the maritime theme by taking in the **3 Museu de Marinha** (Maritime Museum, ► 124–127; left), a huge collection of all things nautical with something for everyone.

1:00pm

The museum's café makes a good stop for a quick lunch or you could head for one of the bars across the road towards the river.

1:30pm

Try and get to the **4 Mosteiro dos Jerónimos** (► 128–132) before the afternoon's coach tours arrive, giving yourself a chance to appreciate this wonderful complex in relative peace. (Alternatively, first take in the Museu dos Coches and backtrack to the Jerónimos later in the afternoon.)

3:00pm

Stroll along to the **5 Museu Nacional dos Coches** (► 133–135; detail on a coach right), pausing for a coffee at the **8 Antiga Casa dos Pastéis de Belém** (► 137).

4:30pm

Time to relax in the **gardens** that front this end of Belém; there are kiosks selling cold drinks and ice cream or you could sit at one of the cafés.

6:00pm

You'll probably be ready to head back to town for the evening, but it's worth checking out what's on offer at the **6 Centro Cultural de Belém** (► 136), one of Lisbon's main venues for music, theatre and dance.

◘ Torre de Belém

Squat and sturdy, yet somehow elegant beyond words, the fantastical shape of the Torre de Belém stands guard over Lisbon's approaches. It's a potent monument to Portugal's past, to the courage of her sea captains, to the vision of the country's kings. It proclaims Lisbon's 16th-century status as capital of a superpower, trumpeting the city's strength and riches to approaching ships. The Golden Age is long since over, but the magic lingers, and this wonderful building, so light, so solid, still resonates with echoes of past glory and contemporary national pride.

Built between 1515 and 1519 by Manuel I, the **Torre de Belém**, dedicated to St Vincent, the patron saint of Lisbon, originally stood on an island well out into the river. It was built as a fortress to safeguard the western approaches to Lisbon's harbour, along with another at Cascais, to the west, and a third at Caparica, on the other side of the Tejo estuary. The great earthquake of 1755 substantially altered the course of the river, and the Torre today stands on the water's edge, though still surrounded on three sides by the sea. It was designed for Dom Manuel by Francisco de Arruda, who had previously worked on Portuguese buildings in Morocco and the Moorish influence is strong in much of the architectural detail. The combination of these elements with Gothic, Venetian and Byzantine touches make it unique and the only completely Manueline building in Portugal, the others were remodelled from earlier buildings or completed later. It lost its original purpose in 1580, when Lisbon was invaded by the Spanish, and was used over the following centuries as a prison and customs house. Neglected and crumbling, it was restored in the 1840s, and declared a National Monument in 1910.

The Torre de Belém was originally built to defend Lisbon's port

Stroll across the walkway which connects it to the shore and you'll find yourself in the hexagonal **bastion**, with the five-storey, 35m-high (115-foot) tower rising on one side. This vaulted chamber has 17 cannon openings and steps leading upwards to an open platform, with Moorish turrets at the corners. It's a lovely place to watch the river before you enter the tower proper. As you do so, look above the portal for the serene Gothic statue of the **Virgin of Calm Voyages** set in a niche with a Manueline baldachin (canopy) above. There's more Manueline decoration on the door leading to the tower and throughout the building. What you'll chiefly notice is the wealth of maritime detail and motifs connected with Dom Manuel himself, particularly the armillary spheres. These represent the globe and were the king's personal badge, as was the cross of the military Order of Christ, once the Templars, who played a major role in all Portuguese military exploits. Don't miss either the intricate stone rope work, so typical of Manueline decoration, which ties a complete knot on the north facade. On the south side, at first-floor level, there's a distinctly Venetian Renaissance loggia which wouldn't look out of place on a palace on the Grand Canal, an insight into Portugal's far-flung trading interests. Four floors up, you'll come to the **chapel**, with its magnificent Manueline rib vault and ever-widening views of the river.

Arcaded windows and Venetian-style loggias on the Torre de Belém

TAKING A BREAK

Walk back to the **Centro Cultural de Belém** for a pause at the café there.

🞣 192 A1 ✉ Avenida de Brasília, Belém
☎ 213 620 034/38; www.mosteirojeronimos.pt or www.ippar.pt/english/monumentos/castelo_belem
🕐 May–Sep Tue–Sun 10–6:30; Oct–Apr Tue–Sun 10–5 (last entry 30 mins before closing)
🎫 Moderate 🍴 Cafés nearby 🚌 729; tram 15
🚊 Belém/Algés

TORRE DE BELÉM: INSIDE INFO

Top tips The stairs up the Torre are **narrow and steep** and you may have to queue for access; not recommended if you have trouble with steps.
• Try and arrive here at 10, when the Torre opens. You'll **avoid the crowds** of coach tourists in this relatively cramped monument.

Hidden gems In the **first-floor chamber** head for the slit of a passageway leading to the northwest corner, peer out of the window and look down. There below, slightly weather-beaten but still bravely scanning the waters, is a stone carving of what's indubitably a rhinoceros. It's Europe's first representation of what was, in the 16th century, a virtually legendary beast, and it's said to have inspired the German artist Albrecht Dürer to produce his famous drawing.

In more depth The Torre de Belém, along with the Mosteiro dos Jerónimos, was designated a **World Heritage Site** by UNESCO in 1983 under two criteria. It's considered to "bear a unique testimony to a cultural tradition and to be tangibly associated with events of outstanding universal significance", putting it up among the world's most publicly recognised treasures.

2 Padrão dos Descobrimentos

Jutting towards the water like the prow of some great ship, the Padrão dos Descobrimentos (Monument to the Discoveries) stands for Portuguese national pride. Its soaring, stark profile, softened by sculptures of the country's most revered historical figures, draws the eye up and out, a symbol of the daring vision of the great explorers. At its base, the wonderful world map marks the voyages; from its highest point, the eye is drawn seawards towards those distant lands.

In 1940, while World War II raged throughout Europe, the dictator Salazar staged the Exhibition of the Portuguese World, a celebration of nationalism designed to distract national attention away from outside events. To this end the Belém district was redeveloped and buildings and monuments erected. The original Padrão was one of these, a temporary construction glorifying the Discoveries on behalf of the Salazar regime. It proved a hit, and in 1960, the 500th anniversary of the death of Henry the Navigator (➤ 8–9) a permanent stone replica was constructed.

Like a ship's prow, the Padrão surges towards the water at Belém

For the best view of the 52m-high (170-foot) **Padrão**, walk to one side, where you'll be able to see how it resembles a ship preparing to sail, her prow already pointed seawards, while a procession of figures lines up behind **Prince Henry** along the rail. It's romantic, it's idealised and there's more than a touch of fascism about its sheer hulking form, but it cannot fail to stir the senses. Henry leads the group; behind him, holding an armillary sphere, are **Dom Manuel I** (1495–1521), during whose reign many discoveries were made, and the figures of the great mariners – **Vasco da Gama**, discoverer of the sea route to India; **Pedro Alvares**, who found Brazil; **Ferdinand Magellan**, the first to circum-

navigate the globe; and **Bartolomeu Dias**, who first rounded the Cape of Good Hope. Their exploits were celebrated by the poet **Luís de Camões** in his work *Os Lusíadas (The Lusiads)*; he's there too, holding a copy of his epic poem, while **Nuno Gonçalves**, painter of this heroic age, stands nearby.

In front of the Padrão stretches a world map, across which, as the sun moves, the shadow of the monument traces the explorers' progress. It's a beautiful thing, with the countries picked out in red marble, the markings of a wind rose running round the outer edge, and the dates of the Portuguese discoveries clearly marked. The Cape of Good Hope, rounded in 1498, is central, a tribute to the government of South Africa who gifted the pavement as a tribute to Prince Henry in 1960.

Inside the Padrão you can take in a **multimedia show** about Lisbon and Belém, though most visitors head straight for the lift that whisks you almost to the top of the monument. Get out the camera to capture stupendous views of the river, Belém, the south bank and the merry sails of the little boats that still use this historic waterway.

TAKING A BREAK

The nearest place is the **Centro Cultural de Belém** (► 136).

Heroic navigators and explorers on the monument

🔢 192 C2 ✉ Avenida de Brasília ☎ 213 031 950; www.padrao
descobrimentos.egeac.pt 🕐 May–Sep Tue–Sun 10–6:30; Oct–Apr Tue–Sun
10–5:50 💷 Inexpensive 🍴 Cafés nearby 🚌 714, 727, 729, 732, 759;
tram 15 🚊 Belém

PADRÃO DOS DESCOBRIMENTOS: INSIDE INFO

Top tips If you've got **young children**, bear in mind that the parapet around the top of the Padrão is too high for them to be able to see over.
• Children will enjoy **"walking round the world"** on the pavement in front of the Padrão.

❸ Museu de Marinha

A stone's throw from Vasco da Gama's departure point for his voyage to India, stands the Museu de Marinha (Maritime Museum), one of the most important of its kind in Europe. This vast collection, housed in a series of galleries, puts Portugal's long maritime history in perspective and sheds light on the actuality of the great sea voyages. Here are ships, royal barges, compasses, globes, maps, guns, uniforms, paintings and photographs – a mind-boggling range of everything connected with the sea, that will fascinate even the most dedicated landlubber.

The Museu de Marinha is housed in the west wing of the **Mosteiro dos Jerónimos** (► 128–132), the extension that was constructed in the 19th century. Founded By King Luís I in 1863, the collection was originally displayed in the Navy Arsenal, later moving to the Palácio Farrobo in the northwest of the city after a fire, before it found a final home at Belém in 1962. A modern pavilion was added to house the largest exhibits, and the site is also home to the **Planetário Calouste Gulbenkian** (Calouste Gulbenkian Planetarium). With over 17,000 items in the collection and over 2,500 on display, the museum can be pretty daunting, and it's best to concentrate on what appeals.

The Maritime Museum is a fine example of Manueline architecture

Walk inside and the first thing you'll see is a tribute, in the form of statues, to the **heroes of the Age of Discoveries**, with Henry the Navigator taking pride of place in the centre of the room. Take time to study the **planisphere** showing how, throughout the 15th century, the routes around the globe opened up, as the Portuguese ventured further and further.

The next room is devoted to the voyages and discoveries, and exhibits include models of the **caravels, navigational instruments and charts**. Efficient compasses, astrolabes for calculating position by the stars, and good charts propelled the explorations and the Portuguese kept them secret, as they did the design and components of their ships. Here too, you'll find **religious statues**, often taken on voyages as a protection against danger. By far the most precious, and perhaps the museum's chief treasure, is a wooden polychrome carving of the *Archangel Raphael*, which accompanied Vasco da Gama on his journey to India in 1497.

As the mariners pushed east, new finds flooded into Portugal, and room 2 is devoted to **Far Eastern exhibits**. Here is Chinese porcelain, which was used for serving the exotic new drinks that arrived in Europe – tea in particular, but also coffee and chocolate from the discovery of what was to become Brazil. There are models of ships used in China and the East Indies, and two fine sets of 16th-century Japanese Samurai armour.

Other rooms have exhibits tracing the **development of merchant shipping**, the Portuguese **fishing fleets** and their exploits off Greenland and Newfoundland, ship building, river boats and the highly specialised local craft used in Madeira and the Azores, both Portuguese possessions. One room is devoted to the construction of an 18th-century ship, and another to superb **globes**, among them a 1645 terrestrial globe made by the most famous of all manufacturers, Willem Jansz Blaeu.

Interesting as these are, most people are more captivated by the room devoted to the **royal yacht** Amélia. Used by the royal family from 1887 to 1910, she was the boat that finally carried the last monarch, King Carlos, to exile, and the royal quarters were later removed from the yacht and are displayed in room 13. The rich wooden panelling and deep upholstery is wonderfully evocative of the joys of 19th-century shipboard life, especially for those at the top end of society. The final part of the collection, housed in a connecting wing, is a huge array of **larger craft**, including others with royal connections in the shape of two 18th-century **ceremonial barges**. One, built for Queen Maria I in the 1780s, was still in use nearly

A Ship for Discovery

There's a lot of talk about the importance of the Portuguese caravel, but what, exactly, made this ship so special? Two things: its speed, and the set of the sails, which meant a caravel could sail close into the wind, rather than relying on a wind coming from directly behind. Portuguese sailors took note of Arab ships, which had high sterns and triangular sails and used these elements in building caravels, which were lighter, faster and more manoeuvrable then earlier ships. They could sail as easily close to the shore as in the open ocean, making mapping easier. Caravels opened up the African coast and the Indian Ocean and helped the Portuguese push their trade routes ever further and further east.

Above: The entrance to the museum

200 years later, when, manned by 78 oarsmen, it carried Queen Elizabeth II of Great Britain during a ceremonial visit to Portugal in 1957. Another exhibit here seems, at first, a bizarre find in a maritime museum – an aeroplane. Step up though, and you'll see this is, in fact, a seaplane, the *Santa Cruz*, in which two Portuguese airmen made the first South Atlantic crossing to Brazil. The year was 1922, when Sacadura Cabral and Gago Coutinho set out from Belém in a Fairey 17 plane to fly the 7,284km (4,527 miles) to Rio de Janeiro. The crossing took nearly four months, with the first two planes, the *Lusitania* and the *Portugal* ditching in mid-ocean. The airmen finally arrived in the Santa Cruz after a nail-bitingly tense crossing that took 62.5 hours' flying time. It's a fitting sequel to the courage of the myriad voyagers commemorated in the museum.

Gulbenkian's Planetarium incorporates special shows for children

TAKING A BREAK

You'll need to leave the museum and walk back to the **Rua de Belém** to find cafés and restaurants.

🚩 192 C2 ✉ Praça do Império, Belém ☎ 213 620 019; www.museumarinha.pt 🕐 Oct–Mar Tue–Sun 10–5; Apr–Sep Tue–Sun 10–6; last entry 30 mins before closing 🍽 Moderate 🍴 Café/bar in museum 🚌 714, 727, 759; tram 15 🚃 Belém

Planetário Calouste Gulbenkian
☎ 213 620 002; www.planetario.online.pt 🕐 Thu 4pm, Sat 3:30pm, Sun 11am, 3:30pm 🍽 Moderate

MUSEU DE MARINHA: INSIDE INFO

Top tips It would take around 1.5–2 hours to see everything in this huge museum, so **plan your visit** using the guide book before you start.
• Don't expect interactive displays or state-of-the-art exhibits; this is an **old-fashioned**, but still **fascinating**, museum.
• The museum is arranged **thematically**, not chronologically, with different rooms devoted to different subjects.
• The most interesting part of the museum are the rooms devoted to the **Age of Discoveries**.

Must see The statue of the **Archangel Raphael**
• The **state barges** in the Pavilhão das Galeotas
• The **astrolobes** and **early maps**

❹ Mosteiro dos Jerónimos

Quite simply, the Mosteiro dos Jerónimos (Hieronymite Monastery) is Lisbon's most beautiful building. This emblematic complex is not only the major masterpiece of Manueline architecture, but also the symbol of Portugal's Golden Age, a massive monument built with gold from the New World. Its monks tended the brave men setting out on the great voyages, and it contains the tomb of the greatest mariner of all, Vasco da Gama. If one building can be said to encapsulate Portugal's architectural and historical achievements, this is it.

The **Mosteiro** was built on the site of an earlier church, dedicated to the Virgin of Bethlehem and founded by Henry the Navigator, where Vasco da Gama spent his last night ashore before setting out on his voyage east in 1497. Dom Manuel I vowed to erect a larger church if the voyage was successful, and building started in 1501. The king visualised the new building as serving both as a burial place for him and his line and as a base where the Hieronymites could provide spiritual support for departing sailors, absolving them of their sins before they faced the dangers ahead. These monks were an Iberian order, with monasteries in both Portugal and Spain; there are still two existing Hieronymite monasteries over the border. Dom Manuel appointed Diogo de Boitaca, the originator of the Manueline style, and João de Castilho, a Spaniard who introduced the Plateresque elements that Manueline was to absorb, as the main architects. Gold coming in from Africa and the East paid for the construction, and the local lias provided the stone. By 1521, the 250 workmen had completed the church, and the entire complex was finished by the end of the century. After the closing of religious houses in 1834 the Jerónimos became state property, and restoration of what was, by then, becoming a dilapidated building, started at the beginning of the 20th century. Granted World Heritage status in 1983, the monastery today is considered one of Portugal's most important monuments.

Below and right: Summer sunlight radiates the Manueline carving on the cloisters of the Mosteiro dos Jerónimos

Before you go into the church, examine the **south facade**, 96m (105 yards) in length, with its exquisite **doorway**. This was designed by João de Castilho, and is dominated by the beautiful image of the Virgin of Belém with the Christ Child in the centre of the arch. She's flanked by four virgin martyrs, four prophets and the twelve apostles, with angels and musicians surrounding them. It's a perfect example of the fusion of Gothic, Renaissance and plateresque which produced Manueline, Portugal's own unique decorative style. The **main west entrance** to the church is now approached from under a covered vault, part of the 19th-century extension which houses the naval museum (▶ 124–127) and the archaeological museum (▶ 136). This portal's wonderful carving, a transition from Gothic to Renaissance, is the work of Nicolas de Chanterenne and shows Manuel I and his second wife, Maria de Castilla, their patron saints, the four evangelists and apostles, all superbly executed, the figures forming a comprehensive and tightly designed entity.

Inside the **church**, walk under the gallery, passing two ornate chapels, and to your left, at the back of the main church, you'll find the **tomb of Vasco da Gama**, while that of **Luís de Camões**, the poet and recorder of the discoveries, lies across the aisle. Da Gama's sarcophagus is supported by lions and decorated with his coat of arms, rope work and six-sailed caravels. Touchingly, he wears a beret with a pompon on top, while his well-clad feet point heavenwards. From here, soaring columns, reminiscent of palm trees, line the **nave** and surge up towards the magnificent **rib-vaulted ceiling**, the heavy decoration on the columns contrasting with the plain lines of the vault and accentuating the spatial tension throughout the building. This contrast is one of the main characteristics of the Manueline style, and there's no better place to experience it than here. Catch it when the morning light falls through the southern windows, and it's easy to see why past worshippers felt close to God in this uplifting space. The nave is flanked by

Above: The present monastery is built over the site of a small church founded by Henry the Navigator

Right: João de Castilho's superb Manueline south doorway

two aisles, and culminates in the **transept**, with more vaulting, here, more than 25m (82 feet) above the ground. The **six transept altars** are rich in detail; one on the left has a fine 15th-century Florentine polychrome terracotta of St Jerome, the patron of the Order of the Hieronymites. The existing **high altar** (1569–1572) replaced an earlier one; it holds the tombs of Dom Manuel and his queen, Maria, and those of João III and Queen Catarina.

You'll need to leave the church to reach the **double-storied cloister**, built between 1517 and 1541. One of the most beautiful and vital pieces of architecture in all Portugal, it embodies the Manueline ability to combine different architectural styles, with elements of Gothic and Renaissance contrasting with its own innovative and ebullient touches, such as the recurring anchors, ropes and maritime motifs, while monarchy is represented by shields and crests, Manuel's armillary spheres and the emblems of the Order of Christ. Don't miss the tiny **confessionals** that open up here, where the seafarers received absolution before setting out on their voyages. It's also home to

Vasco da Gama

Born around 1460, Portugal's super-explorer came from a military, upper-class background, and he was following family tradition when he joined his father, who was mounting an expedition to attempt to open the sea route to the east. In 1497, da Gama senior died and Vasco took over, sailing from Belém. He rounded the Cape, sailed into Mozambique and Mombasa and arrived triumphantly in Calicut (Calcutta) the following year. Back home in 1499, he was richly rewarded with titles, estates and a pension, but the quiet life only lasted until 1502, when he was sent to India to avenge the massacre of Portuguese emigrants. Avenge them he did, firing boats and killing hundreds, before going on to bombard the coast and massacre innocent Hindu fishermen. Back home once more he acted as advisor to the king on Indian matters, a role that led to his appointment in 1524 as Portuguese Viceroy to India. He set sail that year, but died shortly after his arrival in Goa – a man of his times, whose achievements went far to outweigh his faults.

the **refectory**, a simple, vaulted space with marvellous stone rope work and glowing blue-and-white tiles. Each corner of the cloister has a stair leading to the upper level, which, besides being the best place to get an overview of the cloister, gives a wonderful close-up of the fantastical **gargoyles** – crocodiles, angels, birds, lions, rams' heads and even an eagle. On the south side you'll find a door giving access to the church's organ gallery and choir stalls, well worth taking in for its superb view over the interior of the church and for a close-up view of the carving on the columns.

Walk round the cloister on this level and you'll come to the **exhibition space**, beautifully presented in Portuguese and English. It tells the story of the Jerónimos in context of both world events and happenings in Portugal itself from 1501 to 2001.

TAKING A BREAK
Take a break at one of the **cafés** on the Rua de Belém.

✚ 192 C3 ✉ Praça do Império ☎ 213 620 034; www.mosteirojeronimos.pt ◷ May–Sep Tue–Sun 10–6; Oct–Apr Tue–Sun 10–5; last entry 30 mins before closing 💵 Church free, cloisters moderate 🍴 Cafés nearby 🚌 714, 727, 759; tram 15 🚆 Belém

Gardens front the monastery and lead down to the River Tejo

MOSTEIRO DOS JERÓNIMOS: INSIDE INFO

Top tips To reach the monastery from the Padrão, you'll need to **cross the road and railway**. There's an **unsigned tunnel** slightly to the left of the Padrão which brings you out opposite the big fountain in the gardens fronting the monastery.
• As Belém's main site, the monastery is **besieged by tour buses**. Arrive **early**, visit during **lunch time** or wait until **late afternoon** if you want to escape the worst of the crowds.

Must see The south doorway, topped by the image of the Virgin of Belém
• The **tombs** of Vasco da Gama and Luís de Camões
• The **choir stalls**
• View of the **interior** from the gallery
• **Rib and star vaulting** in the nave and transept
• The **cloister** and the **refectory**

⑤ Museu Nacional dos Coches

Portugal's monarchy and nobility demanded precious woods, highly skilled carving, opulent gilding, velvet upholstery and comfort when they travelled, and here, in this extraordinary museum, is gathered the world's largest and most valuable collection of horse-drawn carriages and coaches. The building itself, an 18th-century royal riding school, is a fitting backdrop for these astonishing vehicles and the way of life they exemplify. Small wonder it's the most visited of all Lisbon's museums.

A sumptuous carriage at the National Coach Museum

The Portuguese royal family acquired property in Belém in 1726 which included a riding arena. Sixty years later, this was replaced with today's building, a neo-Classical, two-storey hall 50m (164 feet) long and 17m (56 feet) wide. The upper gallery, decorated with *azulejos*, provided a vantage point for the royal family and the court to watch the equestrian performances in the main hall. It's a magnificent space, its walls and ceiling adorned with paintings and panels depicting all things horsey, and a wonderful setting for the collection. Here are assembled **ceremonial** and **everyday vehicles** used from the 17th to the 19th centuries, a procession of changing designs in the days before the birth of the motor car. The side hall, housing later carriages, was added in 1940.

In the main hall, most of the **coaches** are Portuguese, French and Spanish. The earlier models include **Philip II of Spain's traveling coach**, built at the end of the 16th century, and one of the oldest coaches still in existence. There was no place for the driver, who sat on one of the lead horses. By the 17th century, the coach had evolved into the **Berlin**, whose body was supported by leather straps, a sort of primitive suspension, making travel slightly less bone-shaking. Ceremonial coaches were built right into the 18th century and the museum contains some mind-blowingly opulent examples. Look out for **Maria Anna of Austria's coach**, built for her when she married King João V. The exterior is completely covered with gilded carved wood, rich in symbolism of Anna's virtues and featuring carved figures, back and front, representing the continents of Europe, America, Africa and Asia. There are more geographical allusions on João's gift from the Pope Clement XI to celebrate the birth of a prince; the four continents flank the sides, caryatids represent the seasons at the rear, while the coachman sits supported by a huge gilded seashell. João reciprocated by sending the Pope the **Oceans Coach**, if anything, even more ostentatious, with rear sculptures of the Atlantic and Indian Oceans, gilded figures of Spring and Summer, a gold brocade interior and red velvet paneling. This coach was fully restored in the 1990s and is the best example of just how over-the-top these vehicles must have been when they were new. Nearby are four 18th-century Berlins, intricately decorated and far lighter than the cumbersome coaches; they were built in Portugal and France as ceremonial vehicles for the royal family. Look, too, for the English coach, built in London in 1824. It was last used in 1957 by Britain's Queen Elizabeth II during her state visit to Portugal.

After this, it's something of a relief to move on to the later vehicles in the second hall, some of which are refreshingly plainer. **Cabriolets** made their appearance in the late 18th century and were popular right through the 19th century. They are much lighter and better sprung and were popular for

Painted decoration and coats of arms on some of the coaches on display

Carriage doors on the facade of the museum, which was once a riding school

afternoon outings. There's a charming example from the second half of the 18th century used by the princes and princesses in the grounds of the royal palaces at Mafra (➤ 170–172) and Queluz (➤ 167). About this time too, the **eyeglass chaise** made its appearance, a tough, fast vehicle that could be driven by the occupant, who was protected from the elements by leather curtains, each with a circular glass window – hence the name. In towns, **litters** and **sedan chairs** were popular. The essential difference between them is that litters have side doors for entry and were usually drawn by two mules, while sedan chairs were entered from the front and carried by two runners. Here too, are children's cabriolets; built on a smaller scale, they were often drawn by much-loved ponies and other pets – including well-trained sheep.

All these vehicles are surrounded by equestrian ephemera – paintings, engravings, regalia, livery and processional instruments. There are some wonderful 19th-century advertisements as well; look out for one trumpeting the advantage of English-manufactured "landaus, coupés and Mylords".

TAKING A BREAK

There are **cafés** on the street outside the museum.

🔲 193 D2 ⊠ Praça Afonso de Albuquerque ☎ 213 610 850; www.museudoscoches-ipmuseus.pt 🕐 Tue–Sun 10–6 (last entry 5:30) 💰 Moderate 🍴 Café nearby 🚌 714, 727, 732, 759; tram 15 🚆 Belém

MUSEU NACIONAL DOS COCHES: INSIDE INFO

Top tips Take advantage of the good **English-language information boards** to learn more about the exhibits.
• The museum shop sells a range of goods from all **Portugal's state museums** – china, books, glass and other high-class souvenirs.

At Your Leisure

6 Centro Cultural de Belém

You can't miss the huge, stark block of the Centro Cultural de Belém, usually known as the CCB, which dominates the west side of the open space in front of the Mosteiro dos Jerónimos (► 128–132). Lisbon's premier public art and performance space, it was built in 1992 as the showpiece for Portugal's presidency of the European Union. Designed by Vittorio Gregotti and Manuel Salgado, it was originally criticised for its cost, but soon became one of the city's best-loved venues. With its sweeping, clean lines and lovely terraces overlooking the water, it's a beguiling place to wile away a few hours, take in an exhibition, or enjoy a snack or meal at its excellent café and restaurant. The CCB hosts **major travelling exhibitions** from all over the world in its impressive galleries and has a year-round programme of the music, theatre and dance (► 140), often offering a themed series of events. Even if you don't take in a performance, it's worth a visit and browse in its excellent art-heavy bookshop and the other boutiques.

🔢 192 C2 ✉ Praça do Império ☎ 213 612 400; www.ccb.pt 🕙 Daily 11–8; evening performance times vary 🎫 CCB free; performance and exhibition prices vary 🍴 Café in CCB 🚌 714, 727, 759; tram 15 🚋 Belém

7 Museu Nacional de Arqueológia

Founded in 1893, the National Archaeological Museum holds Portugal's largest collection of archaeological finds, covering the full sweep of Portuguese history, as well as a major Egyptian collection. The museum has been reordering its artefacts for several years, meaning much of the permanent collection is not on view, so check what's on before you visit. You should find plenty to keep you interested in the shape of what is on display and exhibited in the excellent temporary shows. Among the permanent displays is a huge range of **ancient jewellery**, with intricate and beautiful pieces dating from the beginnings of metallurgy to the early Middle Ages. The Iberian peninsula is exceptionally rich in natural metal deposits which provided copper, tin and gold from the earliest times. Don't miss either the **300 Egyptian pieces**, brought to Portugal in the early 20th century. These cover 5,000 years, from 6,000 BC to 400 BC, and include tomb finds, sculpture and jewellery. The MNA also has a fine collection of Roman

The Centro Cultural de Belém

mosaics, with some beautiful pavements from villa sites in the Alentejo.

➕ 192 C2 ✉ Praça do Império ☎ 213 620 000; www.mnarqueologia-ipmuseus.pt 🕐 Mon–Sat 10–6 (last entry 5:45) 💶 Moderate 🍴 Café nearby (CCB) 🚌 714, 727, 759; tram 15 🚇 Belém

8 Antiga Casa dos Pastéis de Belém

You'll find *pastéis de nata* (custard tarts) all over Lisbon, but ask any lisboeta where to get the best and you'll get the same answer: Belém. This beautiful, atmospheric pastelaria, its shelves lined with bottles and its walls tiled in blue and white, has been in business since religious houses were abolished in 1834. Ousted from the nearby monastery, and forced to earn a living, in 1837 a monk sold the recipe of the monastery's most famous pastry to the owner of a nearby store. Day trippers from Lisbon flocked in to sample the exquisite mouthfuls and Domingos Rafael Alvés thrived. He also refused to divulge the recipe, and to this day it's known to only three people. Each morning, at 7am, they shut themselves into the *Oficina do Segredo*

Pasteis de Belém – a little taste of heaven

(Secret Workshop) to make the pastry and the custard filling – enough to fill ovens capable of turning out 1,800 tarts an hour. The Casa expects to sell around 10,000–12,000 tarts every weekday, with the number rising to around 20,000 at the weekend. There are other mouth-watering cakes on offer, but you can't say you've been to Lisbon until you've sampled a *pastel*. Take a seat at one of the wooden tables or stand at the counter, order a couple, sprinkle with cinnamon, and sink you teeth into the crisp pastry and unctuous custard of the best *pastel* in the world – and don't forget to buy a tube of six to take away.

➕ 193 D2 ✉ Rua de Belém 84–92 ☎ 213 637 423; www.pasteisdebelem.pt 🕐 Mon–Sat 8am–11pm, Sun 8am–10pm 🚌 714, 727, 759; tram 15 🚇 Belém

Further Afield

🄭 Igreja da Memória

The Igreja da Memória (Church of the Memory) is, indeed, a memorial church. In September 1758, only three years after the earthquake, the Távora family conspired to murder King Dom José I. They had every reason; the king was suspected of carrying on an affair with the Marquise de Távora and he was shot as he left the family house after an assignation. He survived the attempt, living a further 19 years, and his powerful First Minister, the Marquês de Pombal, pursued the suspects, five of whom were brutally executed at Belém four months later. In memory of the event, the King commissioned the Italian architect Bibiena to build a church on the spot where his life was threatened. Building of this Italianate church, with its pilastered facade and cupola, began in 1760 and finished some 20 years later. The Marquês de Pombal was later buried here.

➕ 193 D4 ✉ Largo da Memória, Calçada do Galvão, Ajuda ☎ 213 635 295 🕔 Mon–Sat 2:30–5 (for visits), Sun 10–11 (Mass only) 🎫 Free 🍴 Cafés nearby 🚌 727 from Belém

🄰 Palácio da Ajuda

The impressive classical facade of the Ajuda Palace hides a secret – walk round to the back and you'll see it's only half a palace, left unfinished in 1807, 12 years after building started, when the royal family fled to Brazil to escape Napoleon's armies. With Napoleon out of the way work began again in 1813, and continued spasmodically, with the royal family living here intermittently during the second half of the 19th century. The palace had its heyday in the 1860s, when Dona Maria Pia, wife of Dom Luís I, had a hand in the interior décor – the over-the-top splendour of some of the rooms dates from her time. Her bedroom, with its rich blue walls, vast chandelier, canopied bed and frescoed ceiling, is particularly grand. Top prize for grandeur has to go to her husband's Throne Room, the highlight of the palace tour.

➕ 193 E4 ✉ Largo da Ajuda, Ajuda ☎ 213 637 095; www.ippar.pt/monumentos/palacio_ajuda 🕔 Thu–Tue 10–5 (last entry 4:30) 🎫 Moderate 🍴 Cafés nearby 🚌 729 from Belém

Where to...
Eat and Drink

Prices
Expect to pay for a three-course meal for one, excluding drinks
€ under €20   €€ €20–€40   €€€ over €40

There are plenty of eateries at Belém, many of them, inevitably, catering for the huge numbers of tourists that arrive here daily. The majority of them are along the Rua de Belém, just east of the Mosteiro dos Jerónimos, and on the Rua Viera Portuense, one block south of here. There are snack bars scattered around the green spaces, good at least for a cold drink, and various self-service places. The best bet is to choose somewhere where the number of locals is high and the menu's short, with a daily special.

BBC – Belém Bar Café €€–€€€
This chic restaurant, housed in a converted warehouse to the east of Belém, offers riverside seating, indoors and out. Great for lunch, it's also a good bet if you decide to stay on in Belém for the evening. Enjoy a delicious dinner of immaculately presented Portuguese cuisine, with specialities such as grilled *Barrosã* beef and *Katif* prawns wrapped in crispy pastry, before joining the young and lively crowd that flocks in as the night wears on. Noise levels at the bar rise and there's often live music and a great atmosphere.

🕂 192 C2 ⊠ Avenida Brasilia, Pavilhão Poente ☎ 213 624 232 ◉ Tue–Fri 12:30–3, 8–midnight; Sat 8pm–midnight 🚊 28; tram 15 Ⓔ Belém

Cafetaria Quadrante €
The terrace, with its tables shaded by olive trees looking out over the river, is the main draw of this café-bar. Coffee, drinks and snacks are served all day, with good sandwiches and a couple of hot dishes at lunchtime. It's popular with students and the crowds attending the exhibitions and cultural events.

🕂 192 C2 ⊠ Centro Cultural de Belém, Praça do Império ☎ 213 622 888 ◉ Daily 10–10 🚊 Tram 15 Ⓔ Belém

O Carvoeiro €€
One block down from the Rua de Belém and overlooking the park, this simple restaurant pulls in tourists and locals alike. You'll find all the meat and fish Portuguese staples on the menu, including freshly grilled sardines, straightforward *bife* (steak) with good chips, and home-made soups. A good place to recharge your batteries in unpretentious surroundings.

🕂 193 D2 ⊠ Rua Vieira Portuense 66–68 ☎ 213 637 998 ◉ Tue–Sat noon–3, Sun noon–3 🚊 Tram 15 Ⓔ Belém

O Caseiro €–€€
If food is described as "Caseiro" you can expect traditional, unpretentious food – literally "home cooking". This attractive restaurant near the Jerónimos Monastery, with its vaulted ceilings and walls hung with air-cured hams and pumpkins, lives up to its name. Simply grilled fish and meat or more elaborate dishes such as oven-roasted lamb or *Açorda de Marisco* (bread stew with prawns) come in generous portions. Try the almond pudding to finish.

🕂 193 D2 ⊠ Rua de Belém 35 ☎ 213 638 803 ◉ Mon–Sat noon–3, 7–10:30; closed Aug 🚊 Tram 15 Ⓔ Belém

Where to...
Shop

The museum-packed suburb of Belém is hardly noted for its retail therapy, but you might want to have a browse in the excellent **museum shops** during your visit.

The main museums, the Mosteiro dos Jerónimos, the Museu de Marinha, the Museu Nacional dos Coches and the Museu Nacional de Arqueológia all have museum shops, selling souvenirs and reproductions. As well as books, china, children's souvenirs and textiles relating to their own collections, they also carry museum reproductions from other places – the beautiful copies of 18th-century porcelain are particularly nice, and you'll find good examples of tiles, faience ware, leather work and jewellery as well.

For something cheap and cheerful you could visit the kiosks and **souvenir stalls** outside the Mosteiro – plenty of tat and kitsch on offer here, or you might want to get the **Antiga Casa dos Pastéis** (▶ 137) to make you up a six pack of custard tarts to take away. The **CCB** (▶ 136) also sells high-quality, design-led souvenirs and books, and has several boutiques around the main entrance.

Music fans should definitely take in **Valentim de Carvalho** (CCB, Praça do Império; tel: 213 624 815), a leading Portugese music retailer with a wide selection of music to suit all tastes – if you're looking for something out of the ordinary, there's a great choice of Brazilian and African CDs.

The CCB is also home to **Coisas do Arco do Vinho** (lojas 7–8; tel: 213 642 031), a trendy wine store with an excellent selection of top-quality wines – the enthusiastic and knowledgeable owners can offer expert guidance.

Where to...
Be Entertained

Belém is home to one of Lisbon's most important performing arts centres, the **Centro Cultural de Belém** (▶ 136). The modern and comfortable theatre hosts a variety of events ranging from classical music and dance to international shows; it has free concerts on weekdays between 7 and 9pm. If you have kids, a weekend visit might be just the thing to keep them interested; there's a monthly programme of events, with English spoken, aimed at families, which features dance, theatre and circus. Look at their website (www.ccb.pt) or ask at the information desk.

For something completely different, you could take to the water. The **Associação Naval de Lisbon** (Doca de Belém, tel: 213 619 480, www.anl.pt), next to the Padrão dos Descombrimentos (Monument to the Discoveries), rents out small boats with or without an instructor, though you'll have to remember to book three days in advance.

For more fresh air and exercise head a bit further west to **Estoril** (▶ 161–163), where there's the option of a day on one of the beaches or a game of tennis at the Clube de Ténis do Estoril (Avenida Conde de Barcelona; tel: 214 662 770), which has 18 courts, a swimming pool and sauna. Estoril is also home to **Golfe do Estoril** (Avenida da Republica; tel: 214 680 176), a beautifully designed two-course complex that's open to non-members.

Parque das Nações

Getting Your Bearings 142 – 143
In a Day 144 – 145
Don't Miss 146 – 151
At Your Leisure 152 – 155
Where to... 156 – 158

Getting Your Bearings

After days spent exploring beautiful old Lisbon, with its steep hills and narrow streets, visitors may wonder where to find the face of the 21st-century city. The answer lies in the east, at the astounding Parque das Nações, a stretch of architecturally ground-breaking waterside development that's home to offices, hotels, residential complexes, a clutch of Lisbon's best attractions and one of its biggest shopping malls. Come here to see contemporary Lisbon, where clean, well-swept promenades run beside the river, trees and plants thrive, state-of-the-art entertainment is on hand and there's a plethora of shops and eating and drinking choices.

The best way to get to the Parque is by metro, and you'll arrive at the Gare do Oriente, Calatrava's iconic railway station, a monument to the best of modern design. From here, take the escalator and walk through the Vasco da Gama mall, a multi-storeyed shopping centre with both Portuguese and international outlets. Cross the road outside and pick up a plan of the Parque at the information kiosk to the left; the Oceanário and the Ciência Viva lie to your right, the Torre Vasco da Gama to your left, and the waterfront gardens straight ahead. If you're planning to explore the whole site it will entail plenty of walking; help's at hand in the shape of a miniature train, or you can hire a bicycle for the day. There are cafés, bars and restaurants everywhere.

★Don't Miss

1 Oceanário ➤ 146

2 Centro da Ciência Viva ➤ 150

At Your Leisure

3 The Waterfront and
  Gardens ➤ 152

4 Torre Vasco da
  Gama ➤ 154

5 Centro Comercial
  Vasco da Gama
    ➤ 154

Page 141: The
Water Wall in
Parque das
Nações

Below: Centro
Comercial
Vasco da Gama

AVENIDA DE BOA ESPERANÇA

Torre
Vasco da Gama **4**

Ave do Atlântico

Jardins
Garcia de Orta **3**

Feira
Internacional
de Lisboa

AVENIDA JOÃO II

AVENIDA DOM

ALAMEDA DOS OCEANOS

Rua do Bojador

AVE DO INDICO

Pavilhão
Atlântico

Centro Comercial
Vasco da Gama **5**

ORIENTE

AVE DO
PACIFICO

Parque das
Nações

Pres do Concelho
de Ministros

AVENIDA JOÃO II

AVENIDA DOM

ALAMEDA DOS OCEANOS

C da Costa

Doca
dos
Olivais

Tejo

Oceanário **1**

AVENIDA DE PÁDUA
DE MEDITERRÂNEO

Centro da
Ciência Viva **2** **3**

Jardim
da Água

Área
de
Lazer

AVE DE   ULISSES

Praça
Prín Perfeito

Teatro
Júlio Verne

Restaurantes
Flutuantes

Rua dos Cruzados

0 ———— 500 m
0 ———— 500 yds

Edifício
Nau

AVENIDA
F PESSOA

ALAMEDA
DOS OCEANOS

Rua N. do

Rua das
Mercandores

Rua das Musas

Porto de
Recreio

Head for the Parque das Nações, a state-of the art leisure complex, to enjoy great shopping and entertainment in an architecturally exciting and beautifully landscaped waterside setting.

Parque das Nações in a Day

9:30am

Head out to the **Parque das Nações** on the metro, taking the green line to Alameda, then changing to the red line to Oriente. When you arrive, take a look at the superb architecture of the station (left), one of Lisbon's most important transport hubs, then head for the information kiosk at the entrance of the site and pick up a map and information leaflet. If you want to rent a bicycle, you'll find them available behind here.

10:00am

Join the first visitors as the ❶ **Oceanário** (► 146–149; left) opens, and spend a few hours exploring one of the world's largest aquariums.

12:00 noon

Take the Teleférico (► 153) from the waterfront near the Oceanário and enjoy a bird's-eye view of the Parque das Nações and the Ponte Vasco da Gama (► 153). When you descend, take a stroll in the Jardins Garcia de Orta with their water features and tranquil planting.

1:00pm

There's plenty of choice for lunch. Near at hand, you could try Passeio do Oriente (Rua da Pimenta 51, tel: 218 956 147, open daily), a cheerful restaurant-bar overlooking the gardens that serves a changing, good-value set menu

2:00pm

Walk past the Pavilhão Atlântico (► 158) and along the Alameda dos Oceanos to ❷ **Centro da Ciência Viva** (► 150–151) a hands-on, interactive science centre that's just as much fun for adults as for kids. (Right: Sun Man sculpture by Jorge Viera.)

3:30pm

Time for some retail therapy in the **5** **Vasco da Gama shopping centre**
(➤ 154), Lisbon's second largest mall, or take in a movie at the 10-screen
cinema, where films are shown in their original language. Take the kids to
the Parque Infantil do Parque do Tejo, a fun playground for all ages, or if
you've hired bikes, why not follow the Passeio do Tejo along the water's
edge for a close-up view of the Ponte Vasco da Gama (➤ 153).

6:00pm

Relax over a drink at an
outdoor café while you
plan the evening.

8:00pm

You could either go back
into town or take in some
of the nightlife at the
Parque, where there's both
eating and entertainment.
There could be a big-name
concert at the Pavilhão
Atlântico, a performance
at the Teatro Luís de
Camões or you could head
for the Casino Lisboa (all
at ➤ 158), where there's
live entertainment, bars
and restaurants to choose
from before you even hit
the gaming areas – not to
mention more than 600
slot machines.

O Oceanário

In terms of showcasing and explaining marine life and the oceans that support it, the Oceanário de Lisboa (Lisbon Oceanarium) has the lot. One of the world's largest aquariums, it has tanks on a scale that give a real glimpse into the underwater world, climate-controlled zones that mimic global ecosystems, and myriad displays, smaller tanks and interactive exhibits. It's beautiful, fascinating and educational, and, with its stress on the future role of the oceans and man's perception of them, it provides some serious food for thought in these days of re-evaluation of humanity's effect on nature.

The Oceanário was one of the key elements of **Expo '98**, the international World's Fair that celebrated the 500th anniversary of the discovery of the sea route to India. The exposition's theme was the oceans, and the aquarium's role was to provide Lisbon with a permanent reminder of Expo by neatly linking the country's maritime past with the future role of the oceans and the public's perception of them. Designed by the American architect Peter Chermayeff, the building itself is a stunner, crouching at the river's edge like some exotic water creature or futuristic underwater machine, but it's the interior that draws the crowds. Step up the ramped bridge to the main building, surrounded by water, and enter the **aquarium**, where **four different ocean habitats** are first seen above the

A shoal of fish in the main tank of the aquarium

water level. The air is full of watery sounds – crashing waves, seabirds' cries, the murmurings of whales and dolphins. Here, in this **vast central tank**, you'll see sharks, rays, undulating flatfish and great schools of smaller fish living at different depths, weaving through the weeds and rock faces and wheeling in tightly packed formations. This central tank, seemingly one but actually subdivided, is surrounded by four areas representing various **oceanic ecosystems**; the Atlantic, the Antarctic, the Pacific and the Indian, mirroring the different zones of the main tank. These exhibits have both **above and below water habitats**, allowing visitors to see birds, animals and vegetation typical of these climatic zones as well as the marine life itself. Around the outer walls are ranged **interactive exhibits**, excellent **displays** and **multimedia galleries** relating to all things maritime and marine and numerous **smaller fish tanks**, each focusing on a different species and illustrating the amazing diversity to be found in each oceanic

The building was designed by Peter Chermayeff

habitat. Everything is clearly labelled in Portuguese and idiomatic English.

Start your visit on the upper level, passing between the different climatic regions, and keeping the central tank on your left. The pick of the bunch on this floor, for most visitors, are the **puffins** and guillemots in the Atlantic, the **Magellan**

The Global Ocean

There may be four oceanic zones in the huge central tank, but the message is clear: that there is in fact only one global ocean and that it's only physiological limitations that prevents all marine life from reaching every corner of the world's seas. The huge central tank appears to be just that, but it's divided by almost invisible panels, giving the illusion that the fish and sea creatures in the tank live in one mass of water. Around 100 species from all over the world appear to share this tank, many of which would never to be found together in the natural environment. It may be disconcerting to see such diverse species together, but it's unforgettable.

Left: Sea anemones add a splash of colour

Right: A ray, one of the inhabitants in the Oceanarium

penguins hopping around the snow in the Antarctic zone and the lithe and streamlined **fish-eating sea otters** of the Pacific. Don't neglect the galleries on the outer walls, which will fill you in on fascinating aspects of man's relationship with the sea and includes exhibits on fishing, ocean products, currents, winds and tides and conservation of every type. Once you descend to the lower level you'll repeat your circular tour, this time viewing the different zones from **beneath the surface**. At this level, sunlight filters through the water onto the weeds and coral and shoals of fish glide silently by – as near to scuba diving as anyone could hope for.

Additional, smaller tanks cover sea habitats as diverse as living **coral reefs** to mangrove forests. Highlights here are the **Australian dragon fish**, their camouflage so perfect they're almost impossible to detect against the weed they live in, the luminous tropical **jelly fish**, vividly coloured **anemones** in pink, blue, green and purple up to 3m (10 feet) across, and an alarming range of **crabs**. There's hard and soft **coral**, illuminated to show its vibrant pinks, oranges and purples, **electric eels** and sinister creatures from the furthest depths. In all, there are over 15,000 animals and plants from 450 different species.

TAKING A BREAK

The Oceanario has a great **ice-cream and coffee shop**, or wander along the promenade to sit at one of the Parque's **open-air cafés**.

➕ 200 B3 ✉ Esplanada Dom Carlos, Parque das Nações ☎ 218 917 002/006; www.oceanario.pt 🕐 Apr–Oct daily 10–7; Nov–Mar daily 10–6 💰 Expensive 🍴 Café on ground floor Ⓜ Oriente

OCEANÁRIO: INSIDE INFO

Top tips If you want to see everything consider purchasing the **Cartão do Parque** (€€€) at the aquarium. It gives access to this, other main sites and discounts elsewhere.
• If you don't feel like walking to the Oceanário, a hop on and off **tourist train** (€) makes the round trip through the Parque between 10–5 (Jul–Sep 10–7). It leaves hourly on the hour from outside the Atlantic Pavilion.
• Waiting time for the Oceanário can be over an hour so **arrive early** at the Parque and head here first.
• The Oceanário has a **large gift shop**, particularly well-stocked with gifts, souvenirs, soft toys and books for children.

Don't miss Rays and hammerhead sharks in the **main tank**.
• Sea otters in the **Temperate Pacific zone**.
• Inca tern, Magellan, macaroni and rockhopper penguins in the **Antarctic zone**.
• Sea urchins and star fish in the **smaller tanks**.
• Tropical fish in the **Tropical Indian zone** and the **smaller tanks**.
• Sea kelp forest in the **main tank**.
• **Mangrove forest** with mudhopper fish.

In more depth The **central tank** measures 1,000sq m (1,196sq yards) and has four 49sq m (59sq yards) acrylic screens dividing the different areas. It holds over 7 million litres (1.5 million gallons) of water and is over 7m (23 feet) deep. To ensure purity, the water is filtrated and treated within the aquarium and continuously pumped through the tanks. Salinity and temperature are adjusted for different areas, depending on the needs of the creatures in that particular zone, and the water quality is analysed daily. Divers clean the tanks every day. Each species is fed according to its needs; tropical fish twice daily, sea otters five times daily, sharks twice a week. Crustaceans, corals, invertebrates, jelly fish and anemones obtain nutrition from microscopic organism and tiny ground particles added to the water in their tanks.

2 Centro de Ciência Viva

A shining example of just what a modern science museum should be, the Centro de Ciência Viva (Living Science Centre) succeeds brilliantly in its mission – to stimulate scientific enquiry. Squarely aimed at the general public, its interactive, state-of-the-art exhibits are, above all, fun, with something for everyone no matter what their age. If you're suffering from cultural overdose after days of art and history, this wonderful play-centre is the perfect antidote.

Living Science's main attractions are theme-centred, drawing on the resources of the world's major scientific institutes. It's housed in the **Pavilhão do Conhecimento** (Knowledge Pavilion), which is approached up a ramp past jets of water. Once inside, head for one of the specialist rooms where everything is clearly labelled in English and Portuguese. Start in the **Exploratorium,** originally designed in San Francisco by Frank Oppenheimer, which focuses on nature and how humans perceive natural phenomena. Here you can experiment with light and colour, making things disappear, or leave just a trace, or learn about wind, vortexes and vacuums. Complex subjects, but so accessible you'll practically have a grasp of quantum

Above and left: Families having fun exploring the interactive displays in the Living Science Centre

physics by the end. Move on then to the **See, Do, Learn** section. Watch, experiment with and touch the 66 brightly coloured, beautifully designed, easy to operate interactive exhibits that teach you about scientific phenomena in everyday life – you can even lie down on a bed of nails and learn that it doesn't hurt because your weight is evenly distributed. Outside here, a metal line stretches across a void which you can cross safely on the **Flying Bicycle**; the counterweight beneath the bike guarantees you won't fall off. Across the hall from here, another room sheds light on the mysteries of sight, perception and light itself, with dozens of interactive exhibits.

Downstairs is the **Mathematics** room, which succeeds in persuading even the numerically challenged that maths is not only relevant, it can even be fun. Down here too is the **Unfinished House**. Kids are encouraged to don overalls, put on a hard hat and get building an unfinished house – though deconstruction is just as feasible. The house, a plastic scaffold, needs walls, panels and tiles; all provided and all lightweight foam and plastic. Wheelbarrows, buckets and pulleys help move the job along and the Construction Boss gives each child its task. Everything has been designed to provide total safety for children from the age of 3 to 6.

This lower level is also home to **temporary exhibitions**, which feature themed interactive displays and quizzes. Once you've left this area, you can settle down in the **media centre** where the friendly staff are happy to help even the most nervous computer user.

TAKING A BREAK

Try one of the terraced cafés along the Parque's main avenues.

➕ 200 B2 ✉ Alameda dos Oceanos, Parque das Nações ☎ 218 917 100; www.pavconhecimento.pt 🕐 Tue–Fri 10–6; Sat–Sun 11–7 💰 Expensive 🍴 Cafés nearby 🚇 Oriente

At Your Leisure

■ The Waterfront and Gardens

Built for Expo '98, the Parque das Nações draws thousands of weekend visitors from the rest of Lisbon. Its attractions are many – it's easy to get to, it's a great shopping, eating and entertainment area and there's lots for kids to do. Another factor that really draws the crowds is the location, for this one of the only places in the city where you can walk peacefully beside the River Tejo, one of Lisbon's great assets.

Until the early 1990s few *lisboetas* came near the area now containing the Parque das Nações. It was an industrial wasteland, scarred by derelict warehouses, an oil refinery and the municipal abattoir. Then the site was chosen as the centre for Expo '98, Lisbon's international World's Fair commemorating the discovery of the sea route to India, an event that both raised the city's profile in international terms and drew its citizens' attention to the eastern areas. A site 2km (1.2 miles) long and covering over 330ha (815 acres) was levelled and construction of the necessary pavilions and arenas began, together with surrounding landscaping and gardens.

Expo ran from May to September 1998 and, once it closed, the site reopened as an urban district renamed the **Parque das Nações** (Park of Nations). Construction is ongoing, with the ultimate aim of creating a large-scale and well-planned residential and business zone, centred on the existing Parque and its huge riverside garden. The area contains two of Lisbon's largest concert venues, smart hotels and a multitude of shops, cafés and restaurants and is served by excellent public transport links via Santiago Calatrava's stunning Estação do Oriente. One of the most enjoyable aspects of the Parque is the greenery and the

One of several spectacular exploding fountains

constant sound of splashing water everywhere, while the waterside location and the promenades and gardens along the river add to the pleasure.

The Tejo here is up to 10km (6 miles) wide and there are terrific views across the water. The most prominent upriver sight is the **Ponte Vasco da Gama**, a huge viaduct and suspension bridge which opened in 1998. It's 17.2km (10.5 miles) long with 11km (7 miles) of its total span over water, and briefly held a starring role as Europe's longest bridge. Its construction and position was hedged with controversy, but it's now an accepted part of the riverscape, and has helped relieve the horrendous traffic jams on the **Ponte 25 de Abril** (➤ 180) downriver. Its graceful arches soar over the salt flats across the water, which form part of the Reserva Natural do Estuário do Tejo, a huge marshland nature reserve that

overlooks the Mar de Palha (Straw Sea), as this part of the estuary is called. The name comes from the straw that was once shipped across the river here, and it's said to be home to the Tágides, the Tejo's own water sprites. More tangible are the huge bird colonies that feed in the **nature reserve**; there are hundreds of species, including one of Europe's largest colonies of pink flamingos. These feed on the mud flats below the bridge and in summer are visible from the east end of the Parque.

Follow one of the waterside walkways east to take in the bridge; you'll stroll first through the **Jardins Garcia de Orta** with their water features and tranquil planting before coming to the expanse of the Casa do Arboreto, where the planting includes exotic shrubs and trees from Portugal's former colonies. This is a great place to cycle if you've rented a bike. Don't miss the Parque's central avenue, the Alameda dos Oceanos. It's the conical fountains, with their ever-changing water displays, that are the main draw here, and take time to visit the **Jardim da Água** at the west end, where ponds are linked by stepping stones and there's a plethora of jets, pumps and fountains. Further west from here another esplanade leads past the marina.

To get a bird's-eye view of all this, you could take the **Teleférico** (cable car), which swoops between the Oceanárium and the Torre Vasco da Gama. It's a fun ride and a great way to get your bearings.

The 145m (476-foot) Torre Vasco da Gama

Shoppers in the Vasco da Gama mall

🔲 200 C5 (Jardins Garcia de Orta); 200 C5 (Jardim da Água)

Parque das Nações
✉ Parque das Nações, Alameda dos Oceanos ☎ 218 919 333; www.parquedasnacoes.pt 🅿 Free 🚇 Oriente

Teleférico
🔲 200 C5 ✉ Operates from Torre Vasco da Gama and west end of marina ☎ 218 956 143; www.parquedasnacoes.pt 🕐 Jun–Sep Mon–Fri 11–8, Sat–Sun 10–9; Oct–May Mon–Fri 11–7, Sat–Sun 10–8 🅿 Moderate 🍴 Cafés and bars nearby 🚇 Oriente

4 Torre Vasco da Gama

A compelling symbol of the Portuguese discoveries, the Torre Vasco da Gama is the eastern counterpoint to the Torre de Belém (▶ 120–121). It was built for Expo '98 as a symbol of the great 15th-century voyages, its very shape representing the sail of the caravel, the ship that made the push across the oceans possible. It was designed by the Portuguese architect Leonor Janeiro and Nick Jacobs of the UK, and the soaring steel structure is Portugal's highest building. The lattice tower rises to 145m (476 feet)

with a three-storey building, which served as the European Union pavilion during Expo '98, at its base. The observation platform and panoramic restaurant are now both closed and the tower's fate remains uncertain. Plans are afoot to expand it and turn it into a stunning waterside luxury hotel.

🔲 200 C5 ✉ Cais das Naus ☎ www.parquedasnacoes.pt 🚇 Oriente

5 Centro Comercial Vasco da Gama

If you live to shop and love malls, the Centro Comercial Vasco da Gama is for you. This huge mall is an integral part of the Parque das Nações complex and there's no choice but to walk through it en route from the station to the other attractions here. Designed by the same firm who built

Lisbon's biggest shopping and leisure complex occupies four floors

the Colombo centre (► 39), Lisbon's biggest mall, the lure of the Vasco da Gama is its position and ease of access, making it simple to combine a few hours' retail therapy with a day out at the Parque. There are four floors of shops, conveniently arranged by type, a busy food court with every type of eating on offer, a 10-screen cinema and the bonus of an upstairs deck where you can recover with a beer while gazing out over the Tejo. Airy and light, with soothing water features, the Centro offers another glimpse into 21st-century Lisbon and its people.

✚ 200 B4 ✉ Avenida Dom João II/Alameda dos Oceanos ☎ 218 930 600; www.centrovascodagama.pt ◉ Daily 10am–midnight ⑪ Food court on 4th floor ⓜ Oriente

For Kids

The Parque das Nações is one of the best **kids' destinations** in Lisbon and, if you have children with you, is the ideal antidote to sightseeing and visiting museums. There's not only the pull of the **Oceanário** (► 146–149) and **Centro da Ciência Viva** (► 150–151), but also **three play areas** (► 158), **bike hire**, the **cable car** (► 153) and masses of space to run round in.

Older children might enjoy a visit to one of the **cinemas** in the Vasco da Gama mall and all ages will probably enjoy the **eateries** here far more than the more sophisticated cuisine on offer in central Lisbon.

The cable car is a fun way to get a bird's-eye view of Parque das Nações

Where to...
Eat and Drink

Prices
Expect to pay for a three-course meal for one, excluding drinks
€ under €20 €€ €20–€40 €€€ over €40

The restaurants listed below are among the best of the dozens of eateries and cafes in the Parque das Nações. In addition, the Vasco da Gama mall has an entire floor of food outlets and restaurants, and there are more within the station complex as you exit the metro.

Agua e Sal €€
Perhaps the nicest of the Parque's eating venues, this elegant restaurant offers the choice of two relaxing terraces or a cool, uncluttered interior. It's open throughout the day, and serves a great choice of grills, all cooked on the charcoal-fired traditional *parrilha*, as well as an imaginative daily special – and lots more besides. The accent is on freshness and quality, with some imaginative twists. Puddings are particularly good; try the chocolate volcano or the pancakes with super-sweet *doce de leite*, a condensed, sweetened milk. The excellent rum-based cocktails make it a popular place for an early evening drink.

➕ 200 B3 ☒ Esplanada Dom Carlos I, Oceanário de Lisboa ☎ 218 936 189 ⊙ Mon–Sat 9:30–midnight, Sun 10–midnight Ⓜ Oriente

Atanvá €€
The accent at this warm and friendly eating house is on the best of Portuguese meat. Enjoy well-hung steaks and the tenderest pork, served simply grilled, or Portuguese specialties such as *bacalhau* (dried cod) or a fragrant *arroz de peixe* (rice and fish). Side dishes include a good selection of bread-based *açordas*, but leave room for the desserts, which range from a light mango mousse to an unctuous chocolate meringue.

➕ 200 C4 ☒ Rua Dua da Pimenta 43–45, Frente Ribeirinha Nord ☎ 218 950 480 ⊙ Daily 12.30–3.30, 7.30–11 Ⓜ Oriente

Brisa do Rio €
It's worth the walk to this well-run restaurant, situated on a street to the east of the main Parque. Inside, you'll find streamlined wood, well-designed lighting, starched linen and sparkling glass, and a menu combining Portuguese and international staples aimed at the locals from the surrounding residential area. Dishes include well-cooked steaks, fresh fish, *bacalhau* and seafood, all prepared with a light touch. Desserts are modern – the mango mousse melts in the mouth.

➕ 200 C4 ☒ Rua Ilha dos Amores L4 ☎ 218 936 035 ⊙ Daily 11am–midnight Ⓜ Oriente

Casino Lisboa €€–€€€
Lisbon's Casino has bars adjoining the gaming area and the choice of three restaurants. Pragma is billed as a gourmet restaurant, offering a seasonal tasting menu and a wine list featuring over 250 different vintages; Spot serves lighter food, salads, pasta and a meat line in sushi; and Atrio specialises in steaks and simple grills. All are well designed, with streamlined fittings and excellent lighting, and there's a high standard of service.

➕ 200 B3 ☒ Alameda dos Oceanos ☎ 218 929 000 ⊙ Mon–Thu 3pm–3am, Fri–Sun 4pm–4am Ⓜ Oriente

Where to...
Shop

El Tapas €–€€

Although this is part of a popular chain, El Tapas is none the worse for that, serving up a wide selection of Spanish mouthfuls as well as some main courses. The staff and the ingredients are all Spanish, so you can be sure the food is the genuine article, and the menu features favourites such as *patatas bravas* (spicy potatoes), *pimentos padrón* (green chillies with garlic), *gambas* (prawns) and *calamares* (squid), as well as a host of cold dishes, including *chorizo* (spicy sausage) and *jamón* (dry-cured ham).

🚹 200 C4 ⊠ Rua da Pimenta 99–101
☎ 218 966 900 🕙 Daily noon–2am
Ⓜ Oriente

Espaço Origens Bio €

Vegetarians and organic food fans will enjoy a drink or a snack at this popular eatery, where the emphasis is on the correct sourcing of its organic ingredients. The menu varies from season to season, but you can always expect fresh, clean-tasting ingredients, using excellent produce. The cold fruit and vegetable juices are particularly good, and there's a wide range of the best of Portuguese cheeses.

🚹 200 B3 ⊠ Alameda dos Oceanos 1.02.1 2A Loja 1 ☎ 218 946 166
🕙 Mon–Sat 12:30–3, 8–11
Ⓜ Oriente

Olá Ice Cream Parlour €

As you emerge after a session at the Oceanário with the children, head for this ice-cream outlet, part of the aquarium complex. The ice cream may be commercial, but it's none the worse for that, and the friendly staff will make up sundaes and floats to order. The smoothies, made with fresh fruit and ice cream, are particularly good, or try one of the ice cream and hot coffee combinations.

🚹 200 B3 ⊠ Esplanada Dom Carlos
☎ 218 917 002/006 🕙 May–Sep daily 10–8; Oct–Apr daily 10–7
Ⓜ Oriente

Sabor a Brasil €–€€

Colourful murals set the tone at this ebullient Brazilian restaurant, where locals kick off the evening with a *caiparinha* or *mojito*, powerful rum-based Brazilian specialities. The food is truly South American, with succulent steaks, fish stews and the hearty bean-based stews so popular across the Atlantic. It's noisy and crowded at weekends, but that all adds to the fun.

🚹 200 B4 ⊠ Alameda dos Oceanos Fracção J ☎ 218 955 143
🕙 11am–midnight Ⓜ Oriente

Status €€

This restaurant, bar and club heaves on Saturday evenings, when it's a popular place for locals to come for straightforward Italian cooking. All the basics are on offer – pasta, risottos, grills and fish; lasagne is very popular. Eat first, then head for the bar as the music gets going.

🚹 200 C4 ⊠ Rua da Pimenta 71–73
☎ 218 951 966 🕙 12:30–3.30,
7:30pm–2am Ⓜ Oriente

The **Centro Comercial Vasco da Gama** is mall heaven for many people, with both international and Portuguese names. Prices are lower in Portugal than in some other European countries, so you may find that goods cost less here than for an identical product in another country. Don't expect designer names – you'll find those on the Avenida da Liberdade, Chiado and El Corte Inglés shopping mall – but for mid-range shopping in pleasant surroundings, this is a great mall.

The biggest stores are **C & A**, for all-purpose men and women's clothing, and **Continente**, a vast hypermarket selling food and drink, electrical goods, clothing, toys and more besides. Women will want to check out **Zara** (level 0, No 202, tel: 218 923 073) for its affordable, up-to-the-minute range and **Mango** (level 1, No 150, tel: 218 951 176) for more of the same. You may be unfamiliar with **Massimo Dutti** (level 1, No 158, tel: 218 955 694), a chain that's strong on men's and women's classic and funky leisure wear and particularly worth a look for knitwear, while **Cortefiel** (level 1, No 26 tel: 218 930 852), another pan-European chain, sells fairly classic women's clothing.

Portuguese shoes are good value – check out **Agostini** (level 0, No 152, tel: 218 955 697). You could stock up on make-up and beauty products at **Sephora** (level 2, 67–71, tel: 218 935 040), a French chain offering all the major skincare and beauty manufacturers' products, also designer scent at keen prices, or try **Perfumes e Companhia** (level 1, 118, tel: 218 951 193). The mall has a creche and children's playground with all the latest internet access throughout the building.

Where to...
Be Entertained

Unlike other city areas, the Parque das Nações offers all-day entertainment for all the family. There are **three children's playgrounds** with slides, swings and the usual equipment, a music playground where kids can activate giant musical instruments and a climbing pyramid – access between them is easy if you **hire a bike** or take the **tourist train** to get around (▲ 149).

There's also **BIL**, a vast bowling alley with 30 state-of-the-art lanes and other facilities (Mon–Thu noon–2am, Fri noon–4am, Sat 11am–4am, Sun 11am–2am; tel: 218 922 521/2), and a **10-screen cinema** with all the latest releases in the original language in the Vasco da Gama Centre (tel: 218 922

280; www.lusomundo.pt, Mon–Fri noon–midnight, Sat–Sun 7:30pm–midnight).

For big-name evening entertainment the **Pavilhão Atlântico** (tel: 218 918 409; www.pavilhao atlantico.pt) is Portugal's largest indoor arena, hosting sporting events and rock concerts – Eric Clapton, Joe Cocker, REM and the Red Hot Chili Peppers have all played here.

There's nightly entertainment at **Casino Lisboa** (tel: 218 929 000; www.casinolisboa.pt, Mon–Thu 3pm–3am, Fri–Sun 4pm–4am), which has more than 1,000 slot machines and 22 gaming tables offering poker, roulette, baccarat, Black Jack and pontoon. Its auditorium has nightly music and dance

shows, and there are live performances in the chill out Arena Lounge. You can start the evening here by eating at one of the three restaurants, **Pragma**, **Spot** or **Atrio** (▲ 156) or enjoying a drink at one of the four bars.

In summer, check out what's on at the **Praça Sony** (Avenida Dom João, tel: 218 919 098), an outdoor arena at the northern end of the Parque. Surrounded by bars, it stages big events in a remarkably cosy atmosphere. If you like Brazilian and Latin music, it's worth the steep prices at **Bugix** (Rua Pedro e Inês, tel: 218 951 181), where Fridays and Saturdays see live rhythms from after midnight until 2.30, followed by DJ sounds until late, late, late.

For something more traditional, bear in mind that the Parque's **Teatro Luís de Camões** (Passeio de Neptuno; tel:218 923 470) offers good entertainment, including performances by the National Ballet, which has its home here.

Excursions

The West Coast 161 – 163
Sintra and Queluz 164 – 169
Mafra 170 – 172

Excursions

Lisbon is particularly blessed in its great range of excursion possibilities, with everything from monumentally grand palaces and sleek coastal resorts to great hiking and wild coastline within an hour or so of the centre.

The one, essential trip every visitor takes is to Sintra, an hour or so northwest of Lisbon. This magical hilltop town, set in deep woodland, comes complete with castles and palaces straight out of Disney. You could combine a trip here with visiting the beautiful royal palace at Queluz, surrounded by some of Portugal's loveliest formal gardens. There are more royal connections at Mafra, an 18th-century palace-cum-convent built with Brazilian gold, outside the city to the north.

In high summer, hop on a train and head down to the coastal towns of Estoril, once a chic resort, and Cascais, where fishing boats are still drawn up on the beach. Beyond here, the coast curves northwards to face the wild Atlantic, whose impressive waves draw serious surfers to the beaches around Guincho. From here, it's just a little further to Cabo da Roca, the westernmost point in continental Europe.

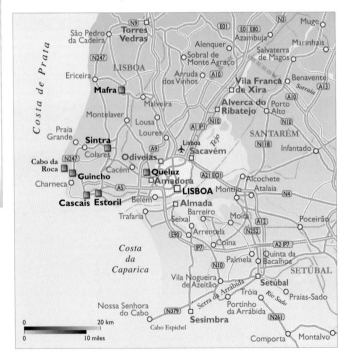

The West Coast

Estoril, Cascais, Guincho and Cabo da Roca

The sun's shining, the water's sparkling, the sky is blue, so hop on the train and head down to explore Lisbon's coast, a wonderful melange of pretty waterfront resort towns, sweeping, deserted beaches and dramatic coastal scenery.

Above: Looking out across Fisherman's Beach, Cascais

Page 159: The *Esplanada* at Estoril

Heading west from Lisbon, the first stop is **Estoril**, synonymous in the mid-20th century with big money, exiled royalty and spies. Watchers and listeners from both sides came to neutral Portugal in World War II, as did deposed monarchs such as Juan Carlos of Spain and Umberto of Italy. Among the intelligence officers was one Ian Fleming; fascinated by the sight of his Yugoslav quarry gambling away his operational funds at the **Casino**, he was later to use the incident as the inspiration for *Casino Royale*. The Casino's still here, and the dice still roll, though nowadays it's the banks of slot machines and extravagant nightly floor shows that really draw the punters. Below the **Casino gardens**, a palm-lined esplanade runs beside the sea and **Tamariz beach**, an unstuffy stretch of clean sand that's popular with locals and visitors.

From here you can easily walk along the seafront to **Cascais**, still as much a **working fishing port** as a busy **resort town** with a thriving marina. The esplanade links three nice **beaches**, popular at the weekend with young lisboetas who come here before hitting Cascais' vibrant

night scene, centred round Rua Frederico Arouca, the main pedestrian thoroughfare, which also has good shopping. Day time visitors can head for the **Museu Conde de Castro Guimarães**, the former home of the Count of Guimarães, which he bequeathed, complete with an eclectic collection of just about everything, to the nation on his death in 1892. From the centre, bus 427 runs to the **Boca do Inferno** (Mouth of Hell), a beauty spot that's seen at its best when stormy weather brings crashing waves.

The casino in Estoril was once popular with spies and exiled royalty

West of Cascais the road heads through a wild and untouched landscape that's hard to credit so near a capital city. Rocky bays, cliffs, clean sweeps of shining sand and undulating wild dunes are the keynotes, and, if you're driving, any sandy cove could make a tempting spot for a bit of **beach combing**.

Surfers and windsurfers favour **Guincho**, 6km (4 miles) from Cascais, where the sands stretch back to the dunes and the Sintra hills (➤ 164) rise up on the horizon. This fantastic **beach** has some of the best windsurfing in Europe, and a string of terrace fish restaurants on the approach road, where you can eat sardines and listen to the surf.

North again, the headland of **Cabo da Roca** lies at the end of the Serra de Sintra, where the hills flatten out to meet the sea. Wild and rugged, with spectacular views up and down the coast, it's the **westernmost point of continental Europe**, situated at a latitude of 38° 47' north and a longitude of 09 30' west°. There's little to see apart from the lighthouse and a monument inscribed with words by Luís de Camões, Portugal's national poet, but it's a worthwhile trip nevertheless, and the tourist office will even sell you a certificate to prove you've stood this far west.

TAKING A BREAK

Pereira (Rua Bela Vista 92, tel: 214 831 215, open Fri–Wed 12–3, 7–10:30, €) is a simple eatery in Cascais providing reasonably priced, traditional cooking with few frills. The menu includes roast kid or duck with rice and other meat options, all served, as always in such Portuguese eateries, in huge portions accompanied by chips and rice. Also in Cascais, the group of eateries known as **Casa da Guia** (Estrada do Guincho, open daily 10–10), are great for lunch or a snack. Options include the **Confeitaria do Monte** and the **Chá da Guia**, both good for quiches, cakes and pastries, and **Dom Grelhas** or **Prazeres da Carne**, where, after watching the sun set from this cliff-top spot above the sea, you could opt for grilled fish and meat dishes.

The rocky headland at Guincho

Tourist Information Estoril
✉ Arcados do Parque ☎ 214 663 813; www.estorilcoast.com
🕐 May–Sep Mon–Sat 9–8, Sat–Sun 10–6; Oct–Apr Mon–Sat 9–7, Sat–Sun 10–6

Tourist Information Cascais
✉ Avenida Combatentes da Grande Guerra 25 ☎ 214 868 204; www.estorilcoast.com 🕐 May–Sep Mon–Sat 9–8, Sun 10–6; Oct–Apr Mon–Sat 9–7, Sun 10–6

Museu Conde de Castro Guimarães
✉ Avenida Rei Humberto de Itália, Cascais ☎ 214 825 401 🕐 Tue–Sun 10–5 💵 Inexpensive

---

THE WEST COAST: INSIDE INFO

Top tips There are **excellent shopping and eating possibilities** in both Estoril and Cascais, so think about staying on for dinner and getting a late train back to Lisbon.
• You could tackle this trip **from either direction** – starting at Estoril to end the day on the west coast, or heading directly to Cabo da Roca and finishing your day at Estoril or Cascais.
• If you're **bathing**, bear in mind that once on the west coast **the water is extremely cold** and **currents very strong** – there are deaths every year on this coast. The **safest bathing** is at Estoril and Cascais.

Getting there Four trains run hourly from **Cais do Sodré to Estoril and Cascais**.
• The journey time to Estoril is 35 minutes.
• Cascais is another 5 minutes down the line, or 20 minutes if you **walk between the two**.
• To **get to Guincho**, take the Scotturb bus No 403 from outside Cascais station for the 30-minute ride to the lighthouse.
• It's worth considering **renting a car** for this trip. The **coastal road** past Guincho to Cabo da Roca is **magnificent** and a car will allow you much more flexibility.
• If you decide to hire for a day, think about **picking up the car in Cascais** to save hassling with the traffic coming out of Lisbon.

When to go Choose a **fine day**; coastal resorts and beaches are no fun in the rain.

Sintra and Queluz

A day in Sintra, once the summer residence of the Portuguese monarchy, is the number one excursion from Lisbon. This World Heritage Site, with its outstanding palaces, gardens and museums, is set amid lushly wooded hills with huge views to the sea. It's made up of three distinct and separate villages, with most of the main attractions in Sintra-Vila. The little town of Queluz, with its fairy-tale royal palace and beautiful gardens, is en route to Sintra.

Sintra

The Romans used Sintra as a defensive position, but it was the Moors who fell in love with this green, well-watered spot, building a palace here in the 9th century. It fell to the Christians in 1147, and became the property of the Kings of Portugal, who retained it until the monarchy's exile in 1910. The palace was both a hunting base and a refuge from Lisbon's summer heat, enlarged and encircled with gardens over the years. Wealthy aristocrats followed, and by the 19th century the Sintra hills were dotted with mansions and huge villas, some of which are still privately owned. With its golf, tennis, riding, and the sea within easy reach, Sintra remains a holiday playground for the well-heeled, who benefit from the retail delights of the boutiques and antique stores in São Pedro de Sintra. There's culture too, in the shape of the International Music and Dance Festival (June–July), one of Portugal's most prestigious.

Two extraordinary conical chimneys, surrounded by a happy blend of Gothic and Manueline architecture with plenty of Moorish touches, dominate the centre of Sintra-Vila. This is the **Palácio Nacional de Sintra**, the 14th- to 15th-century summer pleasure palace largely built by Dom João and his successor, Dom Manuel. A set route through the palace takes in all the main rooms, with tantalising glimpses of hidden courtyards and superb views over the surrounding

Right: The so-called Initiation Well in the gardens at Quinta da Regaleira

Below: The Palácio Nacional de Sintra dominates the heart of Sintra-Vell

countryside. The **Swan's Room**, the main reception chamber during João I's reign and the largest room in the palace, is a magnificently tiled hall overlooking a central patio; its ceiling is decorated with painted swans adorned with golden necklets.. From here, steps lead up to the **Magpie's Room**, a private antechamber whose frieze and ceiling are painted with a flock of jaunty magpies, each holding in its beak the legend "*Por bem*" (For the Best). It was reputedly painted on orders of Dom João to put a stop to the constant gossiping of the court ladies – Philippa of Lancaster, his wife, had heard of his dallying with one of her ladies. From here a succession of smaller, beautifully tiled and decorated rooms and airy corridors leads to the stupendous **Coat-of-Arms Room**, lined with blue *azulejos*, its coffered ceiling displaying the armorial bearings of 72 noble families. The views towards the sea are fabulous; tradition has it that the monarch could watch the fleets

setting out to Africa, Brazil and India from here. At the opposite end of the palace you'll find the **kitchens**, sited, as was
customary, well away from the state chambers. They're home
to the two great chimneys and give an insight into large-scale
medieval catering – which certainly worked efficiently, as the
kitchens are still used for official banquets.

The Throne
Room, one of
the highlights
in the Palácio
Nacional de
Queluz

The **Palácio da Pena**, high above Sintra-Vila, is the most
recent building on this hilltop site, once home to a chapel
with an adjoining late-Gothic cloister, which fell into disuse
after the 1755 earthquake. In 1836, Queen Maria II married
Prince Ferdinand of Saxe-Coburg-Gotha, an enthusiastic
Romantic. He commissioned the German architect von
Eschwege to design today's extraordinary palace, preserved, as
it were, in aspic since the final exile of the monarchy in 1910.
The palace is a **fantasy of the neo-Gothic**, an over-the-top
mix of Manueline decoration, Teutonic embellishments and
Moorish features, built exactly to Ferdinand's vision. Turrets,
cupolas, domes and battlements rear up everywhere and the
interior is no less bizarre, a celebration of late-Victorian taste
where everything that can be decorated is lavishly decorated,
and entire rooms are preserved as if the occupants had just
slipped out for an hour or two. Highlights include some
remarkable stucco work, splendid bathrooms and kitchens,
and some mildly erotic unfinished paintings by Carlos I, last
king of Portugal. The tiled **cloister**, with its simple round
arches, comes as a welcome relief. It's worth exploring the
wooded garden below the palace, an oasis of verdant shade
and soothing water.

Back in town, the **Quinta da Regaleira**, 5 minutes' walk
from Sintra-Vila's main square, is an elaborate private house
that's a fine example of turn of the 20th-century revivalist
neo-Manueline architecture. Bedecked with towers and ornate
stonework, it has some elaborate rooms – look out for the
Rococo wooden ceilings and incredibly detailed mosaic floors,
showing hunting scenes and still lives of dead game. But it's
the **gardens** that steal the show, a maze of paths on a steep
hillside planted with camellias, hydrangeas and tree ferns, and
sprinkled with lakes, fountains, terraces and statuary. They're

full of Masonic themes and imagery, the highlight being the **Initiation Well** with its revolving stone door, approached by moss-covered steps and a tunnel and inspired by the Freemasons and Knights Templars. Near here, kids will love the **Museo do Brinquedo**, a state-of-the-art toy museum with exhibits covering 3,000 years. Down the hill in **Estefânia**, there's serious contemporary art at the **Museu de Arte Moderna**, whose collections cover minimalism, futurism, pop art, kinetic art and more and whose big names include Hockney, Lichtenstein, Warhol and Jackson Pollock.

There's more to see scattered amid the woods and hills, including the **Castelo dos Mouros**, the ruins of a Moorish castle, from whose rocky crags there are extraordinary views up and down the coast. Plantsmen shouldn't miss **Monserrate**, a sprawling garden rich in sub-tropical trees, shrubs and plants, first planted from 1793 to 1799 by William Beckford, a notorious and rich homosexual who fled England to escape hanging. More planting was done under Sir Francis Cook, who built the folly-like mansion and further developed the gardens in the 19th century.

Queluz

It's 30 minutes on the train back to Queluz, home to the elegant, pink-washed, **Palácio Nacional de Queluz**. It too, was originally a hunting lodge, attaining its present form during the reign of Dom Pedro III, who in 1747 embarked on a rebuilding programme. This transformed it into a palace that's considered the country's finest example of rococo architecture, with 18th-century formal gardens to match. Pedro married his niece, the future Queen Maria I, and it was here she spent 27 declining years, driven increasingly mad by grief following the death of her son. One hopes her wretchedness was ameliorated by the charm of her surroundings, whose highlights include the **Music Room**, the **Throne Room** and the **Corridor** with its stunning blue, white and yellow *azulejos*. Best of all perhaps is the **Ambassadors' Room**, with its mirrored columns and black-and-white chequered marble floor. Many of the rooms of this delightful, and surprisingly

The Palácio Nacional de Queluz is surrounded by formal gardens, filled with statuary and fountains

cosy building overlook the **gardens**, laid out with box parterres, tiled walkways lined with topiary, fountains and pools. Much of the statuary is English; John Cheere made **98 lead statues** for Queluz in the 1750s, of which 22 survive, one of Europe's finest collections of such works. The palace grounds house the **Portuguese Royal Equestrian School** and there are summer displays of classical dressage.

Looking out over the forest from one of Sintra Palace's ivy-clad towers

TAKING A BREAK

For a leisurely lunch in Sintra, go to **Tacho Real Sintra** (Rua da Ferraria 4, Vila Velha, tel: 219 235 277, open Thu–Tue 12:30–3, 7:30–10:30) a traditional restaurant where you can enjoy dishes such as *bacalhau*, prawn and beef dishes. It's just 50m (55 yards) from the Palacio Nacional.

Just up the hill from the palace in Queluz is **Palacio del Rei** (Largo Mouzinho de Albuquerque, tel: 214 350 674, open Mon–Sat 12:30–3, 7:30–10). This friendly restaurant is a good option if you choose not to eat at the *pousada* or the palace restaurant. The cooking is straightforward, classic Portuguese, so be prepared for extra-generous portions.

Tourist Information Sintra
✉ Praça da República ☎ 219 231 157/924 700; www.cm-sintra.pt
🕙 Jun–Sep daily 9–8; Oct–May daily 9–7

Palácio Nacional de Sintra
✉ Largo Rainha D Amélia, Sintra ☎ 219 106 840; www.ippar.pt/english/monumentos/palacio_sintra 🕙 Thu–Tue 10–5:30 (last entry 5) 💷 Moderate

Palácio da Pena
✉ Sintra ☎ 219 105 340; www.ippar.pt/english/monumentos/palacio_pena
🕙 Jul to mid-Sep Tue–Sun 10–7; mid-Sep to Jun Tue–Sun 10–5 (last entry 1 hour earlier) 💷 Expensive

Quinta da Regaleira
✉ Rua Barbosa du Bocage ☎ 219 106 650; www.cm-sintra.pt 🕙 Apr–Sep daily 10–8; Nov–Jan daily 10–5:30; Feb–Mar, Oct daily 10–6:30 (last entry 30 mins earlier); guided visits (reserve in advance) 💷 Expensive

SINTRA AND QUELUZ: INSIDE INFO

Top tips If you have plenty of time, you could **take two days** for this excursion, returning to Lisbon each evening. Allow **a day for Sintra** and **half a day for Queluz**.
• If you only have time for one of these, make it **Sintra**.
• Don't think you can walk everywhere in Sintra; the **hills are steep** and **sights scattered**.
• Use the No 434 bus and the **hop on and off Sintra ticket** to get around. You could use it to go on to Cascais via Cabo da Roca, returning to Lisbon on the Cascais line.
• If you **take a taxi to Monserrate** check the price first with the driver as meters aren't always used; approximately €10 should cover it. Taxis wait outside the station and in the Praça de República in Sintra-Vila.

Getting there Rossio station, the downtown departure point for Sintra, is **closed for the foreseeable future**. The best route is to take the metro blue line to Jardim Zoológico, then follow the signs to Sete Rios train station and join the Sintra train there. Trains run every 20 minutes for the 50-minute trip. Queluz is 20 minutes from Lisbon on the same line (30 minutes from Sintra). Get off at Queluz-Belas and follow the signs from the station to the palace, a 15-minute walk.

Getting around Sintra Trains from Lisbon arrive at Estefânia, a 10- to 15-minute walk uphill to Sintra-Vila; São Pedro de Sintra is a further 20 minutes on. The Palácio de Sintra, the Quinta da Regaleira and most other attractions are in Sintra-Vila, with the Palácio da Pena some distance away uphill. A half-hourly **tourist bus links all the main sights**, and it's comparatively simple to get your bearings once you arrive. The gardens of Monserrate call for a taxi, though keen walkers would enjoy the hike.

When to go Leave Lisbon early to see **Sintra and Queluz** at their best.

Museu do Brinquedo (Toy Museum)
✉ Rua Visconde de Monserrate 28 ☎ 219 242 171; www.museu-do-brinquedo.pt 🕐 Tue–Sun 10–6 💷 Moderate

Museu de Arte Moderna
✉ Avenida Heliodoro Salgado ☎ 219 248 170; www.cm-sintra.pt 🕐 Tue–Sun 10–6 💷 Moderate

Castelo dos Mouros
✉ Parque de Sintra ☎ 219 237 300; www.parquesdesintra.pt 🕐 May to mid-Jun daily 9–7, mid-Jun to mid-Sep daily 9–8; mid-Sep to Oct daily 9–7; Nov–Apr daily 9:30–6 (last entry 1 hour earlier) 💷 Moderate

Monserrate
✉ Est de Monserrate ☎ 219 107 806/219 237 300; www.parquesdesintra.pt 🕐 As Castelo dos Mouros 💷 Moderate

Palácio Nacional de Queluz
✉ Largo do Palácio Nacional, Queluz ☎ 214 343 860; www.ippar.pt/english/monumentos/palacio_queluz 🕐 Palace Wed–Mon 9:30–5 (last entry 4:30); gardens May–Sep 10–6; 10–5 Oct–Apr 10–5 💷 Moderate

Mafra

To see just what the gold and diamonds flooding back to Portugal from Brazil paid for, come to Mafra, where the Palácio-Convento offers a taste of royal ostentation on a monumental scale. Built in the hills to the north of Lisbon, the palace dominates a pleasant little town, a perpetual reminder of the wealth and extravagance of its builder.

This vast building, half royal palace, half monastery, was built between 1717 and 1755 by João V, who modelled it on the Escorial outside Madrid in Spain. It was originally intended as a simple convent to honour a vow made on the birth of a royal heir, but building had scarcely started before João and his German court architect, Johann Friedrich Ludwig, had bigger ideas. The final architectural scheme, a fusion of baroque and Italian neoclassical, resulted in a huge basilica, two royal wings and a monastery large enough for 450 monks. Ironically, this grandeur was never intended as a permanent residence; the royal family came to Mafra to hunt and attend religious ceremonies.

More than 50,000 work-men were employed to build this huge palace-monastery

A Few Facts and Figures
- The Palácio is 220m (240 yards) long and 68m (223 feet) high.
- It covers 4ha (10 acres).
- There are 1,200 rooms, 4,700 doors and windows, 156 staircases and 29 courtyards.
- The carillon has 114 bells and is the world's largest.
- The Palácio was constructed by a workforce of 50,000.

A statue of St Francis stands in a niche on the facade of the palace

Tours start in the **monastery**, where you'll be shown the pharmacy, the infirmary, the kitchen and some of the monks' cells. Several of these of these contain instruments of penitence and flagellation straight out of *The Da Vinci Code*, though the tiled images of the Virgin above the monks' beds are more suggestive of the pious life. From here, a door leads into the **palace** proper, where the scale and atmosphere immediately changes to one of baroque magnificence.

Each of the **royal wings** is a mirror image of the other, with identical sets of rooms for the king and queen – two throne rooms, two private chapels, two royal bed-chambers, with a 300m (328-yard) hike between the two, which must have made problems for late night visiting. Between the two wings is the splendid pink and white marble **basilica**, backed by a splendid tiled corridor which gave the royal family a view down into the church on one side while the other gives on to the square fronting the palace. A seemingly endless series of vast apartments eventually leads to the jaw-dropping **Sala dos Troféus**, whose furniture, upholstery and chandeliers are entirely made of antlers and deerskin.

The highlight of all is the **library**, a superb rococo show-piece containing over 35,000 books, among them, many precious incunabula. The books are in fine condition, partly due to specialist care, partly due to low light, steady temperature and low humidity, and also thanks to an active bat population that helps keep book-loving insects under control. It's all truly magnificent, but was once even more so, with gilding everywhere and portraits in the stucco medallions – the ostentation was removed by the Franciscans who took over Mafra in the 19th century.

TAKING A BREAK

There are **bars**, **cafés** and **restaurants** opposite the palace. If you want more than a snack, head for **Sete Sóis** (tel: 261 817 958), a good-value *tasca* with tables outside on the square opposite the main entrance to the palace.

The corridor leading from the monastery to the palace is lined with statues

Tourist Information Office
⊠ Palácio Nacional de Mafra, Torreão Sul, Terreiro Dom João V ☎ 261 817 170; www.cm-mafra.pt ⊙ Daily 9:30–1, 2:30–6

Palácio-Convento de Mafra
⊠ Terreiro Dom João V ☎ 261 817 550; www.ippar.pt/monumentos/ palacio_mafra ⊙ Mon, Wed–Sun 10–5 (last visit 4:30) ✋ Moderate

---

MAFRA: INSIDE INFO

Getting there The best way to get to Mafra is with the **Mafrense bus company** (www.mafrense.pt tel: 261 816 152), whose buses leave the Campo Grande bus terminal roughly twice an hour for the 45-minute journey. Take the metro green line to Campo Grande and follow the signs to the bus station. The Mafrense bus stop is the furthest on the right on the stadium side of the bus station.

When to go Allow **a full half-day for this excursion**, bearing in mind the palace is shut on Tuesdays.

Top tips You can only visit the palace in **accompanied groups**, so you may have to wait a short time for a small group to gather. Visits take 1.25–1.5 hours.
• If you want to hear the **114 bells of the carillon** in action, make sure you visit on a Sunday afternoon in summer, the only time a performance is guaranteed.
• Mafra is the venue for an autumn **International Festival of Music**, when baroque and contemporary concerts take place in the basilica and library. Ask at the tourist office for more information.

Walks & Tours

1 Chiado and the Bairro Alto
  174 – 176
2 Alfama 177 – 179
3 Ferry to Cacilhas and the
  Santuário do Cristo Rei
  180 – 181

1 Chiado and the Bairro Alto

Walk

The Elevador da Glória makes getting around easier

DISTANCE 2.4km (1.5 miles) **TIME** 1 hour straight walking, 2–2.5hours with visits
START/END POINT Praça dos Restauradores ✚ 197 F4

This circular walk, mainly downhill, in central Lisbon gives a taste of two distinctive *bairros* and offers a chance to visit churches, museums, tempting shops and some of Lisbon's most famous cafés.

1–2

Start in the **Praça dos Restauradores** (➤ 53) with the **Palácio Foz**, home to one of Lisbon's main tourist offices, on your left and walk round the corner to the **Elevador da Glória**. This splendid funicular, opened in 1885 and the second to be built in the city, links the slopes of the Bairro Alto with downtown Lisbon. Take a seat for a real Lisbon experience, then turn right at the top of the steps when you get off. A few paces up, on your right, is the garden of the **Miradouro de São Pedro Alcântara**, with its great views over central Lisbon and across to the Castelo. As you leave here, turn left and retrace your steps to walk down Rua São Pedro de Alcântara with the side wall of the **Igreja de São Roque** (➤ 109) on your left.

2–3

Turn left in front of the church and walk round the square to the far corner where you'll see a flight of steps leading down on your left. Go down these, then take the second turning right along the Rua da Condessa, a quiet street with some small workshops and a couple of bars. This leads into the **Largo do Carmo**. This pretty square, with its benches and acacia trees, is home to the **Museu Arqueológico do Carmo** (➤ 61).

When to Go

During shopping hours, particularly the afternoon, when you can pause for a drink and some people-watching at one of the cafés en route.

How to Get to the Start

Metro to Praça dos Restauradores.

Taking a Break

Café A Brasileira (➤ 60–61).

Obelisk in Restaura-dores

site of an earlier one, and the frescoed ceiling above the single nave shows Afonso Henriques, first king of Portugal, vowing to build the original. Just past the Mártires, Rua Serpa Pinto takes you to the **Museu do Chiado** (➤ 60) – you could detour to visit this or simply turn left at the bottom of Sacramento for a drink or coffee at the **Café A Brasileira** (➤ 60–61), a famous Lisbon café.

4–5

With the café behind you, cross the road, walk through the Largo do Chiado and head along Rua D Bragança. A short way along you'll see the Largo São Carlos below you on the left. Take the steps down to the largo and walk in front of the **Teatro Nacional de São Carlos** (➤ 66). This is Lisbon's opera house,

The interior of the Church of São Roque

The headquarters of the GNR occupy a wing of the convent, and it was here that Caetano surrendered during the 1974 Carnation Revolution (➤ 24–25).

3–4

Walk through the square and head down the Calçada do Sacramento to a T-junction with the Rua Garrett, one of Lisbon's ritziest shopping streets. Turn right and walk uphill, taking in the traditional shopfronts along here and the facade of the **Igreja dos Mártires** across the way. The church of Our Lady of the Martyrs was built between 1769 and 1784; like so many Lisbon churches it stands on the

built in the late 18th century and modelled on La Scala in Milan. It has a marvellous rococo interior which you can experience during the winter opera season.

of the rebuild is by Alvaro Siza Vieira, a Porto-based architect who succeeded admirably in retaining a touch of tradition in this historic neighbourhood.

5–6

Past the theatre, continue straight ahead down Rua do Capelo, then turn left along Rua Ivens, a fine street lined with homogenous early 19th-century buildings. This will lead you back to the Rua Garrett. Turn right and you'll see the modern Chiado shopping centre (▶ 65) ahead. This was built during the huge reconstruction programme that followed the catastrophic Chiado fire of 1988; the design

6–7

Turn left at the bottom of Rua Garrett and walk down Rua do Carmo, another classy shopping street. Overhead, you'll see the viaduct of the **Elevador de Santa Justa** (▶ 50), a lift designed and built in 1901 by a fan of Eiffel to link the Baixa with the Largo do Carmo above. You can take the elevator up to reach the Largo do Carmo and enjoy some great city-centre views – turn right down the steps to the entrance. Otherwise, at the bottom of Carmo bear right into the **Rossio** (▶ 52–53).

You can simply walk up through the square to return to the **Restauradores**, bearing left past the station, or lengthen the walk by turning right across Rua Áurea (Rua do Ouro), Rua Sapateiros and Rua Augusta into the **Praça da Figueira**. Turn left here, walk through the square, then left again and back into Rossio and on to Restauradores.

Left: Teatro Nacional de São Carlos
Right: Elevador de Santa Justa

2 Alfama
Walk

The best way to explore the historic Alfama, Lisbon's oldest *bairro*, is on foot. This walk leads up and down the hills that surround it, with the chance to visit some historic churches en route, before taking you right through its very heart.

DISTANCE 3.7km (2.2 miles) **TIME** 1–1.5 hours straight walking, 2–4 hours with visits
START POINT Praça do Comércio ✛ 198 A1 **END POINT** Sé ✛ 198 B1

1–2
Start your walk in the **Praça do Comércio** with your back to the water and head for the far right-hand corner of the square away from the river. Cross the road and walk up Rua da Prata. Take the first right down Rua do

Comércio and cross Rua dos Fanqueiros. Then take the first left and the second right (following the brown signpost) uphill. You'll see the **Igreja da Madalena** on the right; follow the curve of the street up right into Rua de Santo Antonio da Sé; straight ahead you'll soon see the façade of the **Sé** (▶ 72–73).

When to Go
A good walk at almost any time; many people claim the Graça *miradouro* is the best place in Lisbon to watch the sun set.

How to Get to the Start
Metro to Baixa-Chaido, then walk down Rua Áurea (Rua do Ouro) to Praça do Comércio (left).

Taking a Break
Relax at one of the cafés near Miradouro de Santa Luzia or in the Largo das Portas do Sol.

View from the Igreja da Graça

2–3

Keeping the cathedral on your right walk uphill, following the tram lines, along the Rua da Augusta da Rosa. A banner on the wall opposite the cathedral marks the entrance to **Museu do Teatro Romano** (tel: 217 513 200, Tue–Sun 10–1, 2–6; free), dedicated to preserving what little remains of Portugal's only Roman amphitheatre. It was first discovered and surveyed in 1798, but built over, and it was only in 1964 that some stone benches were unearthed and modern excavation started. Most of the theatre is still buried under the surrounding houses, but there's a section of wall visible and the multilingual video will fill you in on the area's evolution. Leave the museum and follow the hill up; the high wall on your right is the Law School, part of the University of Lisbon. Continue uphill through the Largo do Limoeiro and into the Rua do Limoeiro, then take the steps on the right beside the grassy bank to access the **Miradouro de Santa Luzia** (▶ 178).

Tram number 28 at Largo das Portas do Sol

3–4

This splendid viewpoint gets its name from the tiny church of **Santa Luzia**, whose exterior is beautifully decorated with 18th-century *azulejos*. Looking out, the domes and spires over to the left are those of the church of São Estavão. Continue round the left-hand side of the church and up to the **Largo das Portas do Sol**, home to the **Museu-Escola de Artes Decorativas** (Museum of Applied Arts; ▶ 74–76), another *miradouro* with great river views and a statue of São Vicente, patron saint of Lisbon.

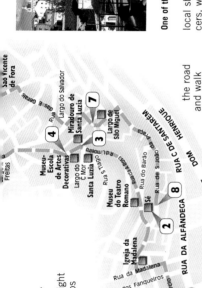

4–5

Take the road – and the tramlines – uphill. Fork left and follow the cobblestones until you see a brown *miradouro* sign pointing right up the Calçada da Graça. This street climbs fairly steeply up to the **Igreja da Graça** (▶ 88), from the front of which there's a superb view over central Lisbon. Look inside before enjoying the views over the Baixa. There's a nice café up here if you want a rest.

5–6

With the church behind you, walk along the south side of the Largo da Graça and right down the steps into the Rua Voz do Operário – look for the tramlines again. Walk down the hill to the church of **São Vicente de Fora** (▶ 80–81) on the left.

6–7

Continue downhill, following the tramlines round a right-hand curve. About 300m (328 yards) on, where the road swings right, cross the road and walk down the Escadinhas das Escolas, a long flight of steps. At the bottom of the steps turn right into the Largo do Salvador where you should fork left and head downhill. These are steep and narrow streets, penetrating into the heart of the **Alfama** (▶ 82–84). Continue down to a tiny square with the Centro Paroquial da Alfama across the corner on the right and turn right beside it to head along a row of

One of the cafés near Miradouro de Santa Luzia

local shops – butchers, bakers and greengrocers, with plenty of vibrant life all around.

7–8

You'll emerge into the **Largo de São Miguel**, a neighbourhood square with a church on the right and a solitary, lofty palm tree in the centre. Walk across the square, keeping the church on the right, and carry straight ahead onto the Rua de São Miguel. This becomes the Rua de São João da Praça, named after the plain 18th-century church. Bear left along the side of the church, gradually heading uphill to emerge on the south side of the Sé.

São Vicente de Fora

Largo do Salvador

Rua

4 Museu-Escola de Artes Decorativas

Miradouro de Santa Luzia **7**

Largo do C Mor
Santa Luzia

Largo de São Miguel **3**

Rua S Tiago

Museu do Teatro Romano

Rua do Barão

Rua de S João da Praça

Sé **8** **2**

RUA C DE SANTAREM

DOM

INFANTE

AVENIDA

Igreja da Madalena

Rua da Madalena

RUA DA ALFÂNDEGA

Rua dos Fanqueiros

RUA DA PRATA

Rua do Comércio

Praça do Comércio **1**

0 — 200 metres
0 — 200 yards

3 Ferry to Cacilhas and the Santuário do Cristo Rei

Tour

It's only a ferry hop across the water to the south bank, where the vast statue of the Cristo Rei spreads its arms towards Lisbon. This tour gives you a taste of the southern shore and the chance to see the entire city spread out, with the Tejo running down to the sea at your feet.

DISTANCE 4.5km (3 miles); walking 1km (0.6 miles) **TIME** 2–3 hours
START/END POINT Cais do Sodré ✚ 197 E2

Lisbon's major bottlenecks during the rush hour and at weekends in summer, when the crowds head for the beaches around Caparica. **Cacilhas** ferry terminal serves the ever-expanding metropolis of Almada.

2–3

Disembark and head left across to the bus

When to Go
Any time during the day except during morning and evening rush hour, but this makes a nice afternoon outing.

How to Get to the Start
Metro to Cais do Sodré.

Taking a Break
Try the café by the Cristo Rei or head west for **Atira-te ao Rio** (Cais de Ginjal 69, tel: 212 751 380), a relaxed Brazilian restaurant.

1–2
Once you're at **Cais do Sodré** (▶ 60) follow the signs for the **Estação Fluvial** and buy a ticket (*bilhete*). Follow signs to the ferry to Cacilhas and grab a seat near an upstairs window. The trip across the Tejo takes about ten minutes and you'll be able to pick out the city highlights receding behind you. Downriver, you can see the **Ponte 25 de Abril**, built in 1966 and then known as the Ponte Salazar. It was Europe's longest suspension bridge when it was constructed. Its four lanes have been upgraded to six, but it's still one of

station to stand No 20 on the far side. Bus No 101 leaves roughly every 20 minutes for the **Santuário do Cristo Rei**; pay the driver as you board. The journey through **Almada** and up to the statue takes around 15 minutes, and on the way you'll pass through the lower, modern area of this busy town. You won't see any sign of the massive statue until you arrive at the top of the hill, where the Christ stands alone on a grassy plateau near the edge of the cliff. If this huge figure reminds you of another, you won't be surprised

The statue of Christ the Redeemer

to learn that it was the famous statue of *Christ the Redeemer* in Rio de Janeiro that inspired its construction. In 1934, just three years after its completion, the Cardinal of Lisbon visited Rio, and was immediately inspired by the South American Christ. Six years later, with most of Europe at war, the Portuguese government vowed to build a similar statue if the country was spared World War II. Portugal remained neutral, and in 1950 building started. The sculptor of this undeniably impressive, but stiff and monolithic figure was Francisco Franco de Sousa; the architect António Lino.

3–4

From the bus stop walk through the central arch of the administrative buildings to the statue. As you approach you really get a sense of its size – the entire structure is 110m (360 feet) tall – the figure of Christ measures 28m (92 feet). Inside, a lift whisks you up to the **observation level**, where you walk through the shop to access the stairs to the viewing platform. There are religious souvenirs for sale, a reminder that, for many Portuguese, the statue is an important national sanctuary and place of pilgrimage. Once outside, you'll be looking down on the Ponte 25 de Abril.

4–5

Across the river to the east lies Lisbon, with the graceful sweep of the **Ponte Vasco da Gama** (➤ 153) marking the city limits. Down river the view stretches past **Belém** (➤➤ 115–140) to the hills of **Sintra** (➤➤ 164–167). Beyond Belém you can pick out the resorts of **Estoril** (➤ 161) and **Cascais** (➤ 161) and, further still, the open sea. Catch the bus back towards old Almada.

5–6

Get off the bus at the 3rd or 4th stop and wander through the old town, which really comes into its own in July, when the town stages Portugal's most important theatre festival. There's another superb view from the *miradouro* behind the **Câmara Municipal** (Town Hall), a fine old church with a pleasant *praça* outside. Either walk back down the hill to the ferry or take the bus. On your way back, you'll have the chance to approach the Baixa as Pombal intended – from the sea, with the Praça do Comércio and the Arco Triunfal acting as the magnificent entrance to the city.

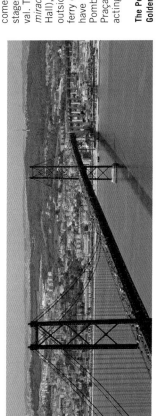

The Ponte 25 de Abril resembles San Francisco's Golden Gate Bridge

Organised Tours

An organised tour is often the best way of getting your bearings in a new city. Lisbon is well served by tour companies offering everything from a city overview by tram to a river cruise, as well as excursions to further-flung places.

Carristur

Lisbon's public transport company operates both regular tours and hop-on hop-off buses, ideal for getting from sight to sight. All leave from the Praça do Comércio.
☎ 213 582 334; www.carristur.pt

Colinas Tour

City-centre tour on a vintage tram, taking in the Baixa, Graça, the Alfama, Chiado, the Bairro Alto and Lapa.
1 hour 20 minutes. Every 30 minutes 10–7 (except 12:30 and 2pm) Jun–Sep; 10, 10:30, 12, 1, 1:30, 3, 3:30, 4, 5, 5:30, 6) Oct–May. Expensive.

Cruzeiros no Tejo €€€

River tours from Terreiro do Paço upriver to the Parque das Nações and down to Belém.

2 hours. Daily 3pm. Expensive.
☎ 808 203 050; www.transtejo.pt

Discoveries Tour

Vintage tram tour through the old city and out to Belém.
1 hour 50 minutes. Daily 11:30, 3:30, 5:30. Expensive.

Lisbon Walker

Four themed accompanied walking tours in English on different areas and aspects of the city, including the Old Town, the post-earthquake city, Chiado and the Bairro Alto, and Legends and Mysteries.
Walks start daily in the Praça do Comércio and last 2–3 hours.
✉ Rua dos Remédios 84 ☎ 218 861 840;
www.lisbonwalker.com

Olispo Tour

Hop on and off this circular route via Bairro Alto, northern Lisbon, Parque das Nações and the riverside.
Daily, on the half hour 10:30–5:30 Mar–Oct; daily 11:30, 1:30, 3:30 Nov–Feb. Expensive.

Tagus Tour

Hop on and off this circular route via Avenida da Liberdade, Praça de Espanha, Estrela, Alcantara, Belém and the riverside.
Every half hour 10:15–5:15 Mar–Jun, Oct; every half hour 9:15–8:15 Jul–Sep; every hour 11:15–4:15 Nov–Feb. Expensive.

Further Afield

There are longer tours to Fátima, Batalha, Nazaré, Alcobaça and Obidos run by:

Cityrama
✉ Avenida Praia da Vitória 12B ☎ 213 191 090;
www.tours.cityrama.pt

Dianatours
✉ Campo Grande 30 B
☎ 217 998 540; www.dianatours.pt

Carris also run daily tours of the whole city and excursions to Sintra via Queluz, Sintra, Cabo da Roca, Guincho, Cascais and Estoril.

Practicalities

Websites

- Welcome to Portugal:
  www.portugal.org
- Portugal National
  Tourist Office:
  www.visitportugal.com

- Lisbon Tourist Office:
  www.visitlisboa.com
- Independent Tourist
  Information:
  www.golisbon.com
- Hotel online booking:
  www.maisturismo.pt

In the UK
Portuguese National
Tourist Office
11 Belgrave Square
London SW1X 8PP
☎ 0845 355 1212

BEFORE YOU GO

WHAT YOU NEED

		UK	Germany	USA	Canada	Australia	Ireland	Netherlands	Spain
● Required	Some countries require a passport to								
○ Suggested	remain valid for a minimum period								
▲ Not required	(usually at least six months) beyond								
△ Not applicable	the date of entry – check beforehand.								
Passport/National Identity Card		●	●	●	●	●	●	●	●
Visa (regulations can change – check before booking)		▲	▲	▲	▲	▲	▲	▲	▲
Onward or Return Ticket		○	○	○	○	○	○	○	○
Health Inoculations (tetanus and polio)		▲	▲	▲	▲	▲	▲	▲	▲
Health Documentation		▲	▲	▲	▲	▲	▲	▲	▲
Travel Insurance		○	○	○	○	○	○	○	○
Driver's Licence (national)		●	●	●	●	●	●	●	●
Car Insurance Certificate		●	●	●	●	●	●	●	●
Car Registration Document		●	●	●	●	●	●	●	●

WHEN TO GO

Lisbon

▭ High season   ▭ Low season

JAN	FEB	MAR	APR	MAY	JUN	JUL	AUG	SEP	OCT	NOV	DEC
15°C	16°C	18°C	19°C	22°C	25°C	27°C	28°C	26°C	22°C	18°C	15°C
59°F	61°F	64°F	66°F	72°F	77°F	81°F	82°F	79°F	72°F	64°F	59°F

☼ Sun   ⛅ Sun/Showers   🌧 Very wet

Temperatures are the average daily maximum for each month. Spring (April to June) and autumn (September to October) are the best times to visit Lisbon as the summer months can be unbearably hot and crowded in the city, although a summer visit could include trips to the resorts of Cascais and Estoril west of Lisbon, or the Caparica coast across the River Tejo. November can be very wet, but January and February herald the first signs of spring, when it's possible to enjoy sitting outside in the middle of the day. Hotel rates tend to be a little lower in these months, making this a good time to visit Lisbon.

In Ireland
Portuguese National
Tourist Office
54 Dawson Street
Dublin 2
☎ 01 670 9133

In the USA
Portuguese National
Tourist Office
590 Fifth Avenue
4th Floor
New York NY 10036-4702
☎ 646/723-0200

In Canada
Portuguese National
Tourist Office
60 Bloor Street West
Suite 1005
Toronto, Ontario M4W 3B8
☎ (416) 921 7376

GETTING THERE

By Air Lisbon's international airport is served by scheduled flights operated by **British Airways** and the Portuguese national airline **TAP-Air Portugal**, with a flight time of around 2.5 hours. Inexpensive flights can be booked from British regional airports via **Avro** (tel: 0871 622 4476; www.avro.co.uk) or with airlines such as **Monarch** (tel: 8700 40 50 40; www.flymonarch.com) and **easyJet** (www.easyjet.co.uk). From the USA TAP has scheduled flights to Lisbon from New York (6.5 hours), with connections to other North American cities.

By Car There are numerous entry points along the border with Spain, with little or nothing in the way of border controls. The main roads into Portugal are from Vigo to Porto, Zamora to Bragança, Salamanca to Guarda, Badajoz to Elvas; you can access the Portuguese motorway system to Lisbon from these towns. From Britain, take a car ferry to Bilbao or Santander in northern Spain, from where it is a drive of about 1,000km (620 miles) to Lisbon.

By Rail There are regular trains to Lisbon from Madrid (10 hours) and Paris (24 hours). A train line from Vigo in Spain crosses the border at Valença do Minho to Lisbon via Porto.

TIME

 Portugal is on Greenwich Mean Time (GMT), the same as the UK, and one hour behind most of continental Europe. During the summer, from the last Sunday in March to the last Sunday in October, the time in Portugal is GMT plus one hour (GMT+1).

CURRENCY AND FOREIGN EXCHANGE

Currency The euro (€) is the official currency of Portugal. Euro coins are issued in denominations of 1, 2, 5, 10, 20 and 50 euro cents and €1 and €2. Notes are issued in denominations of €5, €10, €20, €50, €100, €200 and €500. Note: €200 and €500 notes are not issued in Portugal, but those issued elsewhere are valid.

Foreign currency and travellers' cheques can be changed at banks and exchange bureaux, as well as in many hotels. Exchange bureaux generally offer the best deal, but it pays to shop around and compare commission charges. You will need to show your passport when cashing travellers' cheques. You can also withdraw cash from ATM (cashpoint) machines using your credit or debit card and a PIN (personal identification number). Your own bank will usually make a charge for this service.

Major credit cards are widely accepted in Lisbon, though it is advisable to have small denomination notes to hand as some bars and shops only take cash. It is easier and no more expensive (depending on your credit card charges) to rely solely on plastic, rather than taking travellers' cheques or buying cash in advance.

GMT	Lisbon	USA New York	Germany	Spain	Australia
12 noon	12 noon	7am	1pm	1pm	Sydney 10pm

WHEN YOU ARE THERE

CLOTHING SIZES

UK	Portugal	USA		
36	46	36		Suits
38	48	38		
40	50	40		
42	52	42		
44	54	44		
46	56	46		
7	41	8		Shoes
7.5	42	8.5		
8.5	43	9.5		
9.5	44	10.5		
10.5	45	11.5		
11	46	12		
14.5	37	14.5		Shirts
15	38	15		
15.5	39/40	15.5		
16	41	16		
16.5	42	16.5		
17	43	17		
8	34	6		Dresses
10	36	8		
12	38	10		
14	40	12		
16	42	14		
18	44	16		
4.5	38	6		Shoes
5	38	6.5		
5.5	39	7		
6	39	7.5		
6.5	40	8		
7	41	8.5		

NATIONAL HOLIDAYS

1 Jan	New Year's Day
Feb/Mar	Shrove Tuesday
Mar/Apr	Good Friday/Easter Monday
25 Apr	Day of the Revolution
1 May	Labour Day
May/Jun	Corpus Christi
10 Jun	National Day
15 Aug	Feast of the Assumption
5 Oct	Republic Day
1 Nov	All Saints' Day
1 Dec	Independence Day
8 Dec	Feast of the Immaculate Conception
25 Dec	Christmas Day

OPENING HOURS

○ Shops   ● Post Offices
● Offices   ● Museums/Monuments
● Banks   ● Pharmacies

8am 9am 10am noon 1pm 2pm 4pm 5pm 7pm

☐ Day   ☐ Midday   ☐ Evening

Shops In general 9–12:30, 2:30–7. Large stores and supermarkets are open from around 9–7. Some super-markets stay open until 10 (5 on Sundays). Hypermarkets in malls stay open until 10pm or later.
Offices Generally offices are open 9–12:30, 2–6.
Banks Generally banks are open 8:30–3.
Post offices Mon–Fri 9–6, Sat 9–noon at main branches. In the suburbs, offices may close for lunch.
Museums and churches Lisbon's main museums are mainly open 10–6 and smaller ones 10–1, 2–5, but this can vary, so check before visiting.
Pharmacies They are usually open 9–12:30, 2–7, but duty chemists will be open longer (➤ 188).

EMERGENCY

POLICE 112

FIRE 112

AMBULANCE 112

PERSONAL SAFETY

Violence against tourists is unusual in Lisbon, though you should be careful of bag snatching and pickpocketing on crowded public transport and in some areas.

• Always lock valuables in hotel safety deposit boxes
• Beware of pickpockets in crowded markets, and on crowded buses.
• Do not leave your bag unattended when waiting for a bus or taxi.
• Stick to brightly lit main thoroughfares at night.
• If you are robbed, whatever you do, don't resist.

Police assistance:
☎ **112** from any phone

TELEPHONES

shops displaying the PT (Portugal Telecom) logo. International calls are cheaper between 9pm and 9am and at weekends.
Calls from hotel rooms will invariably attract a heavy premium.
Mobile telephone reception is excellent throughout the city.

There are public telephones on almost every street corner. They take coins, credit cards or phonecards, available from post offices, kiosks and

International Dialling Codes
Dial 00 followed by
UK:	44
USA / Canada:	1
Irish Republic:	353
Australia:	61
Spain:	34

POST

Stamps (*selos*) can be bought at post offices, kiosks and tobacconists. Letters to EU countries will arrive within five to seven days, and to the USA within 10 days. Send urgent mail by *correio azul* and ensure that you post it in a blue post-box. Other postboxes are red.

ELECTRICITY

The power supply is 220 volts AC. Sockets take two-pronged round continental plugs.

Visitors from the UK will need an adaptor, and visitors from the USA will need a transformer for 100–120 volt devices.

TIPS/GRATUITIES

Tipping is not expected for all services and rates are lower than elsewhere in Europe.
As a general guide:
Restaurant bill	(service not included) 10%
Taxis	10%
Tour Guides	half day €3, full day €5
Porters	€1 per bag
Chambermaids	not expected
Toilet attendants	small change

CONSULATES and EMBASSIES

UK
☎ 213 924 000

USA
☎ 217 273 300

Ireland
☎ 213 929 440

Australia
☎ 213 101 500

Canada
☎ 213 164 600

HEALTH

Insurance Citizens of EU countries receive reduced-cost emergency health care with relevant documentation (European Health Insurance Card), but private medical insurance is still advised and essential for all other visitors.

Dental Services The standard of private dental care is generally excellent. Ask at your hotel if you need a dentist. You have to pay for treatment, but your insurance should cover the costs.

Weather The sun is intense at all times of year, and it is possible to burn very quickly, even on cloudy days. Cover up with high-factor sunscreen, wear a hat and drink plenty of water, especially if walking a great deal during the day.

Drugs Chemists (*farmâcia*) are open Mon–Fri 9–1 and 2:30–7, and Sat 9–12:30. Some open through lunch and the late-night duty chemist is posted in pharmacy windows. Pharmacists are highly trained and can sell some drugs that require prescriptions in other countries. However, take adequate supplies of any drugs you take regularly as they may not be available.

Safe Water Tap water is safe but its mineral content may make it taste unpleasant. Ask for sparkling (*água com gás*) or still (*água sem gás*) bottled water.

CONCESSIONS

Young People Most museums have lower admission rates for students (and entry is generally free for children) on production of a passport or valid student identity card.

Senior Citizens Travellers over 65 are usually entitled to discounted admission at museums and reduced fares on public transport. If mobility is a problem, however, getting around can be a bit of a trial (► Travelling with a Disability, right).

TRAVELLING WITH A DISABILITY

Facilities for travellers with disabilities in Lisbon are improving, but many older hotels and public buildings are still inaccessible, and cheaper hotels tend to be on the upper floors of apartment blocks. Cobbled streets are a particular problem for wheelchair users. Some metro stations have platform access by lift. Shopping malls, some museums, the airport and railway stations have specially adapted toilets. Discuss your particular needs with your tour operator or hotel before booking a holiday.

CHILDREN

Hotels and restaurants are generally child-friendly, though younger children won't enjoy the city much. Baby-changing rooms are rare.

TOILETS

There are public toilets in shopping centres, some metro stations and museums. Many bars and cafés have toilets; only use if you have a drink.

CUSTOMS

The import of wildlife souvenirs sourced from rare or endangered species may be illegal or require a special permit. Check your home country's customs regulations.

Useful Word and Phrases

There are two distinctive Portuguese sounds: firstly, the nasalised vowels written with a til (~, like the tilde on Spanish ñ): (so "bread", pão, is pronounced "pow!" with a strong nasal twang; secondly, "s" and "z" are often pronounced as a slushy "sh" (so "banknotes", notas, is pronounced "not-ash"). You will find that while Portuguese is a relatively easy language to read, the pronunciation makes is very difficult for most visitors to understand the spoken language.

GREETINGS AND COMMON WORDS

Yes/No **Sim/Não**
Please **Se faz favor**
Thank you **Obrigado** (male speaker)/
Obrigada (female speaker)
You're welcome **De nada/Foi
um prazer**
Hello/Goodbye **Olá/Adeus**
Welcome **Bem vindo/a**
Good morning **Bom dia**
Good evening/night **Boa noite**
How are you? **Como está?**
Fine, thank you **Bem, obrigado/a**
Sorry **Desculpe/Perdão**
Excuse me, could you help me?
Desculpe, podia ajudar-me?
My name is… **Chamo-me…**
Do you speak English? **Fala inglês?**
I don't understand **Não percebo**
I don't speak any Portuguese **Não
falo português**

EMERGENCY! Urgência!

Help! **Socorro!**
Stop! **Pare!**
Stop that thief! **Apanhe o ladrão!**
Police! **Polícia!**
Fire! **Fogo!**
Go away, or I'll scream! **Vai-se
embora, senão começo a gritar!**
Leave me alone! **Deixe-me em paz!**

NUMBERS

0	zero	15	quinze
1	um	16	dezasseis
2	dois	17	dezassete
3	três	18	dezoito
4	quatro	19	dezanove
5	cinco	20	vinte
6	seis	21	vinte e um
7	sete	30	trinta
8	oito	40	quarenta
9	nove	50	cinquenta
10	dez	60	sessenta
11	onze	70	setenta
12	doze	80	oitenta
13	treze	90	noventa
14	catorze	100	cem

I've lost my purse/wallet **Perdi o
meu porta-moedas/a minha carteira**
My passport has been stolen
Roubaram-me o passaporte
Could you call a doctor? **Podia
chamar um médico depressa?**

DIRECTIONS AND TRAVELLING

Airport **Aeroporto**
Boat **Barco**
Bus station **Estação de camionetas**
Bus/coach **Autocarro**
Car **Automóvel**
Church **Igreja**
Hospital **Hospital**
Market **Mercado**
Museum **Museu**
Square **Praça**
Street **Rua**
Taxi rank **Praça de táxis**
Train **Comboio**
Ticket **Bilhete**
  Return **Ida e volta**
  Single **Bilhete de ida**
Station **Estação**
I'm lost **Estou perdido/a**
How many kilometres to…? **Quantos
quilómetros faltam ainda para
chegar a…?**
Here/There **Aqui/Ali**
Left/right **À esquerda/À direita**
Straight on **Em frente**

DAYS

Today	**Hoje**
Tomorrow	**Amanhã**
Yesterday	**Ontem**
Tonight	**Esta noite**
Last night	**Ontem à noite**
In the morning	**De manhã**
In the afternoon	**De tarde**
This week	**Esta semana**
Monday	**Segunda-feira**
Tuesday	**Terça-feira**
Wednesday	**Quarta-feira**
Thursday	**Quinta-feira**
Friday	**Sexta-feira**
Saturday	**Sábado**
Sunday	**Domingo**

MONEY: Dinheiro

Bank **Banco**
Banknote **Notas**
Cash desk **Caixa**
Change **Troco**
Cheque **Cheque**
Coin **Moeda**
Credit card **Cartão de crédito**
Exchange office **Câmbios**
Exchange rate **Câmbio**
Foreign **Estrangeiro**
Mail **Correio**
Post office **Posto de correio**
Traveller's cheque **Cheque de viagem**
Could you give me some small change, please? **Podia dar-me dinheiro trocado, se faz favor?**

ACCOMMODATION

Are there any...? **Há...?**
I'd like a room with a view of the sea **Queria um quarto com vista para o mar**
Where's the emergency exit/fire escape? **Onde fica a saída de emergência/escada de salvação?**
Does that include breakfast? **Está incluido o pequeno almoço?**
Do you have room service? **O hotel tem serviço de quarto?**
I've made a reservation **Reservei um lugar**
Air-conditioning **Ar condicionado**
Balcony **Varanda**
Bathroom **Casa de banho**
Hot water **Água quente**
Hotel **Hotel**
Key **Chave**
Lift **Elevador**
Night **Noite**
Room **Quarto**
Room service **Serviço de quarto**
Shower **Duche**
Telephone **Telefone**
Towel **Toalha**
Water **Água**

RESTAURANT: Restaurante

I'd like to book a table **Posso reservar uma mesa?**
A table for two, please **Uma mesa para duas pessoas, se faz favor**
Could we see a menu, please? **Poderia dar nos a ementa, se faz favor**
What's this? **O que é isto?**

A bottle of... **Uma garrafa de ...**
Alcohol **Alcool**
Beer **Cerveja**
Bill **Conta**
Bread **Pão**
Breakfast **Pequeno almoço**
Café **Café**
Coffee **Café**
Dinner **Jantar**
Lunch **Almoço**
Menu **Menú/ementa**
Milk **Leite**
Mineral water **Água mineral**
Pepper **Pimenta**
Salt **Sal**
Table **Mesa**
Tea **Chá**
Waiter **Empregado/a**

SHOPPING

Shop **Loja**
Where can I get....? **Onde é que eu posso arranjar...?**
Could you help me please? **Pode-me ajudar, se faz favor?**
I'm looking for... **Estou a procura de...**
I would like... **Queria...**
I'm just looking **Só estou a ver**
How much? **Quanto custa?**
It's too expensive **Acho demasiado caro**
I'll take this one/these **Levo este(s)/esta(s)**
Good/Bad **Bom/Mau**
Bigger **Maior**
Smaller **Mais pequeno**
Open/Closed **Aberto/Fechado**
I'm a size... in the UK **Na Grã Bretanha o meu numero é...**
Have you got a bag please? **Tem um saco, se faz favor?**

TOWN PRONUNCIATION GUIDE

Braga **brag-uh**
Bragança **bra-gan-suh**
Coimbra **queem-bruh**
Évora **e-vor-uh**
Faro **far-ooh**
Fátima **fa-tee-muh**
Lagos **lah-goosh**
Lisboa **leezh-boh-ah**
Marvão **mar-vow**
Porto **port-ooh**
Sagres **sar-gresh**
Tavira **ta-veer-ah**
Vila Viçosa **vee-lah-vee-soh-sah**

Streetplan

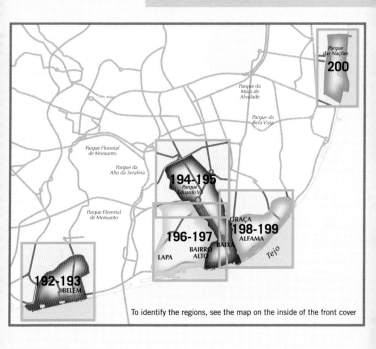

To identify the regions, see the map on the inside of the front cover

City Plan

⎓⎓⎓ Main road		▢	Place of interest
⎓⎓⎓ Other road		*i*	Tourist information
⎓⎓⎓ Minor road		●	Monument
⎓⎓⎓ Narrow road		†	Church
⎯⎯ Railway		✡	Synagogue
●—● Funicular railway		☀	Viewpoint/miradouro
▇ Important building		✉	Post Office
▢ Park		●	Metro station

192–200

0	100	200	300	400	500 metres
0	100	200	300	400	500 yards

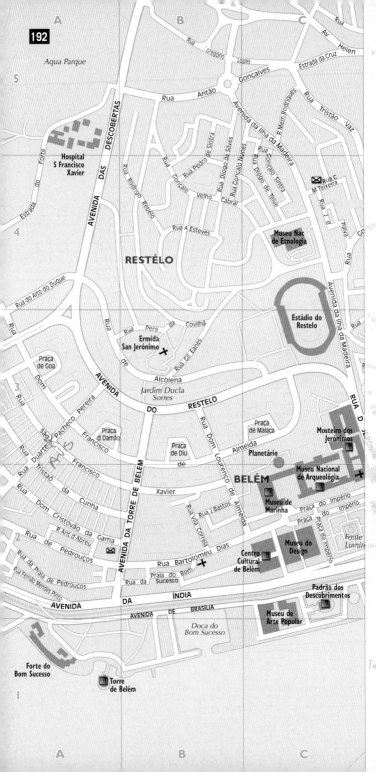

A   B   C

Aqua Parque

Rua Gregório Lopes

AV Helen

Estrada da Cruz

Rua Antão Gonçalves

AVENIDA DAS DESCOBERTAS

Hospital S Francisco Xavier

Estrada do Forte

Avenida da Ilha da Madeira

R Mem Rodrigues

Rua Tristão Vaz

AVENIDA

Rua Rodrigo Rebelo

Rua Gonçalo Velho Cabral

Rua Pedro de Sintra

Rua Diogo de Silves

Rua Gonçalo Sintra

Rua Gonçalo Nunes

Rua Diogo de Teive

Rua C M Teixeira

Rua J d Paiva

Rua A Esteves

Museu Nac de Etnologia

RESTÉLO

Rua do Alto do Duque

Estádio do Restelo

Avenida da Ilha da Madeira

Praça de Goa

Rua Dom

Rua de

Rua Pero da Covilhã

Ermida San Jerónimo ✝

Rua Gil Eanes

AVENIDA

Alcolena

Jardim Ducla Sorres

DO RESTELO

RUA D JERÓNIM

Rua Pacheco Pereira

Praça d Damão

Praça de Malaca

Rua Duarte

Rua Tristão

Rua Dom Cristovão da Gama

Francisco da Cunha

São

AVENIDA DA TORRE DE BELÉM

Praça de Diu

Rua Dom Lourenço de Almeida

Almeida

Mosteiro dos Jerónimos

Planetário

Museu Nacional de Arqueológia ✝

Xavier

BELÉM

Rua de Pedrouços

Rua da Praia de Pedrouços

Rua Fernão Mendes Pinto

R Ant d Abreu

Rua J Bastos

Rua Vila Correia

Museu de Marinha

Praça do Império

Praça do Império

Praça do Império

Fonte Luminos

Rua Bartolomeu Dias

Praia do Bom Sucesso

Centro Cultural de Belém ✝

Museu do Design

DA ÍNDIA

AVENIDA

AVENIDA DE BRASÍLIA

Padrão dos Descobrimentos

Museu de Arte Popular

Doca do Bom Sucesso

Forte do Bom Sucesso

Torre de Belém

A   B   C

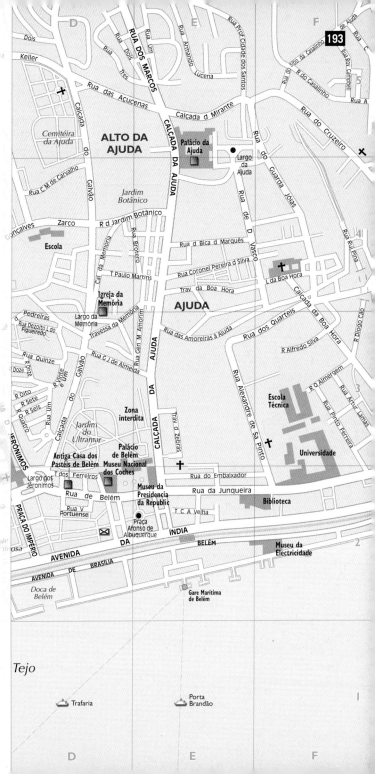

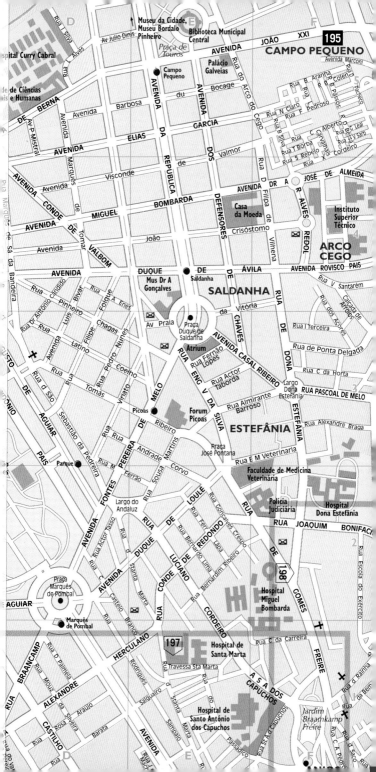

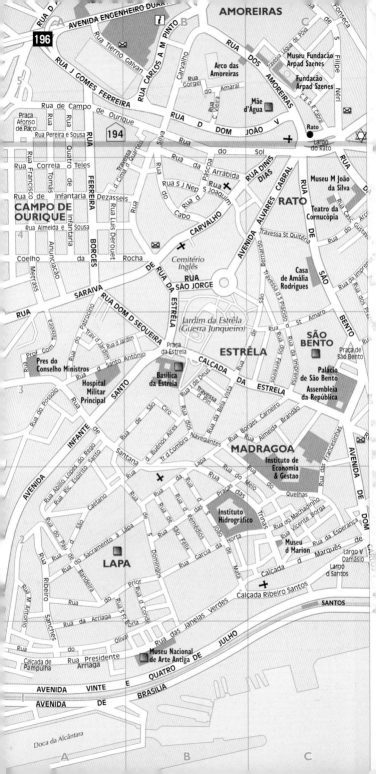

AMOREIRAS

196

AVENIDA ENGENHEIRO DUARTE

RUA J GOMES FERREIRA

RUA TIERNO GALVAN

RUA CARLOS A M PINTO

RUA DOS AMOREIRAS

Museu Fundação Arpad Szenes

Arco das Amoreiras

Fundação Arpad Szenes

Praça Afonso de Paço

Rua de Campo de Ourique

194

Mãe d'Água

Rato

Largo do Rato

Rua Pereira e Sousa

Rua Correia Teles

RUA D DOM JOÃO V

RUA DINIS DIAS

Museu M João da Silva

Rua da Arrábida

Rua S J Nep

Rua S Joaquim

Teatro da Cornucópia

Rua do Cabo

CARVALHO

AVENIDA ALVARES CABRAL

RATO

CAMPO DE OURIQUE

Rua Almeida e Sousa

Infantaria

Travessa St Quitéria

Casa de Amália Rodrigues

SARAIVA

RUA DOM D SEQUEIRA

DE RUA DA ESTRELA

Cemitério Inglês

RUA DE SÃO JORGE

Jardim da Estrêla (Guerra Junqueiro)

SÃO BENTO

Praça de São Bento

Pres do Conselho Ministros

Praça da Estrela

ESTRÊLA

Palácio de São Bento

Hospital Militar Principal

Basílica da Estrela

CALÇADA

DA ESTRELA

Assembleia da República

INFANTE

SANTO

MADRAGOA

Instituto de Economia & Gestão

AVENIDA DE

Quelhas

LAPA

Instituto Hidrográfico

Praças das Trinas

Rua do Machadinho

Museu d Marion

Largo V Damásio

Largo d Santos

Calçada

SANTOS

Calçada Ribeiro Santos

Rua da Arriaga

Rua das Janelas Verdes

Calçada de Pampulha

Rua Presidente Arriaga

Museu Nacional de Arte Antiga

AVENIDA VINTE E QUATRO DE JULHO

BRASILIA

AVENIDA DE

Doca da Alcântara

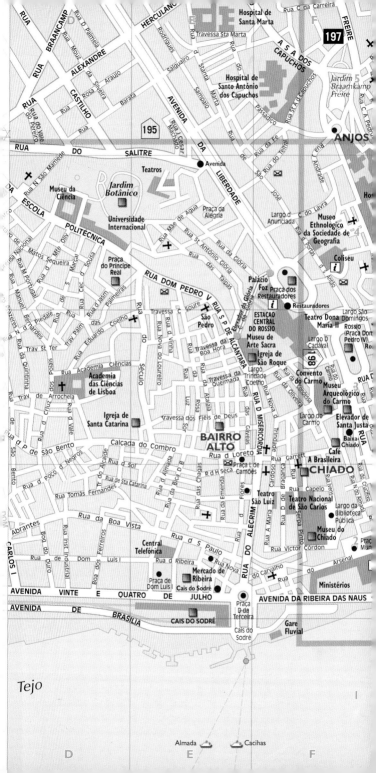

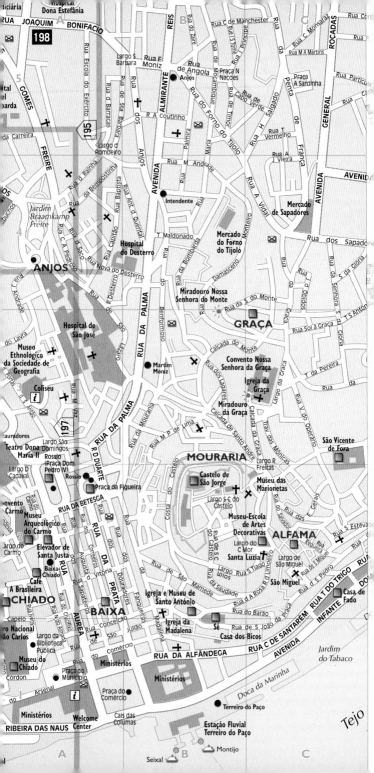

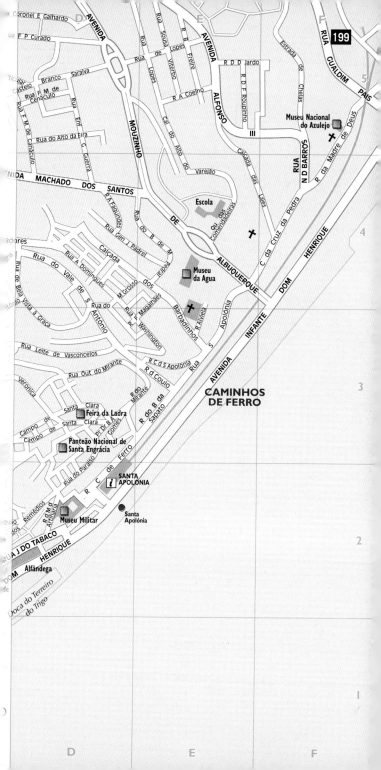

Coronel E Galhardo
ua F P Curado

AVENIDA
D

Rua de Sousa Lopes
E Rua B Lopes
Rua Freire
AVENIDA

Rua de Lopes Vitebro

R D D Jardo
ALFONSO
R D F Roupinho

Estrada de Chelas

RUA GUALDIM PAIS

199
5

Branco
castelo
Saraiva
Rua F M de Cenáculo
Rua F M de Cenáculo
Ent
C Guerra

MOUZINHO

R A Coelho
III
Cal do Alto do

Museu Nacional
do Azulejo
†

RUA N D BARROS
R da Madre de Deus

Rua do Alto da Eira

AVENIDA MACHADO DOS SANTOS
DE

Varelão
Calçada das Lães

C da Cruz da Pedra

RUA DOM HENRIQUE
4

R A Faúndes
Rua do B de M
Escola
Rua Cen J Padrel

Qu das Comendadeiras
†

Calçada
Rua A Domingues
Rua do Vale de S António
M Grosso dos
Rua do
R Ilegível
Museu da Agua
†
R Alviela
Apolónia
Apolónia

ALBUQUERQUE
INFANTE

dores
Rua de Bela Vista a Graça
António
R Washington
Rua Magalhães
Barbadinhos

Rua Leite de Vasconcelos
R C d S Apolónia
Rua
AVENIDA
3

Rua Out do Mirante
R d Couto
R do Mirante

CAMINHOS
DE FERRO

Veronica
santa Clara
Feira da Ladra
santa Clara
R do B da Sapato
Pr do B Cones

Campo de santa
Campo de
Panteão Nacional de
Santa Engrácia
Rua do Paraíso
R C de Ferro

i SANTA
APOLÓNIA

R D M G Artilharia
Museu Militar
Santa
Apolónia
2

RUA J DO TABACO
DOM HENRIQUE
Remédios
dos
evio

Alfândega
DOM
de
Doca do Terreiro
do Trigo

I

D   E   F

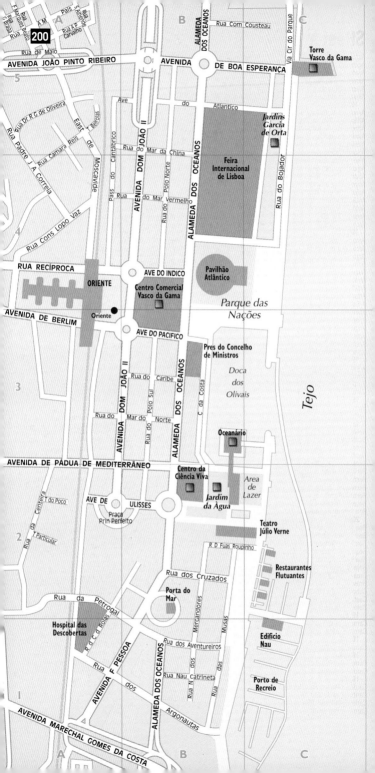

Street Index

Actor Taborda, Rua 195 E3
Açucenas, Rua das 193 D5
Ajuda, Calçada da 193 E3
Alcolena, Rua das 192 B3
Alecrim, Rua do 197 E2
Alexandre de Sa Pinto, Rua 193 E3
Alexandre Herculano, Rua 195 D1
Alfândega, Rua da 198 B1
Alfonso III, Avenida 199 E5
Almirante Barroso, Rua 195 E3
Almirante Reis, Avenida 198 B5
Álvares Cabral, Avenida 196 C4
Alves Redol, Rua 195 F4
Amoreiras, Rua dos 194 B1
Andrade Corvo, Rua 195 E3
Angola, Rua da 198 B5
Anjos, Rua dos 198 B5
Antão Gonçalves, Rua 192 B5
António Augusto de Aguiar, Avenida 195 D3
Arco do Carvalhão, Rua do 194 A1
Arco do Cego, Rue do 195 E5
Arco, Rua do 196 C4
Argonautas, Rua dos 200 B1
Armando Lucena, Rua 193 E5
Augusta Rosa, Rua da 198 C2
Arrábida, Rua da 196 B4
Artilharia Um, Rua 194 B2
Artur Lamas, Rua 193 F3
A Sardinha, Praça 198 C5
Atalaia, Rua da 197 E3
Atlantico, Ave do 200 B5
Augusta, Rua 198 A2
Aurea, Rua 198 A1
Aventureiros, Rua dos 200 B1
Aviador Plácido de Abreu, Rua 194 B2
A Vidal, Rua 198 C4
Barbadinhos, Calçada dos 199 E3
Barbosa Colen, Rua 195 F5
Barbosa du Bocage, Avenida 195 D5
Barracas, Rua d 198 A5
Bartolomeu Dias, Rua 192 B2
B da Sapato, Rua do 199 E3
Belém, Rua de 193 D2
Bempostinha, Rua da 198 A4
Beneficência, Rua da 194 C5
Benformoso, Rua do 198 B3
Bento d Rocha Cabral, C 194 C1
Berlim, Avenida de 200 A3
Berna, Avenida de 195 D5
Bernardim Ribeiro, Rua 195 E2
Bernardo Lima, Rua 195 E2
Betesga, Rua da 198 A2
Boa Esperança, Avenida de 200 C5
Boa Hora, Calçada da 193 F3
Boa Hora, L da 193 F4
Boa Hora, Trav da 193 E4
Boa Hora, Travessa da 197 E3
Boa Vista, Rua da 197 D2
Bojador, Rua do 200 C4
Braancamp, Rua 195 D1
Brasilia, Avenida de 196 B1
Cabo, Rua do 196 B4
Caetano Alberto, Rua 195 F5
Calouste Gulbenkian, Avenida 194 A3
Camara Reis, Rua 200 A5
Camilo Castelo Branco, Rua 195 D2
Campo de Ourique, Rua de 194 A1
Campolide, Rua de 194 A2
Cardeal Cerejeira, Alameda 194 C3
Cardeal Mercier, Rua 194 B5
Caribe, Rua do 200 B3
Carlos A M Pinto, Rua 194 B1
Carmo, Largo do 197 F3

Carmo, Rua do 198 A2
Casal Ribeiro, Avenida 195 E3
Castelo, Costa do 198 B2
Castilho, Rua 195 D1
C de Ferro, Rua 199 D3
C de Manchester, Rua 198 B5
C de Santarém, Rua 198 C1
Cec d Sousa, Rua 197 D4
Centeira, Rua de 200 A2
C F de Sousa, Avenida 194 B2
Chagas, Rua das 197 E2
Chelas, Estrada de 199 F5
Cima d Quarteis, Travessa d 196 B5
Circular do Parque, Via 200 C5
Columbano Borgdalo Pinheiro, Avenida 194 A5
Com Cousteau, Rua 200 C5
Combatentes, Avenida dos 194 B5
Combro, Calçada do 197 E3
Combro, Tr d 198 A3
Comendadeiras, Qu das 199 E4
Comércio, Rua do 198 A1
Conceição, Rua 198 A1
Conde das Antas, Rua d 194 A2
Conde de Redondo, Rua 195 E2
Conde de Valbom, Avenida 195 D4
Conde, Rua d 196 B2
Condessa, Rua da 197 F3
Cons Lopo Vaz, Rua 200 A4
Coronel E Galhardo, Rua 199 D5
Coronel Pereira d Silva, Rua 193 E4
Correeiros, Rua dos 198 A2
Correia Teles, Rua 196 A4
Costa, C da 200 B3
Coulo, Rua d 199 E3
Criuz dos Poiais, Rua d 197 D3
Crucifixo, Rua do 197 F2
Cruzados, Rua dos 200 B2
Cruz da Carreira, Rua 195 F1
Cruz de Pedra, C da 199 F4
Cruz da Santa Apolónia, Rua da 199 E3
Cruz, Estrada da 192 C5
Cruzeiro, Rua do 193 F5
D Duarte, Rua 192 A3
Defensores de Chaves, Avenida dos 195 E3
Descobertas, Avenida das 192 A5
Desterro, Rua 198 A4
Dezoito L do Figueiredo, Rua 193 D3
D Filipa de Vilhena, Rua 195 F4
D Fuas Roupinho, Rua 200 B2
Dinis Dias, Rua 196 C4
Dom Carlos I, Avenida de 197 D2
Dom Cristóvão da Gama, Rua 192 A2
Dom D Jardo, Rua 199 E5
Dom F Manuel d Melo, Rua 194 B2
Dom Francisco de Almeida, Rua 192 A3
Dom João II, Avenida 200 B3
Dom João V, Rua d 194 B1
Dom Lourenço de Almeida, Rua 192 B3
Dom Luís I, Rua de 197 D2
Dom Pedro V, Rua 197 E4
Dom Vasco, Rua da 193 E4
Domingos d Sequeira, Rua 196 A4
Dona Estefânia, Largo 195 F3
Dona Estefânia, Rua de 195 F3
Douradores, Rua dos 198 A2
Doze, Rua 193 D3
D Pacheco, Rua 195 F5
Dr A José de Almeida, Ave 195 F4
Dr Alvaro de Castro, Rua 194 B5
Dr António Cândido, Rua 195 D4
Dr António Martins, Rua 194 A5
Dr Bernardino António Gomes, Praça 199 D3

Dr Júlio Dantas, Rua 194 B4
Dr Nicolau Bettencourt, Rua 194 C4
Dr Rui Gomes de Oliveira, Rua 200 A5
Dr S Teles, Rua 194 C5
Duarte Pacheco Pereira, Rua 192 A3
Duque Cadaval, Largo 197 F3
Duque de Ávila, Avenida 195 E4
Duque de Loulé, Avenida 195 E2
Elias Garcia, Avenida 195 E5
Embaixador, Rua do 193 E2
Emenda, Rua da 197 E2
E M Veterinaria, Rua 195 F3
Enf G Guerra, Rua 199 D4
Engenheiro Duarte-Pacheco, Avenida 194 A1
Engenheiro V da Silva, Rua 195 E3
Escoia do Exército, Rua 195 F2
Escola Gerais, Rua das 198 C2
Escola Politécnica, Rua da 197 D4
Espanha, Praça de 194 B4
Esperança, Rua da 196 C2
Estêvão Pinto, Travessa 194 B4
Estrela, Calcada da 196 C3
Estrela, Praça da 196 B3
Estrêla, Rua da 196 B4
Febo Moniz, Rua 198 B5
Fernando Pessoa, Avenida 200 A1
Fernão Lopes, Rua 195 E3
Fernão Mendes Pinto, Rua 192 A2
Ferr Lápa, Rua 195 E2
Ferreira Borges, Rua 196 A4
Ferreiros, Boa dos 197 D2
Ferreiros, Rua dos 196 C3
Ferreiros, T dos 193 D2
Fialho de Almeida, Rua 194 C4
Fiéis de Deus, Travessa dos 197 E3
Filipe Folque, Rua 195 D4
Flores, Rua d 197 E2
F Magalhães, Rua 199 E4
F Marques Beato, Rua 200 A5
Fontes Pereira de Melo, Avenida 195 D2
Forno do Tijolo, Rua do 198 B5
Francisco Metrass, Rua 196 A4
Frei Manuel de Canáculo, Rua 199 D5
F Roupinho, Rua d 199 E5
Galvão, Calçada do 193 D4
Garcia da Horta, Rua 196 B2
Garrett, Rua 197 F3
General Roçadas, Avenida 198 C5
General Taborda, Rua 194 A2
Gomes Freire, Rua de 195 F2
Gonçalves Zarco, Rua 193 D4
Gorgel do Amaral, Rua 194 B1
Graça, Calçada da 198 C3
Graça, Largo da 198 C3
Graça, Rua da 198 C3
Gualdim Pais, Rua 199 F5
Guarda Jóias, Rua do 193 F4
Helen Keller, Av 193 D5
H Salgado, Rua 198 C5
H Seca, Rua d 197 E2
Ilha da Madeira, Avenida da 192 C3
Ilha do Principe, Rua 198 B5
Ilha São Tomé, Rue 198 B5
Império, Praça do 192 C2
Imprensa Nacional, Rua da 197 D4
Imprensa, Rua da 196 C3
Índia, Avenida da 192 B2
Indico, Ave do 200 B4
Infantaria Dezasseis, Rua de 196 A4
Infante Dom Henrique, Avenida 199 E3
Infante Santo, Avenida 196 A3
Instituto Industrial, Rua 197 D2

I Silva, Rua 195 D5
I Terceira, Rua 195 F3
Ivens, Rua 197 F2
Janelas Verdes, Rua das 196 B2
Jardim Botânico, Rua d 193 D4
J do Tabaco, Rua 199 D2
Jéronimos, Largo dos 193 D2
Jerónimos, Rua d 193 D3
J Gomes Ferreira, Rua 194 A1
João Bastos, Rua 192 B2
João Crisóstomo, Avenida 195 E4
João Pinto Ribeiro, Avenida 200 A5
João XXI, Avenida 195 F5
Joaquim António de Aguiar, Avenida 195 D2
Joaquim Bonifacio, Rua d 195 F2
José Fontana, Praça 195 E3
José Malhoa, Avenida 194 A4
Júlio Andrade, Rua 197 F4
Julio Cesar Machado, Rua 195 E1
Julio Dinis, Av 195 D5
Junqueira, Rua da 193 E2
Lagares, Rua dos 198 B3
Lajes, Calçada das 199 F4
Lapa, Rua da 196 B3
Laranjeiras, Estrada da 194 B5
Largo de Noronha, Rua 194 C5
Latino Coelho, Rua 195 D3
Liberdade, Avenida da 197 E4
Loreto, Rua d 197 E3
Luciano Cordeiro, Rua 195 E2
Luís Bivar, Avenida 195 D4
Luís Derouet, Rua 196 A4
Luz Sor, Rua 197 E3
Machadinho, Rua do 196 C2
Machado Dos Santos, Avenida 199 D4
Madalena, Rua de 198 B1
Madre de Deus, Rua da 199 F5
Mãe de Agua, Rua 197 E4
Marcos, Rua dos 193 E5
Marechal Gomes da Costa, Avenida 200 A1
Maria Andrade, Rua 198 B4
Maria, Rua 198 B5
Marquês da Fonteira, Rua 194 B2
Marquês de Abrantes, Calçada d 197 D2
Marquês de Pombal, Praça 195 D2
Marquês de Ponte de Lima, Rua do 198 B3
Marquês de Sá da Bandeira, Rua 195 D4
Marquês de Tomar, Avenida 195 D4
Marquês Subserra, Rua 194 C2
Meio, Rua do 196 B2
Mem Rodrigues, Rua 192 C5
Memoria, Cal d 193 D4
Memória, Largo da 193 D3
Memória, Travessa da 193 D3
M Ferrão, Rua 195 D2
M Grosso, Rua do 199 D4
Miguel Bombarda, Avenida 195 D4
Mirante, Calçada d 193 E5
Mirante, Rua do 199 D3
Misericórdia, Rua d 197 F3
Moçambique, Rua de 198 B5
Mónicas, Trav das 198 C3
Monte Olivete, Rua do 197 D4
Monte, Calçada do 198 C3
Moscavide, East de 200 A4
Mouraria, Rua da 198 B3
Mouz da Silveira, Rua 195 D1
Mouzinho de Albuquerque, Avenida 199 D5
Musas, Rua das 200 B1
Museu de Artiharia, Rua do 199 D2
M Vaz, Rua 198 A3
Nau Catrineta, Rua 200 B1
Navegantes, Rua dos 196 B3
N d Piedale, Rua 197 D3
Nelson de Barros, Rua 199 F5
Nova do Loureiro, Rua 197 E3

Oceanos, Alameda dos 200 B3
Óuteiro do Mirante, Rua 199 D3
Pacifico, Ave do 200 B3
Padre António Vieira, Rua 194 B2
Padre Joaquim Alves Correia, Rua 200 A5
Pádua de Mediterrãneo, Avenida de 200 A3
Palm, Trav 197 D3
Palma, Rua da 198 B3
Palmeiras, Rua das 197 D4
Páscoa, Rua d 196 B4
Pascoal de Melo, Rua 195 F3
Passadiço, Rua do 195 E1
Pau de Bandeira, Rua do 196 A2
Paulo Martins, T 193 D4
P de São Bento, Rua d 197 D3
Pedreiras, Rua d 193 D3
Pedro de Sintra, Rua 192 B4
Pedro Nunes, Rua 195 D3
Pedrouços, Rua de 192 A2
Penta de França, Rua da 198 C5
Pereira e Sousa, Rua 194 A1
Pereira, T da 198 C3
Pero da Covilhã, Rua 192 B3
Petrogal, Rua da 200 A2
Pin, Travessa d 196 B3
Pinheiro Chagas, Rua 195 D4
Ponta Delgada, Rua de 195 F3
Port Durão, Rua 194 B5
Portas d S Antão, Rua d 197 F4
Possolo, Rua de 196 A3
Praças, Rua das 196 B2
Praia da Vitória, Av 195 E4
Praia de Pedrouços, Rua da 192 A2
Praia do Bom Sucesso, Rua da 192 B2
Prata, Rua da 198 A2
Prazeres, Rua dos 196 C4
Presidente Arriaga, Rua 196 A1
Prin Perfeito, Praça 200 A2
Prior, Rua do 196 B2
Prof Cidade dos Santos, Rua 193 E5
Prof Gom Teixeira, Rua 196 A3
Prof Lima Bastos, Rua 194 A5
Quarteis, Rua dos 193 F3
Quatro de Infantaria, Rua 196 A4
Ramalho Orligão, Rua 194 B4
Rato, Largo do 196 C5
Recíproca, Rua 200 A4
Regueira, Rua 198 C2
Remédios, Rua d 196 B2
Remédios, Rua dos 199 D2
Republica, Avenida da 195 E4
Ressano Garcia, Avenida 194 B4
Restauradores, Praça dos 197 F4
Restelo, Avenida do 192 B3
R Freitas, Largo 198 C2
Ribeira das Naus, Avenida da 197 F2
Ribeira, Rua d 197 E2
Ribeiro Sanches, Rua 196 A2
Ribeiro Santos, Calçada 196 C2
Ric Espírito Santo, Rua 196 A2
Rodrigo da Fonseca, Rua 194 C2
Rodrigo Rebelo, Rua 192 B4
Rodrigues Sampaio, Rua 195 E1
Rosa Araújo, Rua 195 D1
Rosa, Rua da 197 E3
Rovisco Pais, Avenida 195 F4
Roy Campbell, Rua 193 F5
Rui Pina, Rua 193 F4
Saco, Rua d 195 F1
Sacramento à Lápa, Rua do 196 A2
Salitre, Rua do 197 D5
Salvador Alhende, Rua 200 A5
Salvador, Rua do 198 C2
Sampaio Pina, Rua 194 B2
Santa Clara, Campo de 199 D3
Santa Marta, Travessa 195 E1
Santa Quitéria, Travessa 196 C4
Santa Teresa, Trav 197 D3
Santana, Rua de 196 A3

Santo A dos Capuchos, Al 195 F1
São Bento, Rua de 196 C4
São Francisco Xavier, Rua 192 A3
São João da Praça, Rua de 198 C2
São João Nepomuceno, Rua 196 B4
São Joaquim, Rua 196 B4
São Jorge, Rua 196 B4
São José, Rua de 197 F4
São Mamede, Rua de 198 B2
São Miguel, Largo de 198 C2
São Miguel, Rua de 198 C2
São Paulo, Rua d 197 E2
São Pedro de Alcântara, Rua 197 E3
São Sebastião da Pedreira, Rua d 195 D3
São Tiago, Rua 198 C2
Sapadores, Rua dos 198 C4
Sapateiros, Rua dos 198 A2
Saraiva de Carvalho, Rua 196 A4
Saudade, Rua da 198 B2
S do Monte, Rua da 198 C4
S Domingos, Rua de 196 B2
S Dumont, Av 194 C5
Século, Rua do 197 E3
Seis, Rua 193 D3
Senhora S da Gloria, Rua da 198 C3
Serpa Pinto, Rua 197 F2
S Estêvao, Rua 198 C2
Sete, Rua 193 D3
S Filipe Néri, Rua de 194 C1
Sidónio Pais, Avenida 195 D3
Silva Carvalho, Rua 194 B1
Sitio da Casalinho de Ajuda, Rua do 193 F5
S João de Mata, Rua d 196 B2
S Marçal, Rua de 197 D4
Sol à Graça, Rua 198 C3
Sol, Rua do 196 C5
Soure, Travessa C 197 E4
Sousa Martins, Rua 195 E2
T do Trigo, Rua 198 C2
Telhal, Rua do 197 F5
Tierno Galvan, Rua 194 A1
Timor, Rua de 198 B5
Tomás Anunciação, Rua 196 A4
Tomás Borba, Rua 195 F5
Tomás Fernandes, Rua 197 D2
Tomás Ribeiro, Rua 195 E3
Torre de Bélem, Avenida da 192 B2
Torrinha, Azinhaga de 194 C5
Travessa Espanca, Rua 194 C5
Tres, Rua 193 D5
Trés, Rua 194 A3
Trinas, Rua das 196 C2
Trindade Coelho, Largo 197 E3
Tristão da Cunha, Rua 192 A2
Tristão Vaz, Rua 192 C5
T Vermelho, Rua 198 C5
Ulisses, Ave de 200 B2
Um, Rua 193 D3
Um, Rua 193 E5
Vale de Santo António, Rua do 199 D4
Vale do Pereiro, Rua do 195 D1
Vale, Rua d 197 D3
V Chaves, Rua 194 A2
V Damásio, Largo 196 C2
Veronica, Rua da 199 D3
Vicente Borga, Rua 196 C2
Victor Córdon, Rua 197 F2
Vila Correia, Rua 192 B2
Vinha, Rua d 197 E3
Vinte e Quatro de Julho, Avenida 196 A1
Vinte e Um, Rua 193 D3
Viriato, Rua 195 D3
Visconde de Valmor, Avenida 195 D4
Vitor Bastos, Rua 194 A3
Vitória, Rua d 198 A2
V Lusitano, Rua 194 A2

accommodation 34–36
see also individual areas
admission charges 33
airport 30, 185
Alfama 82–84
  Beco do Spirito Santo 84
  Casa dos Bicos 84
  Chafariz do Dentro 82
  Chafariz del Rei 82
  Igreja da Conceição-a-
    Velha 84
  Igreja de São Miguel 83
  Largo de São Miguel 83,
    179
  Rua de São Pedro 83–84
  Santo Estêvão 84
  trams 23
  walk 177–179
Almada 180
Alvares, Pedro 122
Anthony of Padua, St 87–88
Antiga Casa dos Pastéis de
  Belém 137
aquarium 146–149
architecture 16–19
Arco Triunfal 48
Armazéns do Chiado 51
arriving 30–33
Assembleia da República
  110
azulejos (tiles) 14–15
  Museu Nacional do
    Azulejo 85–86
Azurara Palace 74

Bairro Alto 96, 100–101
  Elevador da Glória 100,
    174
  elevadors 23
  Jardim de São Pedro de
    Alcântara 101
  Palácio Ludovice 100
  Praça Luís de Camões
    100
  Rua da Atalaia 101
  Rua do Diário de Notícias
    101
  Rua da Rosa 101
  Rua do Século 100–101
  São Roque 100
  Solar do Vinho do Porto
    100
  trams 23
Baixa 17, 21, 42, 46–49
  Arco Triunfal 48
  Câmara Municipal 47–48,
    181
  Elevador de Santa Justa 23,
    49, 50, 176
  elevadors 23
  Núcleo Arqueológico da
    Rua dos Correeiros 49
  Praça do Comércio 47, 177
  Praça do Município 47–48,
    49

Rossio 47, 52–54, 176
Rua Augusta 48
Rua da Conceição 48–49
  trams 22–23
ballet 40
banks 186
baroque architecture 19
Basílica da Estrela 102–103
basketware 39
beaches 162
Beco do Spirito Santo 84
beer 38
Belém 18, 115–140, 181
  Antiga Casa dos Pastéis de
    Belém 137
  Centro Cultural de Belém
    136
  eating out 139
  entertainment 140
  Igreja da Memória 138
  map 117
  Mosteiro dos Jerónimos
    17, 124, 128–32
  Museu de Marinha
    124–127
  Museu Nacional de
    Arqueológia 136–137
  Museu Nacional dos
    Coches 133–135
  one-day itinerary 118–119
  Padrão dos
    Descobrimentos
    122–123
  Palácio da Ajuda 138
  shopping 140
  Torre de Belém 18,
    120–121
  trams 23
Boca do Inferno 162
Botanical Gardens 109–110
buses 30, 32, 33

Cabo da Roca 162
Cacilhas 180
Caetano, Marcello 24, 175
Café A Brasileira 60–61, 175
cafés 28, 38
Cais do Sodré 60, 180
calçada à portuguesa (paving)
  18
Câmara Municipal 47–48,
  181
Camões, Luís de 101, 123,
  130, 162
car parking 31
car rental 32
car travel 30–31
Carnation Revolution 19,
  24–25, 52
Carris 22, 31
Carvalho, Major Otelo
  Saraiva de 24
Casa dos Bicos 84
Casa de Fado 91

Casa-Museu Amália
  Rodrigues 13
Cascais 33, 161–162, 163,
  181
Casino (Estoril) 161
Casino gardens (Estoril) 161
Castelo de São Jorge 18,
  77–79
Castelo dos Mouros 167, 169
Cathedral (Sé) 19, 72–73,
  177
Cemitério Inglês 103
Centro de Arte Moderna
  62–63
Centro de Ciência Viva
  150–151
Centro Comercial Vasco da
  Gama 154–155
Centro Cultural de Belém
  136
ceramics 39
  azulejos (tiles) 14–15
Chafariz do Dentro 82
Chafariz del Rei 82
Chiado 50–51
  Armazéns do Chiado 51
  Igreja dos Mártires 51
  Largo do Carmo 50–51
  map 175
  Museu Arqueológico do
    Carmo 51, 61
  Museu do Chiado 51, 60,
    175
  Rua Garrett 51
  Teatro Municipal de São
    Luiz 51
  Teatro Nacional de São
    Carlos 51, 175–176
  walk 174–176
children 188
churches 186
cinema 40
climate 184, 188
clothing sizes 186
cobbled streets 18
colonies 6–7
concessions 188
consulates 188
contemporary architecture
  17, 19
Convento do Carmo 50, 61
Convento de Nossa Senhora
  do Monte Carmel 61
credit cards 185
currency 185
customs regulations 188

da Gama, Vasco 6, 9, 122,
  128, 130, 131
dance 40
dental services 188
Dias, Bartolomeu 9, 123
disabilities, travellers with
  33, 188
drinks 38

driving to Lisbon 30–31, 185
drugs 188

earthquake (1755) 15, 17, 20–21, 46
eating out 37–38
  see also individual areas
Eden building 54
electricity 187
Elevador da Glória 100, 174
Elevador de Santa Justa 23, 49, 50, 176
elevadores (funiculars) 23, 32
embassies 188
emergency numbers 187
entertainment 40
  see also individual areas
Estação Fluvial 180
Estefânia 167
Estoril 33, 161, 163, 181
excursions 28, 159–172
  Mafra 170–172
  map 160
  Queluz 167–169
  Sintra 164–167, 169, 181
  West Coast 161–163
explorers 8–9, 122–123, 124
Expo '98 146, 152, 154

fado **13, 40**
  Casa de Fado 91
  Feira da Ladra 89
ferries 32, 180–181
Figueira 52, 53
food and drink 10–11, 37–38, 39
Fundação Calouste Gulbenkian 55
funiculars (*elevadores*) 23, 32

gay and lesbian nightlife 40
ginjinha (bars) 52
Gonçalves, Nuno 123
Graça 88
Guincho 162
Gulbenkian, Calouste 26–27, 55

health 188
Henry the Navigator 8–9, 122, 124

Igreja da Encarnação 51
Igreja da Graça 88, 179
Igreja da Madalena 177
Igreja dos Mártires 51, 175
Igreja da Memória 138
Igreja e Museu de Santo António 87–88
Igreja de Santa Catarina 110
Igreja de São Miguel 83
Igreja de São Roque 109, 174
insurance 184, 188

Jardim da Água 153
Jardim Botânico 109–110
Jardim da Estrela 103
Jardim de São Pedro de Alcântara 101
Jardins Garcia de Orta 153
jewellery 39
João I, Dom 53
José I, Dom 48

Lapa 110
Largo do Carmo 50–51, 174
Largo da Graça 88
Largo das Portas do Sol 178
Largo de São Domingo 53
Largo de São Miguel 83, 179
leather 39
Lisbon Card 33

Madeira wine 11, 38
Madre de Deus 85
Mãe d'Água 111
Mafra 170–2
Magellan, Ferdinand 122–123
Manuel I, King 18, 122
Manueline architecture 17–18, 19
Mariza 13
markets 39
measurements and sizes 186
medical treatment 188
medieval Lisbon 67–94
  Alfama 82–84
  Casa de Fado 91
  Castelo de São Jorge 77–79
  eating out 92–93
  entertainment 94
  Feira da Ladra 89
  Flea Market 89
  Graça 88
  Igreja e Museu de Santo António 87–88
  map 68–69
  Museu da Agua 90
  Museu-Escola de Artes Decorativas 74–76
  Museu Militar 90–91
  Museu Nacional do Azulejo 85–86
  one-day itinerary 70–71
  Panteão Nacional de Santa Engrácia 89–90
  São Vicente de Fora 80–81, 179
  Sé (Cathedral) 72–73, 177
  shopping 93–94
Mercado da Ribeira 60
Mercado de Santa Clara 89
Mesnier de Ponsard, Raul 50
metro 30, 31
Miradouro de Santa Luzia 178
Miradouro de São Pedro Alcântara 174

miradouros (look-outs) 16, 28
Modernist architecture 17, 19
money 185
Monserrate 167, 169
Moorish architecture 19
Mosteiro dos Jerónimos 17, 124, 128–132
Movimento das Forças Armadas (MFA) 24–25
Mudejars 18
Museu da Agua 90
Museu Arqueológico do Carmo 51, 61, 174
Museu de Arte Moderna (Estefânia) 167, 169
Museu Bordalo Pinheiro 63
Museo do Brinquedo (Sintra) 167, 169
Museu Calouste Gulbenkian 55–59
Museu da Carris 23
Museu do Chiado 51, 60, 175
Museu da Cidade 63
Museu Conde de Castro Guimarães (Cascais) 162
Museu-Escola de Artes Decorativas 74–76, 178
Museu de Marinha 124–127
Museu Militar 90–91
Museu Nacional de Arqueológia 136–137
Museu Nacional de Arte Antiga 104–108
Museu Nacional do Azulejo 85–86
Museu Nacional dos Coches 133–135
Museu do Teatro Romano 178
museums 186
music 12–13, 40

national holidays 186
nature reserve 153
neoclassical architecture 17, 19
neo-Manueline architecture 19
nightlife 40
north Lisbon 42–66
  Baixa 46–9
  Café A Brasileira 60–61, 175
  Cais do Sodré 60, 180
  Centro de Arte Moderna 62–63
  Chiado and Santa Justa 50–51
  eating out 64–65
  entertainment 66
  map 43
  Mercado da Ribeira 60

Museu Arqueológico do Carmo 51, 61, 174
Museu Bordalo Pinheiro 63
Museu Calouste Gulbenkian 55–59
Museu do Chiado 60, 175
Museu da Cidade 63
one-day itinerary 44–45
Parque Eduardo VII 62
Rossio, Figueira and Restauradores 47, 52–54, 176
shopping 65–66
Nossa Senhora do Loreto 51
Núcleo Arqueológico da Rua dos Correeiros 49

Oceanário 146–149
opening hours 186
organised tours 182

Padrão dos Descobrimentos 122–123
Palácio da Ajuda 138
Palácio Azurara 74
Palácio Foz 54, 174
Palácio das Janelas Verdes 104
Palácio Ludovice 100
Palácio dos Marquêses de Fronteira 111
Palácio Nacional de Queluz 167–168, 169
Palácio Nacional de Sintra 164–166, 168
Palácio da Pena (Palácio) 166, 168
Palácio Pimenta 63
Panorama of Lisbon 86
Panteão Nacional de Santa Engrácia 89–90
parking 31
Parque das Nações 19, 141–158
Centro de Ciência Viva 150–151
Centro Comercial Vasco da Gama 154–155
eating out 156–157
entertainment 158
map 143
Oceanário 146–149
one-day itinerary 144–145
shopping 157–158
Torre Vasco da Gama 153, 154
waterfront and gardens 152–154
Parque Eduardo VII 62
passports and visas 184
Pavilhão do Conhecimento 150
Pedro IV, Dom 6, 52–53
personal safety 187
Pessoa, Fernando 48, 51

pharmacies 186, 188
PIDE 24, 25
Planetário Calouste Gulbenkian 124
police 187
Pombal, Marquês de 15, 21, 46–47, 100–101
Pombaline architecture 17, 19
Ponte 25 de Abril 153, 180, 181
Ponte Vasco da Gama 153, 181
port 11, 38
Portela airport 30
Portuguese Royal Equestrian School 168
postal services 186, 187
pottery see ceramics
Praça do Comércio 47, 177
Praça Dom Pedro IV see Rossio
Praça da Figueira 53, 176
Praça Luís de Camões 100
Praça do Município 47–48, 49
Praça do Príncipe Real 109
public transport 28, 31–33

Queluz 167–169
Palácio Nacional de Queluz 33, 167–168, 169
Quinta da Regaleira (Sintra) 166–167, 168

Restauradores 52, 53–54, 176
Eden building 54
Palácio Foz 54, 174
restaurants 37
see also individual areas
Rodrigues, Amália 13
Roman city 49
Romanesque architecture 17, 19
Rossio 47, 52–54, 176
Largo de São Domingo 53
Teatro Nacional de Dona Maria 53
Rua da Atalaia 101
Rua Augusta 48
Rua da Conceição 48–49
Rua do Diário de Notícias 101
Rua Garrett 51
Rua da Rosa 101
Rua de São Pedro 83
Rua do Século 100–101

safety 187
Salazar, António Oliveira 24, 122
Santa Justa 50
Santa Luzia 178
Santo Estêvão 84

Santuário do Cristo Rei 180–181
São Bento 110
São Roque 100
São Vicente de Fora 80–81, 179
Saramago, José 48
saudade 12–13
Sé (Cathedral) 19, 72–73, 177
senior citizens 188
shopping 39, 186
see also individual areas
Sintra 33, 164–167, 169, 181
Museu do Brinquedo 167, 169
Palácio Nacional de Sintra 164–166, 168
Palácio da Pena 166, 168
Quinta da Regaleira 166–167, 168
Solar do Vinho do Porto 100
Spanish architecture 17, 18, 19
Spinola, General António 24–25
spirits 38
streets, cobblestones 18
students 188

Tamariz (Estoril) 161
tax-free shopping 39
taxis 30, 32, 33
Teatro Municipal de São Luiz 51
Teatro Nacional de Dona Maria 53
Teatro Nacional de São Carlos 51, 66, 175–176
Teleférico 153
telephones 187
textiles 39
theatre 40
tickets, public transport 32–33
tiles see azulejos
time differences 185, 186
tipping 187
toilets 188
Torre de Belém 18, 120–121
Torre Vasco da Gama 153, 154
tourist information offices 31
tours 182
trains 30, 33, 185
trams 22–23, 32
travelling to Lisbon 30–31, 185

UNESCO World Heritage Sites 121

vegetarian food 38
Vincent, St 83

water, drinking 188
waterfront 152–154
weather 184, 188
West Coast 161–163
western Lisbon 95–114
  Bairro Alto 100–101
  Basílica da Estrela
  102–103
  Cemitério Inglês 103
  eating out 112–113

entertainment 114
Igreja de Santa Catarina
  110
Igreja de São Roque 109,
  174
Jardim Botânico 109–110
Jardim da Estrela 103
Lapa 110
Mãe d'Água 111
map 97

Museu Nacional de Arte
  Antiga 104–108
one-day itinerary 98–99
Palácio dos Marquêses de
  Fronteira 111
Praça do Príncipe Real 109
São Bento 110
shopping 114
wine 11, 38, 39
woodwork 39

Picture Credits

The Automobile Association wishes to thank the following photographers, companies and picture libraries for their assistance in the preparation of this book.

Abbreviations for the picture credits are as follows – (t) top; (b) bottom; (c) centre; (l) left; (r) right; (bg) background; (AA) AA World Travel Library

Front and Back Cover: (t) A Kouprianoff; (ct) A Mockford and N Bonetti; (cb, b) Monica Wells; Spine A Kouprianoff

Alamy © Mark Eveleigh/Alamy 91; © Robert Fried/Alamy 167; © Kevin Foy/Alamy 87l; © Kobi Israel/Alamy 166; © Werner Otto/Alamy 180; © Robert Harding Picture Library Ltd/Alamy 7t; Centro de Ciencia Viva 150t, 150b, 151; Fundação Calouste Gulbenkian 26l, 26c, 26r, 27t, 27l, 27c, 27r, © José Manuel Costa Alves 55t, 57, 59; Getty images 24t, 24b 25; Mary Evans Picture Library 8; Museu-Escola de Artes Decorativas 74, 75, 76.

The remaining photographs are held in the Association's own photo library (AA WORLD TRAVEL LIBRARY) and were taken by

M Birkitt 10, 101t; T Harris 2(3), 18, 28, 41, 77, 78, 118t, 147, 179, 187t; A Kouprianoff 2(5), 6, 9t, 9b, 14, 43, 50, 52/3, 55b, 56, 58, 62, 63, 71t, 80, 81t, 82r, 85, 86t, 86b, 89, 90, 95, 97, 102, 103l, 103r, 104, 105, 106, 107, 109b, 111t, 116/7, 119b, 125, 127, 133, 134r, 135, 163, 168, 170, 171, 172, 175l, 176r, A Mockford and N Bonetti 3(2), 3(3), 3(5), 13, 16/7, 23, 46, 47, 49, 54t, 61l, 72, 81b, 83b, 84, 101b, 141, 142/3, 145t, 145b, 152, 159, 161, 162, 164, 165, 174, 177, 178r, 183; R Newton 24/5bg; Monica Wells 2(1), 2(2), 2(4), 3(1), 3(4), 5, 7b, 11, 12t, 15, 19, 22, 29, 42, 44, 45t, 45b, 48, 54b, 60, 61r, 67, 69t, 69b, 70, 71b, 73, 79t, 79b, 82l, 83t, 87r, 88, 98t, 98b, 99, 108, 109t, 110, 111b, 115, 116, 118b, 119t, 121, 122, 123, 126, 128, 129, 130, 131, 132, 136, 137, 144, 146/7, 148, 149, 153, 154,155t, 155b, 173, 175r, 176l, 178l, 181, 182, 187br, P Wilson 12b, 96, 100, 120, 187bl

Every effort has been made to trace the copyright holders, and we apologise in advance for any unintential ommissions or errors. We would be pleased to apply any corrections in any following edition of this publication.

SPIRAL GUIDE

Questionnaire

Dear Traveller

Your comments, opinions and recommendations are very important to us. So please help us to improve our travel guides by taking a few minutes to complete this simple questionnaire.

You do not need a stamp (unless posted outside the UK). If you do not want to remove this page from your guide, then photocopy it or write your answers on a plain sheet of paper.

Send to: The Editor, Spiral Guides, AA World Travel Guides, FREEPOST SCE 4598, Basingstoke RG21 4GY.

Your recommendations...

We always encourage readers' recommendations for restaurants, night-life or shopping – if your recommendation is used in the next edition of the guide, we will send you a FREE AA Spiral Guide of your choice. Please state below the establishment name, location and your reasons for recommending it.

_____

_____

_____

_____

_____

Please send me AA Spiral _____
(see list of titles inside the back cover)

About this guide...

Which title did you buy?

_____ **AA Spiral**

Where did you buy it? _____

When? m m / y y

Why did you choose an AA Spiral Guide? _____

_____

_____

_____

_____

Did this guide meet your expectations?

Exceeded ☐   Met all ☐   Met most ☐   Fell below ☐

Please give your reasons _____

_____

_____

_____

_____

continued on next page...

Were there any aspects of this guide that you particularly liked?

____

____

____

____

____

Is there anything we could have done better?

____

____

____

____

About you...

Name (Mr/Mrs/Ms) _______________

Address _______________

____

_______________ **Postcode** _______________

Daytime tel no _______________ **email** _______________

Please *only* give us your email address and mobile phone number if you wish to hear from us about other products and services from the AA and partners by email or text or mms.

Which age group are you in?

Under 25 ☐ **25–34** ☐ **35–44** ☐ **45–54** ☐ **55–64** ☐ **65+** ☐

How many trips do you make a year?

Less than one ☐ **One** ☐ **Two** ☐ **Three or more** ☐

Are you an AA member? Yes ☐ **No** ☐

About your trip...

When did you book? mm/ y y **When did you travel?** mm/ y y

How long did you stay? _______________

Was it for business or leisure? _______________

Did you buy any other travel guides for your trip? ☐ **Yes** ☐ **No**

If yes, which ones? _______________

____

Thank you for taking the time to complete this questionnaire. Please send it to us as soon as possible, and remember, you do not need a stamp (unless posted outside the UK).

The information we hold about you will be used to provide the products and services requested and for identification, account administration, analysis, and fraud/loss prevention purposes. More details about how that information is used is in our privacy statement, which you'll find under the heading "Personal Information" in our terms and conditions and on our website: www.theAA.com. Copies are also available from us by post, by contacting the Data Protection Manager at AA, Fanum House, Basing View, Basingstoke, RG21 4EA. We may want to contact you about other products and services provided by us, or our partners (by mail, telephone) but please tick the box if you DO NOT wish to hear about such products and services from us by mail or telephone.

☐